A HANDBOOK FOR DEVELOPING MULTICULTURAL AWARENESS

SECOND EDITION

Paul Pedersen

AMERICAN
COUNSELING
ASSOCIATION

5999 Stevenson Avenue
Alexandria, VA 22304

10 9 8 7 6 5 4 3 2 1

American Counseling Association
5999 Stevenson Avenue
Alexandria, VA 22304

Director of Communications
Jennifer L. Sacks

Acquisitions and Development Editor
Carolyn Baker

Production/Design Manager
Michael Comlish

Copyeditor
Heather Jefferson

Library of Congress Cataloging-in-Publication Data

Pedersen, Paul, 1936-
   A handbook for developing multicultural awareness/Paul Pedersen.—2nd ed.
     p.   cm.
   Includes bibliographical references and index.
   1. Cross-cultural counseling. 2. Minorities—Counseling of. 3. Ethnopsychology.
I. American Counseling Association.
II. Title.
BF637.C6P336   1994
158'.3—dc20   93-33195
                                            CIP

*Dedicated to Anne Bennett Pedersen,
the source of the motivation as well as
many of the ideas for developing a multicultural
awareness*

CONTENTS

PREFACE

Counselors who disregard a client's cultural context are unlikely to interpret a client's behavior accurately. The same behavior across cultures might have a different interpretation, just as different behaviors might have the same interpretation. Therefore, developing multicultural awareness is essential for all counselors to accurately interpret the meaning of cultural similarities and differences.

The counselor has only two choices: to ignore the influence of culture or attend to it. In either case, however, culture will continue to influence a client's behavior with or without the counselor's awareness. Therefore it seems likely that the current trend toward multicultural awareness among counselors will have as great an impact as a "fourth force" in the helping professions of the next decade as Carl Rogers' "third force" of humanism had on the prevailing psychodynamic and behavioral systems.

Multicultural awareness provides a safe and accurate approach to managing differences across groups in a multicultural population. Multicultural awareness is safe because it provides a third "win-win" alternative to judgments of right or wrong between two culturally different persons in conflict. Multicultural awareness increases accuracy because it interprets behaviors in the context of the culturally different client's intended meaning. Culture is not a vague or exotic label attached to faraway persons and places, but a personal orientation to each decision, behavior, and action in our lives.

The importance of culture has been most evident in minority groups' political struggle for equity. Culture has provided the rationale and "roots" for unifying and defining populations of Blacks, Asian Americans, Hispanics, Native Americans, and—more recently—Whites. The same model also has coalesced support among the elderly, gender groups, physically handicapped, gays and lesbians, and many others. The importance of culture is broader than indicated by any one or two of these special interest groups, however. Culture provides a metaphor to better understand differences between groups of people as they relate to one another. Perhaps more importantly, culture provides a metaphor for understanding different perspectives within each of us as our different social roles compete, complement, and cooperate with one another in our decisions.

Some terms as defined in this book may be unfamiliar to the reader. In most cases, the terms can be understood from the context in which they appear, but it may be useful to review some of the more basic definitions as used in this book.

Culture is defined inclusively. Kroeber and Kluckhohn (1952) found over 150 different definitions of culture. Culture is described as the things a stranger needs to know to behave appropriately in a specific setting. Likewise, Geertz (1973) took a broad definition when he spoke of culture as "thick description" in the tradition of Max Weber and, more recently, systems theories. We spin webs of significance that we call culture. The analysis of culture is both an experimental science in search of rules and an interpretative study in search of meaning.

Multicultural counseling is a situation in which two or more persons with different ways of perceiving their social environments are brought together in a helping relationship. The term *multicultural* tends to be preferred over *cross-cultural, intercultural,* or *transcultural* because it describes a variety of groups with co-equal status rather than comparing one group to another. By implying comparison, the terms *cross-cultural, intercultural,* or *transcultural* implicitly suggest that one culture is better than the other.

Race refers to a pseudobiological system of classifying persons by a shared genetic history or physical characteristics such as skin color. The many emotional and political implications of the term *race* have led to its frequent misuse. The term *race* too often has promoted myths of superiority of one group over another (Mason, 1986; Yinger, 1986).

Ethnicity includes a shared sociocultural heritage that includes similarities of religion, history, and common ancestry. Ethnicity is important to individual and family identity as a subset of culture. In the past, *ethnicity* more frequently has referred to non-White groups, but more recently White ethnic groups have also emerged as separate ethnic groups.

Minority generally refers to a group receiving differential and unequal treatment because of collective discrimination. Minority is frequently defined by the condition of oppression rather than by numerical criteria. In this sense, women are sometimes classified as a minority even when they are a numerical majority.

Transcultural goes beyond culture to include the more universal constructs of before birth, after death, and religious philosophical concepts.

Counseling is defined broadly to include the full range of formal and informal means of helping others. In a multicultural setting, the functions of counseling are frequently present even though the traditional counseling relationship may be absent.

Before I begin to discuss the process of multicultural development, it is important to consider some of the more controversial questions in the literature about the concept called "culture" and the culture-learning process. It is also important to identify the assumptions behind this book's approach to describing multicultural development for each of the more controversial questions.

1. How Is "Objective" Culture Different from "Subjective" Culture?

Objective culture refers to the visible "point-at-able" artifacts or behaviors that are culturally learned or derived, and that can be objectively identified or pointed at by both persons within and outside a given culture. *Subjective culture* refers to the internalized feelings, attitudes, opinions, and assumptions that members of a culture hold, which, although profoundly important to the culture, are difficult to verify. To work with a culture, it is important to go beyond its more obvious objective and verifiable symbols toward the more subjective perspective its members hold.

2. Is the Concept "Culture" Broadly or Narrowly Defined?

The narrow definition of *culture* is limited to ethnographic variables such as nationality and ethnicity, although it may include language and religion. A broader "social system" definition of culture includes: (a) demographic variables such as age, gender, and place of residence; (b) status variables such as social, educational, and economic levels; and (c) affiliation variables that may be formal memberships or informal affiliations. Each element within the full range of demographic, status, and affiliation factors functions in ways similar to ethnographic categories to define a person's cultural identity. On occasion, any of these factors may be more salient to someone's personal cultural orientation than the ethnographic features. Therefore, it seems reasonable to include the full range of social system variables within the broad definition of *culture.*

3. Are Cultural Differences More Important Than Cultural Similarities?

Both cultural similarities and differences are equally important in the multicultural perspective. By overemphasizing differences in a separatist perspective, groups become exclusionary and stereotyped toward one another, which results in competition, conflict, and a lack of cooperation. By overemphasizing similarities in a universalist perspective the more powerful groups tend to dominate the less powerful groups and impose their perspective on the "melting pot." By emphasizing both the particular differences and the universal similarities at the same time, it is possible for culturally different persons or groups to find common ground without giving up their important and uniquely defining values, beliefs, and behaviors.

4. Is Culture Learning Best Pursued Through the "University Model" or Through More "Experiental" Learning?

The university model of didactic, lecture-based classroom teaching is certainly one of the valuable ways a person can learn about another culture. However, for persons unfamiliar with the culture, the experiential methods seem to have worked more efficiently (Harrison & Hopkins, 1967). Experiential methods place emphasis on less formal, field-based experiences and a two-way interaction between teachers and learners. Because both methods have their place, this book seeks to identify those conditions when formal training may be better than informal training experience, as well as those conditions where experience is indeed the best teacher.

5. Can Culture Learning Take Place as a General Process Independent of Any Specific Cultural Context?

Culture-general approaches teach about principles that apply to all multicultural contact whenever and wherever it may occur. Culture-general approaches emphasize self-awareness, flexibility, and increased tolerance of cultural differences. Culture-specific and culture-general training approaches complement one another in providing a full range of multicultural development for the person being trained.

As in the first edition of this book, the 12 chapters are divided into three sections. Chapters 1–4 focus on appropriate awareness of culturally learned assumptions and "starting points" on which all of our thinking is based. Chapters 5–8 focus on accurate knowledge and comprehension of necessary facts or gathering of necessary information about culture based on an appropriate level of awareness. Chapters 9–12 focus on effective skills to take action based on an appropriate level of awareness and accurate information. This three-level developmental sequence, around which this book is organized, models an approach for education and training as well as research and organizational communication in a variety of settings. Although the book emphasizes counseling functions—broadly defined—the activities, insights, and general guidelines apply to communication skills in a variety of settings. Wherever there is purposive communication across or among culturally different groups or people in which help is being provided or exchanged, counseling functions can be appropriate to facilitate a psychoeducational and developmental process.

The first four chapters emphasizing awareness focus on the importance of culturally learned assumptions that control behavior. Chapter 1 demonstrates the importance and the utility of defining culture inclusively. By looking at both similarities and differences, it becomes possible to identify "common ground" across cultures without forcing one or both groups or persons to sacrifice their cultural differences. This necessarily complex and dynamic process is described in terms of cultural salience and culturally learned patterns in behavior.

Chapter 2 describes the three-stage developmental progression from awareness to knowledge to skill. A comprehensive sequence is described to develop awareness, knowledge, and skill in training and education. Examples of training approaches emphasizing awareness, knowledge, or skill are also provided.

Chapter 3 demonstrates the importance of cultural bias in counseling and suggests ways to control or change those biases. Examples of unintentional racism are identified and discussed. Ten examples of cultural bias are discussed that reflect Western attitudes, and non-Western alternatives are presented. The construct of "balance" is offered to combine Western and non-Western approaches to counseling.

Chapter 4 provides structured experiences for identifying culturally learned assumptions. The importance of implicit assumptions is demonstrated, barriers to accurate communication across cultures are discussed, and specific strategies are presented to discover implicit culturally learned assumptions in behavior.

The next four chapters focus on the importance of specific and accurate facts and information based on appropriate awareness for intentional multicultural counseling. Chapter 5 describes the process of developing a cultural identity. Culture shock is discussed as essential to the "encounter" with other cultures that leads people to a sense of their own unique cultural identity. The importance of power relationships in racism and prejudice is documented, and alternative models of racial/ethnic identity development are described.

Chapter 6 focuses on cultural patterns and relationships between individuals and groups. Beginning with the separation of fact and inference, two contrasting approaches to cultural systems are presented. The first approach describes culture as something objective that people "discover" and that results in dispositions much like traits toward culture-specific behavior. The second approach describes culture as something subjective that people "construct" based on experiences to explain their behavior. A Cultural Grid is provided that combines elements of both alternative approaches.

Chapter 7 guides the reader toward significant research sources on multicultural counseling theory and practice. A historical framework is described for reviewing research from the multiethnic, international, conceptual, and theoretical perspectives. The counselor's and the client's viewpoints are described separately in the discussion of research on multicultural counseling.

Chapter 8 provides a critique of ethical guidelines for professional counselors from a multicultural perspective. Measures of ethical equity are reviewed, and historical trends regarding ethical guidelines are discussed. The dangers of cultural encapsulation are discussed and documented in the American Psychological Association (APA) and American Counseling Association (ACA) ethical guidelines for counselors.

The final four chapters focus on developing skills to apply appropriate awareness and accurate knowledge to the ultimate objective of developing multicultural counseling skills. Chapter 9 describes a conceptual framework for multicultural counseling skills. The importance of including informal as well as formal counseling strategies is described. Basic competencies of multicultural counseling skill are identified. Strategies for developing multicultural skill through training are discussed in terms of experiential/didactic and culture-specific/general approaches. The "balance of power" in multicultural counseling is described to clarify outcome measures of multicultural counseling skill.

Chapter 10 describes the Triad Training Model as one possible design for developing multicultural counseling skill. The origin and development of a model based on the internal dialogue of culturally different clients and counselors is described. Variations of the Triad Training Model are presented, and strategies for using the Triad Training Model in training are described. Guidelines for using the Triad Training Model are suggested.

Chapter 11 focuses on four dimensions of multicultural skill training using the Triad Training Model. The importance of perceiving the problem from the client's cultural viewpoint, recognizing resistance in specific rather than general terms, diminishing defensiveness of culturally different counselors, and recovery after doing or saying the wrong thing are described and documented.

Chapter 12 reviews the published competencies for developing multicultural counseling skills. The need for measurable competencies is discussed emphasizing awareness, knowledge, and skill outcomes. Assessment strategies; tests for measuring multicultural awareness, knowledge, and skill; and the applications of multicultural counseling competence are discussed.

This handbook is not intended to compete with or displace the many other publications on multicultural counseling. Rather, it is intended to guide the reader toward specific publications and resources and to complement those many other sources of awareness, knowledge, or skill. For that reason, a great many ideas, models, and strategies are not discussed in depth, but enough information is presented for the reader to determine where to go next in the search for multicultural counseling resources.

Many persons helped contribute to this handbook. First of all, the sources cited in the volume deserve credit for their extensive publications. No doubt other valuable authors have been inadvertently omitted from this rapidly growing literature on multicultural counseling as our awareness of resources grows and develops. Mark Hamilton and his staff at the American Counseling Association deserve credit for their support and encouragement in this second edition. Finally, Sue Kelly, who helped type and organize these materials, deserves credit for her hard work. My hope is that this book leads readers to ways that multiculturalism can make their tasks easier rather than harder, and can increase their satisfaction in working with other cultures.

PART I

Awareness of Multicultural Assumptions

CHAPTER 1

The Rules of Multiculturalism

Major objective:

1. To demonstrate the utility of defining culture inclusively.

Secondary objectives:

1. To demonstrate the importance of both similarities and differences.
2. To demonstrate the necessity of accepting cultural complexity.
3. To demonstrate the ever-changing dynamic characteristics of culture.
4. To demonstrate the cultural salience of ethnographic, demographic, status, and affiliations.

Before we were born, cultural patterns of thought and action were already being prepared to guide our lives, influence our decisions, and help us take control of our lives. We inherited these cultural patterns from our parents and teachers who taught us the "rules of the game." As we developed awareness of other people and cultures, we learned that "our" culture was one of the many possible patterns of thinking and acting from which we could choose. By that time, most of us had already come to believe that our culture was the best of all possible worlds. Even when we recognized that the new ways were better, it was not always possible to replace our cultural habits with new alternatives. Therefore, the primary enemy of multiculturalism is our exclusive reliance on the "self-reference criterion" by which we measure the goodness or badness of others exclusively according to ourselves and our own "natural" perspective.

1. Cultural Similarities and Differences

Multiculturalism presents us with a paradox because it requires us to look at how we are the same and how we are different at the same time. The multicultural perspective is one of the most important ideas in this century because it emphasizes both the ways that we are each unique *and* the ways that we share parts of our identity with others. Alternative views of culture have made three serious mistakes:

1. The "melting pot" metaphor made the mistake of overemphasizing the ways we are the same and ignoring differences. This has usually resulted in the more powerful groups imposing their perspectives on everybody else.

2. The overemphasis of differences has resulted in stereotyped and disconnected "special interest" cultural groups in an exclusionary perspective while ignoring the common ground of shared interests, which makes the welfare of each group important to each other group.

3. The assumption that one must select either the universalist or the particularist viewpoint has resulted in a false choice because both are important to define the cultural context accurately and comprehensively. Each cultural perspective is unique, but each perspective also shares overlapping features with each other group like overlapping fish scales. We can best understand the cultural perspective by focusing one eye clearly on the part that is shared and the other eye on the part that is unique in a cross-eyed but accurate perspective.

Some views of multiculturalism proceed from the assumption of radical cultural relativism—that each culture is unique and different and that all cultures are equal in value. Others evaluate all cultures according to a single, absolute measure of truth. Just as cultural relativism defines each culture in its own terms, customs, symbols, norms, and beliefs, cultural absolutism assumes a universal measure of normal psychological functions and the ways those functions relate to behavior. The universalist position assumes that the same psychological processes are operating in all humans independent of culture. Patterson (1978b, 1986) took a universalist position in criticizing counselors for modifying counseling to fit different cultures. Although counseling needs to be modified for clients of different ages, genders, experiences, and social backgrounds to fit the different expectations of clients, Patterson disputed the need for different sets of skills, emphasis, and insights for use in each culture, emphasizing that the "context" is multicultural, not the counseling "process." As Draguns (1989) pointed out, this criticism constructively raises questions about the limits of cultural accommodation and the universal versus the particular perspective of counseling.

The rhetoric in support of cultural differences and multicultural counseling has been written into documents of counselor accreditation, certification, licensure, and professional identity for many years. According to the exclusionary definition of *culture*, these statements have been perceived as political favors to the special interests of one group or another. However, according to the inclusionary definition of culture, multiculturalism goes beyond the self-interests of any particular group to redefine the basis of identity for both the counselor and the client, regardless of his or her skin color, age, gender, socioeconomic status, or affiliation. The argument on which much of the previous rhetoric has been based has been largely humanitarian or ethical. The argument from an inclusionary definition of culture is based on the functional accuracy necessary for good counseling without diminishing the ethical or humanitarian imperative.

The revolution of culturally different consumers has been most pronounced in educational settings. The schools were battlegrounds for civil rights, textbook censorship, and social change, and now the pressure is on to deal with cultural diversity among the students and community. "This movement for diversity has been dubbed multiculturalism and has become a major force in American education, from city to suburban elementary schools, from high schools to universities" (Cohen, 1990, p. 76).

The multicultural revolution has also led to a phenomenon of "politically correct" or PC behavior. Philosophically, PC means the subordination of the right to free speech to the right guaranteeing equal protection under the law. The PC position contends that an absolutist position on the First Amendment (you may slur anyone you choose) imposes a hostile environment for minorities and violates their right to an equal education. Promotion of diversity is one of the central tenets of PC. The content of PC is in some ways not controversial. Who would defend racism? What is distressing is that tolerance is having to be externally imposed rather than internally developed, substituting one repressive orthodoxy with another (Ravitch, 1990).

There is still a greater danger in the discussion of PC: the polarization of alternatives into either–or categories. Both the advocates and the opponents of PC are in danger of oversimplifying multiculturalism by presuming a single "correct" orthodoxy.

The real issue in schools is not whether there will be multiculturalism. The rapidly changing ratio of minority to majority culture people guarantees a multicultural future. The question is, what kind of a multiculturalism will survive? Ravitch (1990) described two polarized features: "Two versions presently compete for dominance in the teaching of American culture. One approach reflects cultural pluralism and accepts diversity as a fact: the other represents particularism and demands loyalty to a particular group. The two coexist uncomfortably, because they are not different by degree. In fact, they are opposite in spirit and in purpose" (p. 44).

There is a potential for error by both the particularist and the universalist perspectives. Whereas the particularist perspective may define culture too narrowly and result in ethnocentric exclusion by culturally defined special interest groups, the universalistic perspective may result in the continued domination by the more powerful majority culture at the expense of minority cultures.

D'Souza (1991) provided a recent example of polarized thinking in his documentation of failures in affirmative action programs at U.S. universities. Although the many failures of affirmative action programs are readily apparent, D'Souza ignored the need for positive strategies that offer better alternatives. D'Souza provided many examples of how simplistic solutions and "cosmetic" changes fail through his own equally simplistic criticism, which ignores the underlying multicultural reality that stimulated affirmative action in the first place. Polarized thinking suggests the possibility of easy answers or obvious wrongdoing while ignoring the complexity of changes that will be required by multiculturalism. Although the "right" way to accommodate multiculturalism remains unclear and the "wrong" ways have not worked, we will never be able to return to an "earlier age," as the more conservative perspective of D'Souza seems to advocate. D'Souza is right about one thing. The worst, and perhaps the best, is yet to come.

Miles (1989) pointed out that it is a mistake to limit the parameters of racism by reference to skin color. The extensive evidence of racism and related exclusionary practices requires that we define *racism* broadly to include sexism, ageism, and nationalism as well as the exclusionary practices associated with these ideologies. Miles rejected Katz's (1978) definition of *racism* as a "White person's problem" for being simplistic in its disregard for the differential definitions of power across situations. At the same time, he supported Katz's contention that Whites have been socialized into a perspective that presumes White superiority. Every attempt to reduce culture and cultural differences according to skin color alone has resulted in simplistic, stereotyped, or polarized alternatives that disregard the necessary complexity of multiculturalism.

Haq (1993) compiled a report for the UN Human Development Program showing that citizens of some developing countries are better off than American Blacks or Hispanics, whereas U.S. Whites rank Number 1 in the world on a quality-of-life index. The report ranks 173 countries on differences in life expectancy, education, and purchasing power, including the analysis of ethnic and gender groups within many of those countries. The United States ranks sixth (after Japan, Canada, Norway, Switzerland, and Sweden), although U.S. Whites top the list if they are considered separately. Conversely, U.S. Blacks rank 31st or about the same as Trinidad and Tobago, and U.S. Hispanics rank 35th or about the same as Latvia and Estonia. The report describes the United States as one country with two nations, separated by their access to productivity. Women are a majority of the world's population, but have access to only a small share of the development opportunities. At the same time, U.S. White women are ranked slightly ahead of U.S. White men due to a longer life expectancy and greater educational attainment despite lower wages and employment rankings. We are multicultural, but our resources are not fairly distributed.

Ramirez (1991) presented a model based on five characteristics of a multicultural orientation. First, there is a striving for the maximum development of the person through self-actualization. Second, there is adaptability to different environments and the "cognitive flex" to adapt to be effective. Third, there is the challenge of leadership roles in diverse groups finding innovative solutions for resolving conflict in groups with diverse memberships. Fourth, there is a commitment to changing groups, cultures, and nations to guarantee social justice for all persons. Fifth, there is the motivation to get the most out of life by celebrating diversity in experiences. Multicultural counseling is important because it contributes to a multicultural society where peace, cooperation, and understanding become the norms without sacrificing the inclusion of cultural differences in the process.

2. Culture Is Complex and Not Simple

Complexity is a friend not an enemy because it protects us from our own reductionistic assumptions. This process is most apparent in our use of scientific theories. In attempting to understand complexity, we develop simplified models that can be explained and understood but that reflect only selected aspects of reality. Our imbedded rationality requires that we construct simplified models of complex reality to explain things. If we behave rationally with regard to the model, we assume the behavior is appropriately explained in the real world. The danger is that we confuse simple explanations and labels with a more complex reality. We normally have little tolerance for the confusion of aggregate, mixed-up, unsorted, undifferentiated, unpredictable, and random data. We naturally move quickly to sort, order, and predict simplified patterns from the chaos (Triandis, 1975).

Rather than resort to the "digital model" where alternatives are sorted in either–or categories with discrete criteria, the more complex analog or family resemblance alternative is preferred. The analog approach describes natural categories through prototypes of the same "family" within a continuum of increasing or decreasing similarity of membership (Rosch, 1975). The clearest metaphor to this phenomenon is color membership, where each color represents a prototype surrounded by colors of decreasing similarity. The analogy makes boundary judgments difficult because of a "fuzzy" characteristic in overlapping family memberships, but it allows variation both within and between categories without rigidly imposing judgments of correct or incorrect evaluation.

By perceiving the world from a narrow or rigid frame of reference, we ignore the complex reality around us in the illusion of simplicity. Alternatively, the principle of complementarity (Bohr, 1950) suggests that many phenomena can be understood only from a variety of different perspectives. Theories of cognitive complexity suggest that people who are more cognitively complex are more capable than others of seeing these multiple perspectives. Likewise, research in adult development suggests that cognitive complexity is related to broader and more advanced levels of development. Bohr used the principle of complementarity to prove that sometimes light may be regarded as a particle and sometimes as a wave, so that both quantum and wave theories are necessary to explain the "real" nature of light. The principle has likewise proved itself useful in gastroenterology, ecclesiology, literary criticism, the philosophy of science, organizational behavior, economics, and political science. Science has long accepted genetic diversity as essential to the survival of a species.

Some persons are able to tolerate complexity better than others. These people are either better at differentiating and perceiving several dimensions in a range of alternatives or integrating and seeing complex connections between different sources. People who are more complex are able to see many different dimensions, classifications, theories, or alternatives to explain a situation. Because reality tends to be complex, those who are able to identify more alternatives are more likely to see correctly and make more appropriate decisions, although this process requires a high tolerance for ambiguity. In *The Crack Up*, Scott Fitzgerald's (1945) essay about his own mid-life crisis, he suggested that the test of a first-rate intelligence is the ability to hold two opposed ideas in the mind at the same time and still retain the ability to function.

Culture's complexity is illustrated by the hundreds, or perhaps even thousands, of culturally learned identities, affiliations, and roles we each assume at one time or another. The dynamic nature of culture is demonstrated as one alternative cultural identity replaces another in salience. A counselor must keep track of the client's salient cultural identity because it changes even within the context of an interview). There is considerable interest in broadening the categories of culture in the developmental counseling literature (Stoltenberg & Delworth, 1987) and from the social-cognitive perspective (Abramson, 1988). Counselors develop their competence through stages of progressively more complex and adaptive facility in making decisions and processing information (Pedersen, 1990).

Complexity involves the identification of multiple perspectives within and between individuals. For example, Can the counselor perceive a problem from the multiple viewpoints of a culturally different client in the many different and changing culturally learned roles that the client fills from time to time and place to place (Draguns, 1989)?

The following 10 examples of observable and potentially measurable counseling behaviors are rooted in traditional theories of counseling on the one hand

and are particularly relevant for the complexity of multicultural counseling on the other hand.

1. *The Clear and Separate Identification of Multiple but Conflicting Cultur- ally Learned Viewpoints Between Persons in the Interview Is Necessary.*

Research on empathy in counseling (Goldstein & Michaels, 1985) has al- ready demonstrated the importance of distinguishing different viewpoints in the interview. If two culturally different viewpoints are in conflict, we need not assume that one is right and the other is wrong. The multicultural perspective for a proper understanding is unique in allowing both viewpoints to be right within their own cultural contexts.

2. *The Clear and Separate Identification of Multiple but Conflicting Cul- turally Learned Viewpoints Within Persons in the Interview Is Necessary.*

Behavioral approaches to counseling suggest that the same individual may take on different culturally relevant roles or identities, depending on the situa- tion (Tanaka-Matsumi & Higginbotham, 1989). Stereotyping results when a counselor assumes that all persons of a particular ethnic group, nationality, gender, or age will always have the same perspective. This conflict in roles may be the reason for seeking counseling.

3. *The Ability to Accurately Relate the Actions of Different Persons in the Interview in Ways That Would Explain Their Behavior from Their Own Cultural Perspective Is Necessary.*

The ability to take another person's perspective has been an important goal of gestalt therapists and a tool for psychodrama in counseling. It is also essen- tial in accurate assessment (Lonner & Ibrahim, 1989). However, the more cul- turally different the counselor is from a client, the more difficult it will be for the counselor to take that culturally different perspective (Pedersen, Fukuyama, & Heath, 1989).

4. *The Ability to Listen and Store Information Without Interrupting the Cli- ent for Introduction Later When Culturally Appropriate in the Interview Is Necessary.*

An important microskill emphasized by Ivey (1988) includes aspects of careful listening and basic attending skills. Listening requires counselors to tolerate silence and to suspend judgment until all perspectives of a culturally different client are thoroughly understood. Sometimes keeping silent, although appro- priate, can be very difficult for a counselor. Otherwise counselors may unfairly impose a self-reference criterion.

5. *The Ability to Shift Topics in Culturally Appropriate Ways Is Necessary.*

Pattern recognition allows the counselor to lead the client toward increased insight by knowing when a cultural topic is salient to the client's point of view. Ivey (1988) described this as "observation of client verbal tracking and selective attention" (p. 75). This skill presumes knowledge of the client's culture so that each behavior can be matched with the client's culturally learned expectation and value.

    6. The Accurate Labeling of Culturally Appropriate Feelings in Specific Rather Than General Terms Is Necessary.

Ivey (1988) discussed the microskill "reflection of feeling" as the foundation of a client's experience. Being specific and accurate in labeling a culturally different client's feelings requires learning new cues, signals, and patterns of emotional expression. Accurate feelings are at least as important as accurate facts in good counseling technique, even though this may be more difficult in a multicultural context. Lopez (1989) discussed how wrong attributions, assumed base rates, selective memory, and self-confirming hypothesis testing result in bias against culturally different clients.

    7. The Identification of Culturally Defined Multiple Support Systems Is Necessary for the Client Outside the Interview.

Recent attention to natural support systems as potential resources in counseling is encouraging (Pearson, 1985). In many cultures, these support systems are the preferred source of counseling through informal methods and in an informal context.

    8. The Ability to Identify Alternative Solutions and Anticipate the Consequences of Each Solution Is Necessary.

Decisional counseling and other problem-solving or decision-making approaches to counseling are particularly useful in cultures where the counselor is perceived as a teacher and a source of authoritative knowledge (Ivey, Ivey, & Simek-Morgan, 1993).

    9. The Ability to Identify the Culturally Learned Criteria Being Used to Evaluate Alternative Solutions Is Necessary.

The personal constructs being applied by culturally different clients are based on culturally learned assumptions. Without knowing these culturally learned criteria, the counselor cannot accurately interpret or evaluate a client's behavior (Neimeyer & Fukuyama, 1984).

    10. The Ability to Generate Insights for the Other Person from the Other Person's Culturally Learned Perspective(s) in the Interview That Explains the Situation Is Necessary.

Many theories of counseling are based on insight by the counselor as well as the client, using skills such as interpretation, reflection of feeling, and reflection of meaning (Brammer, 1988; Hackney & Cormier, 1988; Ivey, 1988). Accurate insight presumes a high level of awareness, knowledge, and skill in the multicultural context.

The 10 examples of cultural complexity discussed as counseling skills are already familiar features of the counseling literature, but not as they apply to multicultural counseling. Rather than separate the multicultural perspective as a special branch of counseling, it is important to see it as a viewpoint and perspective applicable to all areas of counseling.

3. Culture Is Dynamic and Not Static

The construct of balance was defined by Heider (1958), Newcomb (1953), and McGuire (1966) in consistency theory *as the search for an enduring consistency in an otherwise volatile situation.* Cognitive balance was achieved by changing, ignoring, differentiating, or transcending inconsistencies to avoid dissonance (Triandis, 1977). From another more complicated perspective, however, dynamic balance can be described as a tolerance for inconsistency and dissonance rather than for resolving differences.

In this more complicated and asymmetrical definition of *dynamic balance*, the task of counseling may be to find meaning in both pleasure and pain, rather than to resolve conflict in favor of increased pleasure. Social change in this context is perceived as a continuous and not an episodic process. Balance as a construct seeks to reflect the complex and sometimes asymmetrical metaphors of organic systems in holistic health. Problems, pain, and otherwise negative aspects of our experiences may also provide necessary resources for the dark side of healthy functioning in an ecological analysis of psychological processes (Berry, 1980).

There is evidence that successful cross-cultural therapy systems have a tendency to compensate for the social context by restoring and maintaining a balance of opposites. Wittkower and Warnes (1974) suggested that cross-cultural preferences in therapy depend on etiological views and ideological differences, which is why they claimed psychoanalysis gained ground in the United States in the context of strong individualism, work therapy in the Soviet Union because of Marxist ideology, and Morita therapy in Japan because of culturally imposed rigid self-discipline. Tseng and Hsu (1980) furthered discussed how therapy compensates for culturally different features, so that highly controlled and overregulated cultures might encourage therapies that provide a safety valve release for feelings and emotions, whereas underregulated or anomic cultures would encourage therapies with externalized social control at the expense of self-expression. Lin and Lin (1978) attributed mental illness to harmful emanations affecting the yin and yang when they are disturbed or "out of balance."

Watts (1961) compared counseling to a social game based on conventional rules that define boundaries between the individual and the cultural context. It is then the duty of a therapist to involve participants in a "counter game," which restores a unifying perspective of ego and environment, so that the people can be liberated and a balanced context restored. In some cases, balance has been restored through therapy by bringing in a "mediator" as a third person in addition to the counselor and client. Bolman (1968) advocated the approach of using two professionals, one from each culture collaborating in cross-cultural counseling, with traditional healers as co-counselors. Weidman (1986) introduced the concept of a "culture broker" as an intermediary for working with culturally different clients.

In many non-Westernized systems, there is less emphasis on separating the person from the presenting problem than in Western cultures. There is less tendency to locate the problem inside the isolated individual, but rather to relate that individual's difficulty to other persons or even to the cosmos. Balance describes a condition of order and dynamic design in a context where all elements, pain as well as pleasure, serve a useful and necessary function. The non-Western emphasis is typically more holistic in acknowledging the reciprocal interaction of persons and environments in both their positive and negative aspects.

Success is achieved indirectly as a by-product of harmonious two-directional balance, rather than directly through a more simplistic one-directional alternative. In a one-directional approach, the goal is to make people feel more pleasure and less pain, more happiness and less sadness, and more positive and less negative. In the two-directional alternative, the goal is to help people find meaning in both pleasure and pain, happiness and sadness, negative and positive experience. In the Judeo-Christian tradition, God not only tolerates the devil's presence but actually created demonic as well as angelic forces in a balance of alternatives.

The restoration of value balance provides an alternative goal to the more individualized goal of solving social problems. In the context of value balance, social change is perceived as a continuous and not an episodic process, taking place independently both because of and despite attempts to control that change. Value balance is a process rather than a conclusive event or events. In a similar mode, the problems, pain, and other negative aspects of education provide necessary resources for creating a dynamic value balance.

Balance as a construct for multicultural counseling involves the identification of different or even conflicting culturally learned perspectives without necessarily resolving that difference or dissonance in favor of either viewpoint.

Healthy functioning in a multicultural or pluralistic context may require a person to simultaneously maintain multiple, conflicting and culturally learned roles without the opportunity to resolve the resulting dissonance. The following 10 examples of observable and potentially measurable counseling behaviors, although rooted in traditional theories of counseling, also provide valuable "balance" skills for multicultural counseling.

1. The Ability to See Positive Implications in an Otherwise Negative Experience from the Client's Cultural Viewpoint Is Necessary.

Ivey (1988) emphasized the importance of a "positive asset search" in counseling. It would be simplistic for a provider to assume that the negative experiences of culturally different clients are not also related to positive outcomes and consequences.

2. The Ability to Anticipate Potential Negative Implications from an Otherwise Positive Experience to Provide Multiple Perspectives Is Necessary.

The counseling implications of rational-emotive therapies and of reality therapy are discussed by Corey (1991) and elsewhere in the counseling literature. Each solution that a counselor brings to a culturally different client will almost certainly also have potential negative effects that must also be considered from the client's viewpoint.

3. The Ability to Articulate Statements of Meaning to Help Interpret or Integrate Positive and Negative Events in a Constructive Way Without Requiring the Client to Resolve the Dissonance in Favor of One or Another Culture Is Necessary.

The role of the counselor is to help clients articulate the meaning of an otherwise difficult situation for their lives and for their futures. Tolerance for ambiguity is emerging as an important characteristic of multiculturally skilled persons (Kealey, 1988; Ruben & Kealey, 1979). The meaning of each event will include both positive and negative elements that must be understood in a cultural context. Ivey's (1988) microskill "reflection of meaning" requires counselors to explore basic and often conflicting concepts in their multiple cultural identities.

4. The Ability to Avoid Simple Solutions to Complex Problems and Acknowledge the Complicated Constraints of a Client's Cultural Context Is Necessary.

Ivey (1988) described the "premature solution" as the most frequent mistake of beginning counselors. This is even more true in a multicultural setting. It is useful to anthropomorphize the problem as both a friend and an enemy to help counselors better understand the complexity of problems in culturally different settings from the client's viewpoint.

5. Sensitivity to How Collective Forces Influence an Individual's Behavior and Increase Alternative Interpretations Is Necessary.

Ivey (1988) frequently pointed out how traditional counseling is biased toward an individualistic perspective. In a more collectivist culture, the welfare of the unit or collective forces may be more important than the welfare of an individual. Good multicultural counseling may require balancing the welfare of the individual client against the welfare of these collective forces in a way that satisfies the individual and the collectivity.

6. Sensitivity to the Changing Power of the Person Being Interviewed Over Time as a Result of Counseling Is Necessary.

Strong (1978) described social influence theory's contribution to understanding the importance of power in counseling. Power is culturally defined, and good multicultural counseling is sensitive to whether counseling is enhancing or diminishing a client's power.

7. Sensitivity to How the Changing Power of the Person Being Interviewed Across Different Topical Areas, Which Reduces Stereotyping, Is Necessary.

Differentiation by counselors requires them to note changes in social influence and power across topics as well as across time. A good multicultural counselor should be able to identify areas of expertise as well as areas of deficiency in a culturally different client. The importance of self-esteem and the destructive effects of perceived helplessness apply especially to a client attempting to cope in a culturally unfamiliar context (Pedersen et al., 1989).

8. Sensitivity to the Changing Power of the Person Being Interviewed in Culturally Different Social Roles, Which Is Essential to Understand Change, Is Necessary.

Clients who function at an adequate level in some roles may not function adequately in other roles. Lopez (1989) pointed out how counselor bias frequently disregards differences in role functioning ability. Is the counselor sensitive to the different power level of a client across cultures and roles?

9. The Ability to Adjust the Amount of Influence by the Interviewer, Which Can Facilitate the Independent Growth of the Other Person, Is Necessary.

To facilitate a balanced perspective, the counselor needs to provide enough, but not too much, control influence or power as defined by the cultural context. If the counselor exerts too much control on a strong client, the client may rebel and reject the counselor as more troublesome than the problem. If the counselor exerts too little control toward a weak client, the client may abandon the counselor as inadequate and unable to provide the necessary protection (Pedersen, 1981a, 1984a, 1986; Strong, 1978).

10. The Ability to Maintain Harmony Within the Interview Is Necessary to Demonstrate a Culturally Inclusive Perspective.

Lambert (1981) pointed out that good rapport consistently emerges as a necessary but not sufficient condition of good counseling in the research across all settings. Ivey (1988) also commented on the importance of counseling techniques being measured by their contribution to a harmonious rapport between client and counselor, even though they may be from different cultural backgrounds. Ivey suggested that, like a samurai swordsman, good counselors must go beyond the imitation of technique and integrate their skills into their own natural style.

Although the construct of dynamic balance is elusive, the preceding 10 examples of observable counselor behaviors describe some of the essential aspects as applied to multicultural counseling. These examples are rooted in the traditional counseling research literature and are not, by themselves, controversial. Because these examples are familiar, they may provide a conceptual bridge for counselors to develop multicultural counseling skills with culturally different clients.

4. Multiculturalism Is Inclusive and Broadly Defined

The multicultural perspective seeks to provide a conceptual framework that recognizes the complex diversity of a plural society, although at the same time it suggests bridges of shared concern that bind culturally different persons to one another. The ultimate outcome may be a multicultural theory, as Segall, Dasan, Berry, and Poortinga (1990) suggested. "There may well come a time when we will no longer speak of cross cultural psychology as such. The basic premise of this field—that to understand human behavior, we must study it in its sociocultural context—may become so widely accepted that all psychology will be inherently cultural" (p. 352). During the last 20 years, multiculturalism has become recognized as a powerful force, not just for understanding exotic groups but also for understanding ourselves and those with whom we work.

Multiculturalism has more often been regarded as a method than as a theory. If multiculturalism refers exclusively to narrowly defined culture-specific categories such as nationality or ethnicity, then multiculturalism might best be considered as a method of analysis. The multicultural method can then be applied to the encounter of specific cultural groups with one another and also emphasizing the culture-specific characteristics of each group.

However, if multiculturalism refers inclusively to broadly defined social-system variables such as ethnographics, demographics, status, and affiliations, then multiculturalism might better be considered a theory. In that case, the underlying principle of multicultural theory would emphasize both the culture-specific characteristics that differentiate and the culture-general characteristics that unite in the explanation of human behavior. The accommodation of both within-group differences and between-group differences is required for a comprehensive understanding of complicated cultures (Pedersen, 1991a).

By defining *culture* broadly, to include demographic variables (e.g., age, gender, place of residence), status variables (e.g., social, educational, economic), and affiliations (formal and informal), as well as ethnographic variables such as nationality, ethnicity, language, and religion, the construct of "multicultural" becomes generic to all counseling relationships. The narrow definition of *culture* has limited multiculturalism to what might more appropriately be called a "multi-ethnic" or "multinational" relationship between groups with a shared sociocultural heritage that includes similarities of religion, history, and common ancestry. Ethnicity and nationality are important to individual and familial identity as one subset of culture, but the construct of culture—broadly defined—goes beyond national and ethnic boundaries. Persons from the same ethnic or nationality group may still experience cultural differences. Not all Blacks have the same experience, nor do all Asians, all American Indians, all Hispanics, all women, all old people, nor all disabled persons. No particular group is unimodal in its perspective. Therefore, the broad and inclusive definition of *culture* is particularly important in preparing counselors to deal with the complex differences among and between clients from every cultural group.

Just as differentiation and integration are complementary processes, so are the emic (culture-specific) and etic (culture-general) perspectives necessarily interrelated. The terms *emic* and *etic* were borrowed from *phonemic* and *phonetic* analyses in linguistics describing the rules of language to imply a separation of general from specific aspects. Even Pike (1966), in his original conceptualization of this dichotomy, suggested that the two elements not be treated as a rigid dichotomy but as a way to present the same data from two viewpoints. Although research on the usefulness of emic and etic categories has been extensive, the notion of a "culture-free" (universal) etic has been as elusive as the notion of a "culture-pure" (totally isolated) emic. The basic problem facing counselors is how to describe behavior in terms that are true to a particular culture while at the same time comparing those behaviors with a similar pattern in one or more other cultures (Pedersen, 1984b). Combining the specific and general viewpoints provides a multicultural perspective. This larger perspective is an essential starting point for mental health professionals seeking to avoid cultural encapsulation by their own culture-specific assumptions (Sartorius, Pedersen, & Marsella, 1984).

Although Sue (1990) favored a culture-specific approach to multicultural counseling, he acknowledged some legitimate criticisms of advocating culture-specific techniques for counseling minority clients: (a) They foster a technique-oriented definition of counseling devoid of a conceptual framework; (b) counselors and therapists may be limited in their ability to adopt a different counseling style; (c) the technique approaches may be distal to the goal of effective therapy; and (d) by describing characteristics of each ethnic group, we may be guilty of perpetuating stereotypes.

There is a strong argument against the broad definition of *culture*. Triandis, Bontempo, Leung, and Hui (1990) distinguished between cultural, demographic, and personal constructs. Cultural constructs are those shared by persons (a) speaking a particular dialect; (b) living in the same geographical location during the same time; and (c) sharing norms, roles, values, associations, and ways to categorize experience described as a "subjective culture" (Triandis, 1972). This view contends that demographic level constructs deal with these same topics but are shared only by particular demographic groups within a culture, such as men and women or old and young. Personal level constructs belong to still another category of individual differences and cannot be meaningfully interpreted with reference to demographic or cultural membership.

The problem with this perspective is that it tends to be arbitrary in defining the point at which shared constructs constitute cultural similarity because, as Triandis et al. (1990) pointed out, "We cannot expect that 100% of a sample agrees with a position. We decided arbitrarily, that if 85% of a sample shares the construct, it is cultural. Similarly, if 85% of the men share it, we consider it gender linked. If less than 85% share the construct we might examine if it is shared by the majority of a sample but if less than 50% of a sample share the construct, we definitely do not consider it shared" (p. 304).

Likewise, Lee and Richardson (1991) made a persuasive argument against the broad definition of *culture*. They argued that the term *multicultural* is in imminent danger of becoming so inclusive as to be almost meaningless. The broad definition includes all constituent groups that perceive themselves as being disenfranchised in some fashion. This has resulted in diffusing the coherent conceptual framework of multiculturalism in training, teaching, and research. "As the term has been increasingly stretched to include virtually any group of people who consider themselves 'different' the intent of multicultural counseling theory and practice has become unclear" (Locke, 1990, p. 6). In responding to Fukuyama's (1990) argument for a more universalist emphasis of culture for understanding the complex interacting systems of society, Locke suggested that the broad view of multicultural at best serves as a prologue for a narrow or "focused" perspective.

A view of multicultural counseling that does not direct attention toward the racial/ethnic minority groups within that culture is but an attempt to eliminate any focus on the pluralistic nature of that culture. "Such a system views cultural differences as no more than individual differences" (Locke, 1990, p. 24).

Cultural differences are not the same as individual differences. Brislin (1990) distinguished cultural aspects from individual differences by looking at seven indicators. Individual differences describe some but not all people in a society, and the members of that society can be graded on a distribution according to individual differences of "intelligence," for example. On the other hand, cultural aspects include: (a) the part of a way of life that people make, (b) ideas transmitted from generation to generation, (c) identifiable childhood experiences resulting in internalized values, (d) socialization of children into adults, (e) consistent patterns of concepts and practices, (f) cultural patterns that are maintained despite mistakes and slipups in the system, and (g) a feeling of helplessness or bewilderment that results when cultural patterns are changed.

The distinction between individual differences and cultural differences is real and important. The cultural identities to which we belong are no more or less important than are our individual identities. Skin color at birth is an individual difference, but what that skin color has come to mean since birth is cultural. Although culture has traditionally been defined as a multigenerational phenomenon, the broad definition of *culture* suggests that cultural identities and culturally significant shared beliefs may develop in a contemporary horizontal as well as vertical historical time frame and still be distinguished from individual differences.

Poortinga (1990) defined *culture* as shared constraints that limit the behavior repertoire available to members of a sociocultural group in a way that is different from individuals belonging to some other group. Segall et al. (1990) affirmed that ecological forces are the prime movers and shapers of cultural forms, which in turn shape behaviors. "Given these characteristics of culture, it becomes possible to define it simply as the totality of whatever all persons learn from all other persons" (Segall et al., 1990, p. 26). Culture is part of the environment, and all behavior is shaped by culture, so it is rare (perhaps even impossible) for any human being ever to behave without responding to some aspect of culture.

Another application of the broad inclusive definition of *culture* is "cultural psychology," which presumes that every sociocultural environment depends for its existence and identity on the way human beings give it meaning and are in turn changed in response to that sociocultural environment. Cultural psychology studies the ways that cultural traditions and social practices regulate, express, and transform people in patterned ways. "Cultural psychology is the study of the ways subject and object, self and other, psyche and culture, person and context, figure and ground, practitioner and practice live together, require each other, and dynamically, dialectically and jointly make each other up" (Shweder, 1990, p. 1).

Culture provides a unique perspective, in which two persons can disagree without one being right and the other being wrong when their arguments are based on culturally different assumptions. It becomes possible for a counselor to identify a "common ground" between two culturally different people whose expectations and ultimate goals are the same even though their behaviors may be very different. Even the same individual may change his or her cultural referent group during the course of the interview—from emphasizing gender to age to socioeconomic status to nationality or ethnicity to one or another affiliation. Unless the counselor is skilled enough to understand that each of these changing salient cultures requires a different understanding and interpretation of that person's behavior, the counselor is not likely to be accurate in assessing the person's changing behavior. The same culturally learned behavior may have very different meanings for different people and even for the same person across time and situations.

Another application of the broad definition is a Cultural Grid, described in chapter 6, which provides a framework for integrating same and/or different behaviors with same and/or different expectations. Behavior is not data until and unless the behavior is understood in the context of the person's culturally learned expectations. Similar behaviors may have different meanings, and different behaviors may have the same meaning. It is important to interpret behaviors accurately in terms of the intended expectation. If two people share the same expectation (e.g., for success, accuracy, fairness, or safety), they do not have to display the same behaviors to get along with one another. In this paradigm, *cross-cultural conflict* is defined as an interaction in which two persons have the same expectation (e.g., for trust, respect, success, or sharing), but different behaviors.

Smiling is an ambiguous behavior, for example. It may imply trust and friendliness, or it may not. The smile may be interpreted accurately, or it may not. Outside of its culturally learned context, the smile has no fixed meaning. Two persons may both expect trust and friendliness, even though one is smiling and the other is not. Similar culturally learned expectations based on ethnographic, demographic, status-related, or "affiliation" variables frequently cut across the boundaries of narrowly defined cultural groups. If these similar expectations are undiscovered or disregarded, then differences of behavior are presumed to indicate differences of expectation, which result in conflict. However, if the two culturally different persons understand that they really have the same expectations even though their behaviors may be very different, they may agree to disagree or recognize that they are both approaching the same goal from different directions in complementary ways. The obvious differences in behavior across cultures are typically overemphasized, whereas the more difficult to discover similarities of expectations are typically underemphasized.

Frequently we hear about how multiculturalism or cultural differences present problems to counselors and counseling, usually in the form of quotas or measures of imposed equity. Culture has frequently been seen as a barrier to counseling, rather than as a tool for helping counselors be more accurate and as a means to facilitate good counseling. As long as our understanding of cultures is limited to labels for exotic cultures (narrowly defined), the generic relevance of culture and multicultural counseling is not likely to be appreciated.

However, multiculturalism needs to be understood in a perspective that does not replace or displace traditional theories by invalidating them. Multiculturalism should complement, rather than compete with, traditional theories of counseling. Taking the broad definition of *culture*, it is difficult for a counselor to be accurate and skilled according to any theory without in some way accounting for the ever-changing cultural salience in his or her client's perspective.

5. The Dangers of Ignoring Culture

The tendency to depend on one authority, one theory, and one truth has been demonstrated to be extremely dangerous in the political setting. It is no less dangerous in a counseling context. The encapsulated counselor is trapped in one way of thinking that resists adaptation and rejects alternatives. By contrast, a broader definition leads counselors toward a more comprehensive understanding of alternatives and a more complete perspective of one's own beliefs. The broader inclusive perspective offers liberation to the culturally encapsulated counselor. By ignoring cultural differences, counselors are placed in danger of being inconsistent.

Although counseling has traditionally emphasized the importance of freedom, rational thought, tolerance, equality, and justice, it has also been used as an oppressive instrument by those in power to maintain the status quo (Sue & Sue, 1990). Whenever counseling is used to restrict rather than foster the well-being and development of culturally different persons, counselors are participating in overt or covert forms of prejudice and discrimination. The culturally different client approaches counseling with caution, asking, "What makes you, a counselor/therapist, any different from all the others out there who have oppressed and discriminated against me?" (Sue & Sue, 1990, p. 6).

Ponterotto and Casas (1991) documented the perception that "the majority of traditionally trained counselors operate from a culturally biased and encapsulated framework which results in the provision of culturally conflicting and even oppressive counseling treatments" (pp. 7–8). Counseling training programs are often presumed to be defenders of the status quo, stimulating considerable criticism regarding counseling research by racial and ethnic minority groups. Multiculturalism, the power of cultural bias, and the recognized importance of cultural awareness has been widely recognized for a long time, especially among authors from a minority background such as DuBois (1908).

There is a history of moral exclusion when individuals or groups are perceived as nonentities, expendable, or undeserving (Opotow, 1990). This exclusionary perspective has been described as a form of encapsulation. Wrenn (1962, 1985) first introduced the concept of "cultural encapsulation" for counseling. This perspective assumes five basic identifying features. First, reality is defined according to one set of cultural assumptions and stereotypes, which become more important than the real world. Second, people become insensitive to cultural variations among individuals and assume that their view is the only real or legitimate one. Third, everyone has unreasoned assumptions that they accept without proof and protect without regard to rationality. Fourth, a technique-oriented job definition further contributes toward and preserves the encapsulation. Fifth, when there is no evaluation of other viewpoints, there is no responsibility to accommodate or interpret the behavior of others except from the viewpoint of a self-reference criterion.

Even multicultural counselors have been culturally encapsulated. Ponterotto (1988) summarized many of the criticisms leveled at cross-cultural research on counseling regarding methodology in its disregard for cultural complexity. First, there is no conceptual theoretical framework. Second, there is an overemphasis on simplistic counselor–client process variables, although important psychosocial variables are disregarded. Third, there is overreliance on experimental analogue research outside the "real-world" setting. Fourth, there is disregard for intracultural within-group differences. Fifth, there is overdependence on student samples of convenience. Sixth, there is continued reliance on culturally encapsulated measures. Seventh, there is a failure to adequately describe the sample according to cultural backgrounds. Eighth, there is a failure to describe the limits of *generalizability*. Ninth, there is a lack of minority cultural input. Tenth, there is a failure of responsibility by researchers toward minority subject pools. Many, if not all, of these weaknesses have resulted from a narrow definition of culture and disregard for the broad definition.

Culture can provide stability and explanations of the events around us without resulting in encapsulation. Once we have created a set of culturally learned beliefs or truths, we are able to explain the world around us in relation to these beliefs. Thus, the concept of culture has an important function in all organizations. Schein (1991) described the process of creating an organizational culture. First, a single person (founder) has an idea for a new enterprise. Second, the founder brings in one or more other people and creates a core group that shares a common vision with the founder. That is, they all believe that the idea is (a) a good one; (b) workable; (c) worth running some risks for; and (d) worth the investment of time, money, and energy that will be required. Third, the founding group begins to act in concert to create an organization by raising funds, obtaining patents, incorporating, locating space, and so on. Fourth, others are brought into the organization as partners and employees, and as a common history begins to be built. If the group remains fairly stable and has significant shared learning experiences, it will gradually develop assumptions about itself, its environment, and how to do things to survive and grow.

Defining culture broadly rather than narrowly helps avoid the problems of encapsulation. First, the broad definition allows and forces counselors to be more accurate in matching a client's intended and culturally learned expectation with the client's behavior. Second, a broad definition helps counselors become more aware of how their own culturally learned perspective predisposes them to a particular decision outcome. Third, a broad perspective helps counselors become more aware of the complexity in cultural identity patterns, which may or may not include the obvious indicators of ethnicity and nationality. Fourth, the broad definition encourages counselors to track the ever-changing salience of a client's different, interchangeable cultural identities within a counseling interview.

Whether multiculturalism emerges as a truly generic approach to counseling or whether it emerges as a fourth force with an articulated impact on counseling equivalent to behaviorism, psychodynamics, and humanism, culture does provide a valuable metaphor for understanding ourselves and others. It is no longer possible for good counselors to ignore their own cultures or the cultures of their clients through encapsulation. However, until the multicultural perspective is understood as making the counselor's job easier instead of harder, and increasing rather than decreasing the quality of a counselor's life, little real change is likely to happen.

6. Conclusion

The development of multicultural awareness begins with an awareness of the rules. The rules highlighted in this chapter are: (a) multicultural perspectives emphasize each group's similarities and differences at the same time; (b) multicultural perspectives are necessarily complex; (c) multicultural perspectives are dynamic for each person, place, and time; and (d) multiculturalism is broadly inclusive and not narrow.

The inclusive multicultural perspective of emphasizing both similarities and differences has inhibited research on multicultural aspects of counseling because our measures of culture are inadequate. It is easier to ignore culture or limit the cultural perspective to either similarities or differences. Breaking this first rule of multiculturalism has resulted in false and inadequate/incomplete choices. The controversy over "political correctness" reflects the inadequacy of this false dichotomy where both sides of the argument are wrong. The argument supporting an objectively "correct" view of each culture rightly protects the unique and different perspectives of each cultural group against insult but wrongly presumes that culture is defined by these objective guidelines. The argument against political correctness rightly emphasizes the need to find common ground across cultures but wrongly presumes that cultural differences are unimportant.

The rules of inclusiveness, complexity, and dynamic balance are described as essential to an understanding of culture for multicultural counselors. Examples are provided to show how these constructs are grounded in the research literature about psychological counseling. At the same time, these three constructs suggest a new direction for multicultural counseling that challenges some of the assumptions of traditional counseling theory.

First, a tolerance for logical inconsistency and paradox suggests a subjective definition of knowledge to supplement the more familiar rules of objective, rational logic. Second, the primary importance of relationships and collectivism contrasts with the more familiar bias toward individualism. Third, the implicit or explicit differentiation between modernization and westernization ignores the possibility that other cultures may have good solutions to our problems. Fourth, the implicit assumption that change and progress are good is challenged by clients having to deal with change as *both* good and bad at the same time. Fifth, the metaphor of a natural ecological setting reminds us of the many unknown and perhaps unknowable mysteries of relationship among people and their environment. Sixth, the absolute categories of problem and solution and success and failure are brought into question as inadequate. Seventh, the need to apply familiar counseling concepts to the less familiar multicultural settings is emphasized. Eighth, the need for new conceptual and methodological approaches to deal with the complexities of culture is apparent. Ninth, the need for a grounded theory of multicultural counseling is essential to all counselors and is not an exotic or specialized perspective.

To escape from what Wrenn (1985) called *cultural encapsulation*, counselors need to challenge the cultural bias of their own untested criteria. To leave our assumptions untested or, worse yet, to be unaware of our culturally learned assumptions is not consistent with the standards of good and appropriate counseling.

CHAPTER 2

Developing Multicultural Awareness, Knowledge, and Skill

Major objective:

1. To describe a three-stage developmental progression from awareness to knowledge to skill.

Secondary objectives:

1. To describe the six stages of developing a training design.
2. To describe examples of multicultural awareness training.
3. To describe examples of multicultural knowledge training.
4. To describe examples of multicultural skill training.

Developing multicultural awareness is not an end in itself, but rather a means toward increasing a person's power, energy, and freedom of choice in a multicultural world. Multicultural awareness increases a person's intentional and purposive decision-making ability by accounting for the many ways that culture influences different perceptions of the same solution.

Culture is not external but is "within the person," and it is not separate from other learned competencies. Therefore, developing multicultural awareness is a professional obligation as well as an opportunity for the adequately trained counselor. Millions of people today live and work in a culture other than their own. People who live in another culture are likely to become multicultural in their awareness of alternative values, habits, customs, and life-styles that were initially strange and unfamiliar. Sometimes they have learned to adjust even more profoundly and effectively than they realize. They have learned to respond in unique ways to previously unfamiliar situations and come up with the right answers without always being aware of their own adjustment process.

This handbook is an attempt to review the development of multicultural awareness. Readers should benefit from this awareness in two ways. First, reviewing the influence of their own multicultural identity helps readers already living in another culture to better understand the constant changing of their own viewpoint; second, they are able to anticipate the right questions to ask as they adapt their life-styles to multicultural alternatives. Increased awareness provides more freedom of choice to persons as they become more aware of their own multiculturalism.

1. Three Stages of Multicultural Development

When multicultural training programs fail, they fail in three ways. Some of the programs emphasize "awareness" objectives almost exclusively. As a result, the participants become painfully aware of their own inadequacies or the inadequacies of their environment and the hopelessly overwhelming problems the group faces in bringing about equitable change. Trainees who overdose on awareness are frustrated because they do not know what to do with the awareness they have gained in terms of increasing their knowledge or information and learning appropriate action.

A second way that programs fail is by overemphasizing "knowledge" objectives. Teaching programs that overemphasize knowledge about a culture through lectures, readings, and excessive accumulation of information fail unless the student is already aware of the importance of this knowledge as the basis for developing skills in applying the accumulated knowledge. These programs provide large amounts of information through readings, lectures, and factual data regarding a particular group or topic. The participants are frustrated because they do not see the need for this information, and because they are not sure how to use the information once it has been gathered.

A third way that programs fail is by overemphasizing "skill" objectives. Teaching that overemphasizes skill without providing appropriate awareness and documented knowledge about the culture may be implementing change in the wrong or culturally inappropriate directions. Participants in these programs emerge with the capability of changing other people's lives, but they are never sure whether they are making changes for the better. Without the benefit of awareness and knowledge, misapplied skills may make things worse. Each of the three stages builds on the former toward a comprehensive and balanced perspective that fits both the culture studied and the student's own development.

Multicultural development, as presented in this handbook, is a continuous learning process based on three stages of development. The "awareness" stage emphasizes assumptions about cultural differences and similarities of behavior, attitudes, and values. The "knowledge" stage expands the amount of facts and information about culturally learned assumptions. The "skills" stage applies effective and efficient action with people of different cultures based on the participants' clarified assumptions and accurate knowledge. Multicultural counselors need to be trained in awareness, knowledge, and skill to develop multicultural competency. A five-step training program is described to suggest guidelines for such training (Center for Applied Linguistics, 1982).

2. Needs Assessment

The first step in structuring an orientation or training program is a needs assessment of the group's level of: (a) awareness, (b) knowledge, and (c) skill. Assessing the level of a student's awareness is an important first step. Awareness is the ability to accurately judge a cultural situation from both one's own and the other's cultural viewpoint. The student should be able to describe a situation in a culture so that a member of that culture agrees with the student's perception. Such an awareness would require an individual to have:

- ability to recognize direct and indirect communication styles;
- sensitivity to nonverbal cues;
- awareness of cultural and linguistic differences;
- interest in the culture;
- sensitivity to the myths and stereotypes of the culture;
- concern for the welfare of persons from another culture;
- ability to articulate elements of his or her own culture;
- appreciation of the importance of multicultural teaching;
- awareness of the relationships between cultural groups; and
- accurate criteria for objectively judging "goodness" and "badness" in the other culture.

Assessing a student's level of knowledge becomes important once the student's awareness has been corrected and judged to be adequate. If awareness helps the student to ask the "right questions," then knowledge provides access to the "right answers." The increased knowledge and information should clarify the alternatives and reduce the ambiguity in a student's understanding about a culture. Learning the language of another culture is an effective way to increase one's information. Anticipating preconceptions and stereotypes from another culture's viewpoint requires knowledge about the myths and widely "understood" perceptions from that culture's viewpoint. It is also important to know the right way to get more information about the culture in question so that the teaching/learning resources are appropriate.

In a needs assessment to determine the student's level of knowledge about a culture, the following questions provide guidelines for measuring knowledge awareness:

- Does the student have specific knowledge about the culturally defined group members' diverse historical experiences, adjustment styles, roles of education, socioeconomic backgrounds, preferred values, typical attitudes, honored behaviors, inherited customs, slang, learning styles, and ways of thinking?
- Does the student have information about the resources for teaching and learning available to persons in the other culture?
- Does the student know about his or her own culture in relation to the other culture?
- Does the student have professional expertise in an area valued by persons in the other culture?
- Does the student have information about teaching/learning resources regarding the other culture and know where those resources are available?

A great deal of information is necessary before the student can be expected to know about another culture. Some assessment of the student's level of knowledge prior to training is essential so that the teacher can fill in any gaps with accurate factual information that allows the student to proceed with an accurate and comprehensive understanding of the other culture.

Assessing the level of a student's skill becomes important once the student's informed awareness is supplemented with factual data about the other culture. Skill becomes the most important stage of all and therefore requires a great deal of preparation in teaching about awareness and knowledge. By teaching a skill, the teacher is enabling the student to "do" something that he or she could not do before. It is possible to measure the things a student now can do effectively that he or she could not do before. Skill requires the student to do the right thing at the right time in the right way and provides the final test of whether the teaching has been effective after all.

Skills are difficult to evaluate. Sometimes the suggested solution is not credible to all persons in the other culture. Skill requires the ability to present a solution in the other culture's language and cultural framework. Skill requires the student to test stereotypes against real and present situations, and to modify them accordingly. Skill requires the student to seek agreement on evaluation criteria and to implement change that causes an improvement.

In a needs assessment to determine the student's level of skill development, a teacher might examine several aspects:

- Does the student have appropriate teaching/learning techniques for work in the other culture?

- Does the student have a teaching/learning style that is appropriate in the other culture?
- Does the student have the ability to establish empathic rapport with persons from the other culture?
- Is the student able to receive and accurately analyze feedback from persons of the other culture?
- Does the student have the creative ability to develop new methods for work in the other culture that go beyond what the student has already learned?

3. Objectives

Once the needs of participants for training have been analyzed, the next step is to design appropriate objectives for a training plan. The relative emphasis on awareness, knowledge, or skill depends on the results of the needs assessment. An awareness objective changes the person's attitudes, opinions, and personal perspectives about a topic. The primary need may be to help a group discover its own stereotypical attitudes and opinions. Usually the awareness objectives focus on a person's unstated assumptions about another culture or about themselves in relation to the other culture.

Once clearly stated training objectives are identified, it is useful to look at the awareness, knowledge, and skill aspects of each objective. Therefore, we may look at the matrix where the same objective has an awareness aspect, a knowledge aspect, and a skill aspect. Figure 1 indicates these two ways of viewing training objectives.

The awareness objectives for multicultural training focus on changing the students' attitudes, opinions, and personal perspectives about themselves and the other culture so that these elements are in harmony with one another. Specific objectives for multicultural teaching might be based on several important elements of awareness:

- Is the student aware of differences in cultural institutions and systems?
- Is the student aware of the stress resulting from functioning in a multicultural situation?
- Does the student know how rights or responsibilities are defined differently in different cultures?
- Is the student aware of differences in verbal and nonverbal communication styles?
- Is the student aware of significant differences and similarities of practices across different cultures?

In identifying the training objectives for a particular group, it is useful to proceed from an analysis of their awareness needs to their knowledge or information needs and finally to their skill needs. It is important to identify the needs from the group's viewpoint rather than those of outsiders.

FIGURE 1
Three Components of Multicultural Training Objectives

		Component	
Objective	Awareness	Knowledge	Skill
1			
2			
3			

The knowledge component for developing multicultural objectives focuses on increasing the amount of accurate information available to the student. Having developed a correct and accurate awareness of the other culture, students enrich that awareness by testing attitudes, opinions, and assumptions against the body of factual information they now control. The students' level of awareness is certain to increase in direct proportion to the extent of their knowledge about the other culture. Specific objectives for multicultural teaching might be based on several knowledge perspectives:

- Does the student know about social services and how they are delivered to needy and deserving members of the culture?
- Does the student know about the theory of culture shock and stages of cultural adaptation as they relate to the other culture?
- Does the student know how the other culture interprets its own rules, customs, and laws?
- Does the student know patterns of nonverbal communication and language usage within the other culture?
- Does the student know how differences and similarities are patterned in the other culture and how priorities are set in different critical situations?

The skill objective for developing multicultural objectives focuses on what the students now can do. If any of the previous teaching about awareness and knowledge is missing or inadequate, the students may have difficulty making right decisions in multicultural communication. If awareness has been neglected, they may build their plan on wrong assumptions. If knowledge has been neglected, they may describe the cultural situation inaccurately. If skill has been neglected, they may change a situation in counterproductive directions. Specific objectives for developing multicultural objectives for skills might be based on several important prospectives:

- Is the student able to gain access to social services and resources that satisfy his or her basic needs?
- Is the student able to cope with stress and manage difficulties in the new culture?
- Is the student able to understand consequences of behavior and choose wisely among several options that the other culture presents?
- Is the student able to use the culture's language to react appropriately to others from that culture?
- Is the student able to function comfortably in the new environment without losing his or her own cultural identity in the home culture?

These are a few examples of skill objectives that must be assessed to make sure that the student has been taught to communicate in the other culture. Many additional skills should be developed for each specific situation.

4. Design Techniques

The next step in developing a training program is to design a plan that shows how the identified objectives will be carried out in such a way that the identified needs will be met. There are many different ways to match techniques with awareness, knowledge, or skill objectives. Some examples follow.

Techniques to Stimulate Awareness

- Experiential exercises such as role plays, role reversals, and simulations
- Field trips
- Critical incidents
- Bicultural observation and experiences
- Questions, answers, and discussion
- Case studies and critical incidents

Teaching increased awareness frequently relies on experiential exercises such as role plays, role reversals, or simulations of multicultural interaction. Other approaches include field trips to areas where the culture exists normally on a day-to-day basis. Sometimes critical incidents or brief case studies from the culture can be analyzed to increase a student's awareness of the culture. A resource person or informant from the culture enables effective bicultural observation, whereby both individuals and groups may exchange questions and answers in a thorough discussion. Almost any approach that (a) involves the student's basic assumptions, (b) tests the student's prevailing attitudes, and (c) elicits the student's implicit opinions about the culture serves to increase the student's awareness.

Techniques to Impart Knowledge

- Guided self-study with reading list
- Lecture and discussion
- Panel discussion
- Audiovisual presentations
- Interviews with consultants and experts
- Observations

The increase of multicultural knowledge frequently relies on books, lectures, and classroom techniques. Guided self-study with a reading list also is an effective way to help students increase their knowledge. Panel discussions about the other cultures help students absorb more information relevant to their particular situation. Audiovisual presentations, when available, provide valuable knowledge. Interviews with consultants or resource persons and experts knowledgeable about the other culture help students fill in gaps where accurate information might otherwise be impossible to secure. Simply observing persons from the other culture in their daily activities is an important means for learning about the culture, providing the student knows what to look for in the culture.

Increasing knowledge about multicultural skills takes many forms. Modeling and demonstrating a skill is an effective means to develop students' skills. When available, audiovisual resources provide important feedback to students both about how the skill is performed in the other culture and how they are doing in modeling that skill. Supervising students' work in the other culture provides a valuable ongoing means of assessing developing levels of skill. The opportunity to practice new skills and behaviors enables students to improve their skills in a variety of different situations.

Techniques to Develop Skills

- Modeling and demonstration
- Using video and media resources for feedback
- Supervising
- Practicing a new behavior pattern
- Practicing writing skills

5. Training Approaches

The fourth step in developing a training package is the actual implementation of a training design. After determining the date, time, place, and cost of the training, the trainer needs to draft an agenda, check supplies, and locate physical facilities for training. Trainers need to select resource participants or guest speakers and gather relevant resource materials. Preparation should include assembling packets or workbooks so that all the information conveyed to trainees verbally is also available in writing for later clarification. Finally, the trainer needs to develop evaluations of the workshops.

Most workshops begin in more or less the same way. There is an introduction with some attempt to break the ice. This might include a formal welcome from an official host or an informal welcome by the workshop leader. A discussion of the group's objectives and expectations ensues, as well as sharing of the trainer's objectives and expectations. Then the agenda is reviewed so that all participants know what is likely to happen in sequence; this helps them to review the materials in their workshop packet for any necessary clarification. The better trainees are prepared to work with one another, the more positively they are likely to view the training experience.

Once these general group-building tasks have been completed, the workshop may begin by emphasizing a balance of appropriate objectives focused on awareness and planning data. Each of these three alternative components (awareness, knowledge, and skill) suggest a different training format. Figure 2 presents an example of how each stream would differ in training cultural orientation (CO) providers to work with refugees.

FIGURE 2
Three Alternative Cultural Orientation Training Sequences

I.   Introduction/ice breaker
     A. Formal welcome by official, or
     B. Informal welcome by workshop leader

II. Discussion of group expectations
     A. Group objectives
     B. Leader/trainer objectives

III. Review of agenda

IV. Review of materials or packet

Note: From *Providing Effective Orientation: A Training Guide* (p. 12) by P. Pedersen with staff from Center for Applied Linguistics, Refugee Services, 1982, Washington, DC: Center for Applied Linguistics. Copyright 1982 by the Center for Applied Linguistics. Adapted by permission.

Awareness Focus

OBJECTIVE: In training, you should help the CO providers to become aware of the contrast and conflict between their background and that of the refugees.

    V. Introduction to the experiential exercise *Bafa Bafa*
       A. Processing *Bafa Bafa*
    VI. Reactions to *Bafa Bafa* as a training method and how the group experience relates to meeting the above objective
    VII. Divide into groups of twos or threes to write their own critical incidents relating to their professional and personal interaction with the recipients of CO
    VIII. Presentation and discussion of the critical incidents
    IX. Application of awareness gained during the workshop to professional activities
    X. Evaluation
    XI. Adjournment

Knowledge Focus

OBJECTIVE: In training, you should help the CO provider to have knowledge of the refugee resettlement process including institutions at national, regional, and local levels.

    V. An overview of the refugee resettlement process to be given by the trainer or a knowledgeable resource person
    VI. Panel discussion of the resettlement process. Resource persons might include: local Volag director, local welfare agency, local social service agency contracted by federal or state government, and representation of MAAs
    VII. Question and answer period
    VIII. Panel member representing the local welfare agency presents and distributes a directory of social services in the area
    IX. Application of knowledge gained during the workshop to professional activities
    X. Evaluation
    XI. Adjournment

Skills Focus

OBJECTIVE: In training, you should help the CO provider to be skilled in working with interpreters and cultural informants.

6. Evaluation

The last step of a training sequence is to evaluate whether the persons you trained have met your objectives in awareness, knowledge, and skill. This is called "formative" evaluation. Another kind of evaluation is a long-term and much more complicated evaluation to verify whether your objectives were appropriate and met the long-term needs of your group. This second type of evaluation is called "summative" evaluation.

Evaluation methods range from informal discussions over wine and cheese to formal written evaluations of long-term changes in productivity determined by random work samples. However you proceed, you should allow room for evaluation in your training activities. These data are valuable to your trainees in giving them feedback on their accomplishment, valuable to you in demonstrating the strength or weakness of your design, and valuable to those sponsoring the training activity as a basis for making decisions. Some criteria for evaluating follow.

Students are trained to increase their *awareness* so they:

- appropriately recognize the valued priority they give to basic attitudes, opinions, and assumptions;
- accurately compare their own cultural perspective with that of a person from the other culture;
- sensitively articulate their own professional role in relation to the other culture;
- appropriately estimate constraints of time, setting, and resources in the other culture; and
- realistically estimate the limit of their own resources in the other culture.

Students are trained to increase their *knowledge* so they:

- understand the process of institutional change in the other culture at local, national, and regional levels;
- cite the relevant literature of the other culture;
- identify similarities and differences of their own home culture and the other culture;
- identify referral resources in the other culture; and
- select key resource persons from the other culture for more information.

Students are trained to increase their *skill* so they:

- efficiently plan, conduct, and evaluate training about the other culture;
- accurately assess the needs of persons from the other culture;
- utilize the talents of interpreters and cultural informants from the other culture;
- observe, understand, and accurately report about culturally learned behaviors in the other culture; and
- interact, advise, and appropriately manage their assigned task in the setting of the other culture.

Multicultural development is presumed to proceed from an awareness of attitudes, opinions, and assumptions to a knowledge of facts and information to skill in taking the appropriate action. However, most persons being trained are at different stages of development. Some trainees require more emphasis on awareness, some on knowledge, and others can proceed directly to skill development.

7. Examples of Multicultural Awareness Training

Training is an attempt to increase a person's alternatives for being accurately understood in a wide variety of cultures. Multicultural training of counselors must be responsive to the variety of cultures within the client and the counselor as well. The benefits of multicultural training are measured by their relevance to real-life situations. The more culturally defined alternatives or strategies a counselor possesses, the more likely it is that the counselor will identify the right choice in culturally different settings (Pedersen & Ivey, in press). A variety of multicultural training approaches have been used to prepare counselors to work in other cultures. These various approaches can be classified according to their emphasis on awareness, knowledge, or skill as the primary focus. An examination of examples for training help clarify the specific emphasis at each developmental level.

Awareness requires the ability to accurately see a situation from your own and the other person's perspective. Several multicultural counselor training approaches emphasize awareness through experiential learning, cultural awareness, and specific cultural values clarification.

Through experiential learning, participants "experience" the effect of cultural similarities and differences through their own involvement with others. The assumption is that increased involvement in the life-style of culturally different people through field trips and direct or simulated contact will increase the trainee's accuracy of judgments, attitudes, and assumptions about other cultures. A counselor educator facilitates this involvement by providing a "safe" setting in which the trainee can take risks. Having a significant intercultural experience through immersion, field trips, or role playing is not enough, however. The trainee needs to analyze the effect of that experience to "capture" the resulting insights for future reference.

Cultural immersion requires the trainee to live and work in another culture and learn by experience alongside culturally different persons. Any contact with culturally different persons or groups can provide the opportunity for learning through immersion. Some counselors have become highly skilled without any formal training by learning through their own mistakes and triumphs. Unguided immersion is an effective training approach, although learning from experience without any preparation tends to be expensive in time, money, and emotional stress for the client as well as the counselor.

Field trips provide trainees with a less traumatic example of experiential training through brief visits to other cultures on their home turf. Many aspects of a host culture can be learned by observation but cannot be "taught" through abstract principles. Trainees visiting a host culture can become participant observers in that host culture in their own home context. By observing host culture people cope with problems and make decisions, the trainees are able to recognize culturally distinctive patterns of activity. To be effective, field trips require skilled debriefing to help the trainees articulate what was learned. There are two types of field trips possible. The first type is organized around a specific agenda. These field trips need to be organized around a specific focus to illustrate or challenge specific attitudes, opinions, and assumptions from one or both cultures. The second type is to deliberately avoid any agenda or expectation before the experience, and to let the insights grow out of the interaction itself.

Role playing is another frequently used experiential training approach in which an individual learns about other cultures by taking on the role of a person from that culture. The experience of becoming someone from the other culture—to the extent that this is possible—often changes a participant's level of awareness. This approach usually relies on articulate and authentic resource persons from the host culture to guide the trainee. It is easy to find resource persons who are authentic but not articulate, or articulate but not authentic. It is more difficult to find resource persons who are both articulate and authentic. When asked how they manage to do such a good job, skilled but untrained resource persons frequently respond, "I can't tell you or teach you how to do it but I can demonstrate for you what I would do if you give me a problem situation." In any case, the trainer must provide careful structures to guide the learning through role playing, both to provide a safe context in which the role player might take risks and to generate insights about the other culture.

Experiential approaches to awareness training are expensive and require highly skilled trainers as well as cooperative host culture resource persons. Experiential training works when participants feel safe enough to take risks. If the experience becomes unsafe, trainees experience high levels of stress that might be counterproductive to training and potentially dangerous to the participants. Sometimes the awareness is focused on several insights, and at other times it is focused on a specific culture.

Culture-general approaches help people articulate their own implicit cultural attitudes, opinions, and assumptions about themselves. Self-awareness emphasizes the values of a person's home culture as contrasted with the values of many other cultures. The emphasis is usually on areas of general similarity and difference. People's own cultural values are frequently so familiar that they are not explicitly aware of them. For example, in some cultures the importance of individualism is not seen as "cultural," but simply "the way things naturally are." Brislin, Cushner, Cherrie, and Yong (1986) described 18 culture-general themes for training illustrating culture-general experiences (1–5), knowledge areas (6–13), and ways to organize information (14–18). These themes include: (1) anxiety, (2) disconfirmed expectancies, (3) belonging, (4) ambiguity, (5) confrontation with one's prejudices, (6) work, (7) time and space, (8) language, (9) roles, (10) importance of the group and importance of the individual, (11) rituals and superstitions, (12) hierarchies of class and status, (13) values, (14) categorization, (15) differentiation, (16) in-group–out-group distinction, (17) learning style, and (18) attribution.

Culture-specific approaches require training in the specific values of a particular target culture. Culture-specific training is usually limited in focus to the particular target group and has a very specific focus. For example, learning the language of a host culture is an important culture-specific way to learn about the attitudes, opinions, and assumptions in that particular culture. Other examples include the behaviors, expectations, and values of that particular culture. Most professional counseling associations have indicated that counselors who work with specific other cultures without culture-specific awareness about that culture are behaving in an unethical manner.

A variety of other awareness training approaches focus on the trainee's self-awareness and awareness of the trainee's home culture. This awareness emphasizes both similarities and differences by contrasting the home culture with one or more other cultures. The emphasis of awareness training is always on re-evaluating the trainee's attitudes, opinions, and assumptions about his or her own culture and other cultures.

8. Examples of Multicultural Knowledge Training

Increasing the counselor's knowledge about other cultures is another popular focus for multicultural training. Knowledge training means having correct and sufficient information about one's own culture as well as target cultures. The most frequently used knowledge training approaches are through publications and reading materials, as well as audio and visual media presenting the other cultures to the trainee in terms of facts and information.

Classroom training emphasizes lectures, group discussions, written materials, and media presentations to help trainees increase their information about other cultures. Trainees are provided with factual information about the host culture to understand their own role as outsiders. These facts might relate to: (a) socioeconomic, political, or social structures; (b) the climate and physical setting; (c) the decision-making styles and habits; or (d) the values underlying daily behavior. Classroom training provides models and structures for organizing, classifying, and analyzing other cultures.

The facts are most useful if trainees are highly motivated to learn the new information and see an immediate relevancy of these facts for their own situation. It is essential that the factual data be based on an awareness of why the data are important to trainees. Unless the trainees have adequate awareness, trainees are unmotivated to learn information about the other cultures. Trainees who have achieved awareness of the target culture in relation to themselves are prepared to document that awareness in the facts and information describing similarities and differences. With appropriate preparation, trainees can become highly motivated to increase their knowledge through fact- and information-oriented training.

Attribution training is a second form of knowledge-based training that has proved to be successful. Attribution training methods guide the trainee to explain behavior from the host culture's viewpoint, rather than from their own self-reference criterion. Presented with a critical incident or paragraph-length description of an event, the trainee chooses between several alternative explanations "attributed" to the incident. One of the attributed explanations offered to the trainee is more accurate than the others for specific reasons. Trainees are coached to select the most accurate and appropriate attribution through practice in analyzing a series of critical incidents. This method assumes that train-ees learn a culture's implicit patterns of decision making through attribution training, where they can generalize from the critical incidents to unfamiliar cultures and situations. Brislin et al. (1986) provided 100 critical incidents using attribution training methods in a culture-general approach.

The best known application of attribution training is the "culture assimila-tor" developed by Triandis and others. Many different culture assimilators have been designed for specific cultures and social groups, resulting in a great deal of research and evaluation data (Triandis, 1975). Leong and Kim (1991) de-scribed an intercultural sensitizer for counselors based on the cultural assimi-lator model. There is probably more data on the culture assimilator than any other cross-cultural training approach. Culture assimilators provide a structured series of incidents and alternative responses in a specific cultural context with a series of explanations or attributions. One of the alternative attributions is more accurate and appropriate than the others. Each alternative is matched with explanations to explain the rightness, wrongness, and consequences of each choice. To the extent that culturally accurate and appropriate attributions can be determined for each situation, the culture-specific culture assimilator has been extremely successful.

In addition to the formal knowledge-training approaches, there is also an informal alternative where the individual, who has achieved a high level of awareness, looks for his or her own answers. One sign of having achieved awareness is increased sensitivity to the implicit culture learning in all reported facts and information. People are accumulating cultural facts and information whether they are aware or not as they are socialized by the media and sources of facts or information. Self-guided training provides purpose to the accumulation of facts and information through reading, observation, and reflective experiences. These facts may be accumulated about a specific other culture, one's self, or cultures that generally contrast with one's own understanding. A purposive program for self-guided learning about other cultures can be an inexpensive and effective approach. If "awareness" training articulates the questions we should be ask-ing, then "knowledge" training guides us toward comprehensive answers to those questions.

9. Examples of Multicultural Skill Training

Multicultural skill goes beyond "knowing" what needs to be done toward being able to actually do it. Skill training provides the multicultural counselor with the strategies to match the right method to the right situation in the right way at the right time. Because multicultural skills are based on awareness and knowledge, they require cognitive comprehension and affective sensitivity, as well as behavioral facility to interact with the client's complex and dynamic cultural context. There are many different examples of these more comprehensive and "general" multicultural skill-training approaches.

Cognitive or behavioral modification training depends on identifying rewards or goals in the client's cultural context from the client's viewpoint. Once you find out what the client wants, it is easier to teach the client acceptable ways to get it. When the client moves to an unfamiliar culture, the strategies that used to work might not work as well, and new or unfamiliar ways of thinking or acting need to be learned to reach the more familiar goal of respect, friendship, trust, or success. If the new ways of thinking and acting can be matched with the client's agenda, and can be shown to work better than the old ways, the client can be persuaded to try them. For this training to work, the counselor needs to know the client's agenda, the problems and opportunities in the client's cultural context, and the ways of thinking or acting that would be appropriate and effective.

Training approaches that are focused on affective or "feeling" goals also depend on structured interaction between the client, the culture, and the method. This training can occur in either a real-life or simulated setting where skills can be practiced and rehearsed with feedback. In the safety of a simulated encounter, the client can learn to deal with risky or dangerous feelings but avoid the consequences of hurting people. As the client becomes more skilled in dealing with dangerous feelings in the new cultural context, he or she becomes more confident to try out skills in real-world settings.

Microskills training has also proved effective in multicultural settings (Ivey, 1988; Pedersen & Ivey, in press). By dividing the more general skill areas into smaller "micro" units, the client learns step by step how to increase his or her skill. These skills build on "attending behaviors" through "influencing skills" toward "integrative skills." The client–trainee "builds" or "constructs" a hierarchy of skills toward the ultimate goal of becoming a skilled counselor. As the microskills become progressively more difficult and complicated, the client builds on basic foundation skills toward more advanced skills. There is more empirical research data supporting the effectiveness of microskills training than any other skill-building method in the literature.

Structured learning is another social behavioral method used in building multicultural skills (Goldstein, 1981). This method focuses on practical skills and abilities to do a necessary function or achieve a valued goal in the client's cultural context. Structured learning proceeds through a sequence of steps. First, the skill is presented and discussed. Second, the skill is demonstrated with an opportunity for clarification. Third, the skill is rehearsed and practiced in role playing with feedback. Fourth, the skill is transferred to the real-world setting.

Culture-general skill training assumes a foundation of international or multicultural attitudes, opinions, and assumptions that apply to different cultures. The previously mentioned and other popular methods of counselor training can be applied to the multicultural setting, provided they are based on appropriate multicultural awareness and accurate multicultural knowledge. These culture-general methods document the ways in which different groups share some of the same values and expectations, even though they display very different behaviors.

Culture-specific skill training also provides strategies that target a specific group, problem, identity, or role. Large amounts of specific factual knowledge and information help document the ways in which each group's behavior is different and distinct, even though they share some of the same values and expectations. There are many examples in the literature of culture-specific skill training for groups defined by nationality, ethnicity, religion, language, age, gender, region, socioeconomic status, educational background, and an almost unlimited number of other formal or informal affiliations. The culture-specific focus may be on the group's identity, a specific problem, or any other carefully defined context. Culture-general and culture-specific skill-training approaches complement one another. In any multicultural setting, there are both cultural similarities and cultural differences on which to focus.

10. The Developmental Sequence

The three-stage developmental sequence described in this chapter and demonstrated in this book provides a convenient structure to organize the necessary elements of multicultural training. The three stages were originally designed by staff (Paul Pedersen, Anthony Marsella, and Derald Wing Sue) of a National Institute of Mental Health training project at the University of Hawaii from 1978 to 1981 entitled "Developing Interculturally Skilled Counselors" (DISC; Pedersen, 1981b). This three-step approach is best known through the definition of *multicultural counseling competencies* (Sue, Bernier, Durran, Feinberg, Pedersen, Smith, & Vasquez-Nuttall, 1982), which is discussed later in this book.

Awareness provides the basis for accurate opinions, attitudes, and assumptions. It is essential to first become aware of implicit priorities given to selected attitudes, opinions, and values. Awareness presumes an ability to (a) accurately compare and contrast alternative viewpoints, (b) relate or translate priorities in a variety of cultural settings, (c) identify constraints and opportunities in each cultural context, and (d) clearly understand one's own limitations. A well-defined awareness becomes essential for teaching, research, training, direct service, and consultation. If the awareness stage is overlooked in multicultural training, the knowledge and skills—however accurate and effective—may be based on false assumptions. However, if training does not go beyond awareness objectives, the clients may be frustrated by seeing the problems but not being able to change things.

Knowledge provides the documentation and factual information necessary to move beyond awareness toward effective and appropriate change in multicultural settings. Through accumulated facts and information based on appropriate assumptions, it is possible to understand or comprehend other cultures from their own viewpoint. The facts and information about other cultures is available in the people, the literature, and the products of each culture at the local, national, and regional levels. The second stage of gaining knowledge helps people access those facts and that information, directs people to where the knowledge can be found, and identifies reliable sources of information to better understand the unfamiliar culture. If the knowledge stage is overlooked in training, the cultural awareness and skill—however appropriate and effective—may lack grounding in essential facts and information about the multicultural context, and the resulting changes may be inappropriate. However, if training does not go beyond the collection of facts and information about other cultures, the clients may be overwhelmed by abstractions that may be true but are impossible to apply in practice.

Skill provides the ability to build on awareness and apply knowledge toward effective change in multicultural settings. Trained people become skilled in planning, conducting, and evaluating the multicultural contexts in which they work. They assess needs of other cultures accurately. They work with interpreters and cultural informants from the other culture. They observe and understand behaviors of culturally different people. They interact, counsel, interview, advise, and manage their tasks effectively in multicultural settings.

11. Conclusion

Just as culture is complex but not chaotic, so should multicultural training be guided by learning objectives that reflect the needs of both the student and the multicultural context. Teaching multicultural counseling and communication needs to include any and all methods relevant to the multicultural context from that culture's viewpoint. Training designs need to be comprehensive enough to include both culture-general and culture-specific perspectives. The developmental sequence from awareness to knowledge to skill provides an eclectic framework for organizing the content of multicultural training and a rationale for educational development in multicultural settings.

CHAPTER 3

Culturally Biased Assumptions and the Alternatives

Major objective:

1. To demonstrate cultural biases in counseling and what can be done to change them.

Secondary objectives:

1. To identify 10 examples of frequently encountered cultural biases in counseling.
2. To identify non-Western alternative perspectives/assumptions about counseling.
3. To describe the construct of individualism and its consequences.
4. To examine unintentional racism.

It is high time that we recognize cultural biases in our conventional thinking as having little to do with "Eastern" or "Western" geography and a great deal to do with social, economic, and political perceptions of power. There are perhaps as many Western thinkers in Eastern parts of the world as there are Eastern thinkers in the Western hemisphere. In strictly numerical terms, it is increasingly true that the Western viewpoint is the more "exotic," although until recently it has been the more powerful. Despite that numerical advantage, social scientists—including psychologists—depend on textbooks, research findings, and implicit psychological theory based almost entirely on Euro-American, culture-specific assumptions. These assumptions are usually so implicit and taken for granted that they are not challenged even by fair-thinking, right-minded colleagues. The consequences of these unexamined assumptions are institutionalized racism, ageism, sexism, and other examples of cultural bias.

1. Culturally Biased Assumptions

This chapter attempts to identify the most frequently encountered examples of cultural bias that keep coming up in the literature on multicultural counseling and development. The examination of culturally learned assumptions must become a more important part of the curriculum in the development of counseling for a multicultural world if we wish to emphasize accuracy in our assessments and appropriateness in our applications.

The first such assumption is that we all share the same single measure of "normal" behavior. There is a frequent assumption that describing a person's behavior as normal reflects a judgment both meaningful and representative of a particular pattern of behaviors. There is an implicit assumption that the definition of normal is more or less universal across social, cultural, economic, and political backgrounds.

Behaviors labeled *normal* change according to the situation, the cultural background of the person or persons judged, and the time period during which a behavior is displayed or observed. Many psychological research projects disregard multicultural backgrounds that have influenced the definition of *normality*. Our own complex but not chaotic patterns describe our own personal cultural orientation in ways that make normal fluid rather than fixed.

A second assumption is that individuals are the basic building blocks of all societies. The presumption is that counseling is primarily directed toward the development of individuals rather than units of individuals or groups, such as the family, the organization, or society. If we examine the jargon used in counseling, our preference for the welfare of individuals becomes quickly evident. The criteria of self-awareness, self-fulfillment, and self-discovery are important measures of success in most counseling. The constructs of person in personality, individuality in measuring achievement and aptitude, and separation from the group in developing abilities all presume that a counselor's task is to change the individual in a positive direction, even, perhaps, at the expense of the group in which that individual has a role. In some cultures, the welfare of an individual counselor or client is frustrated by the conflicting agenda of a group in which the counselor or client is a member or where collectivism is more important than individualism.

While teaching English as a second language in Indonesia, I was asked why English speakers always capitalize the first person singular ("I") in writing English. I confessed that, because I was no expert in English as a Second Language (ESL), I really had no idea why the letter "I" was capitalized when referring to the first person singular. The students smiled at me and said knowingly that they already knew why. They assumed it was because English speakers are so thoroughly individualistic that the capitalization of first person singular comes naturally.

In Chinese culture, it would be normal and natural to put the welfare of the family before the welfare of any individual member of that family. To speak of an individual's health and welfare independently of the health and welfare of the family unit would not make sense in that context. Individual counseling has even been described as destructive of collectivistic societies in promoting the individualistic benefits of individuals at the expense of the social fabric. It is important for counselors to work comfortably and skillfully in both these cultures where the primary emphasis is on the welfare of the individual and in those cultures that emphasize the value of the unit.

A third assumption is that only the problems defined within a framework of the counselor's expertise or academic discipline boundaries are of concern to the counselor. There is a tendency to separate the identity of counselor from that of psychologist, sociologist, anthropologist, theologian, or medical doctor. Unfortunately, the multicultural problems a client faces are not inhibited by any of our artificial boundaries. The research literature in our various disciplines frequently overlaps. Questions in one discipline or field can be matched to answers suggested by a complementary discipline or field. Wrenn (1962, 1985) warned of cultural encapsulation, owing to the substitution of symbiotic stereotypes for the real world that disregards cultural variations among clients and dogmatizes a narrowly defined technique-oriented job definition of the counseling process.

For example, in many cultures the important questions related to mental health relate to questions of life (or before life) and death (or after death). If the client believes in reincarnation, then which person are we considering? The persons they were, are, or will become may each be a legitimate focus of a conversation if, indeed, it is possible to separate these identities at all. Once again, it is important for counselors to become skilled in going beyond the boundaries of their own "self-reference criteria" to examine the problem or issue from multiple culturally different perspectives. Kleinman (1978, 1980) described how frequently a medical doctor may take the limited "disease" perspective in dealing with a patient as a "malfunctioning unit," whereas the patient is more likely to take the broadly defined "illness" perspective where a particular problem has a systems-wide impact on the patient's family, friends, and total surrounding context. The self-imposed boundaries we place on our counseling roles are culturally learned and must be widened as we move from one culture to another.

A fourth assumption, in our use of professional jargon, is that others understand our abstractions in the same way as we intend. Concepts such as "good" or "bad" have little meaning for high-context cultures without putting the concept in a contextual setting. Because the more powerful and dominant cultures in our century have tended to be a low-context culture, there is a tendency to use abstract concepts such as "fairness" or "humane," which, outside of a particular context, are difficult to understand. Although low-context abstractions are useful shortcuts in conveying an idea, they may foster misunderstandings and inaccuracies in high-context cultures (Hall, 1966).

A fifth assumption is that independence is desirable and dependence is undesirable. As part of our emphasis on individualism, there is a belief that individuals should not be dependent on others, nor should individuals allow others to be dependent on them. If a counselor encounters "excessive" dependence in a counselee, he or she is likely to see the elimination of that dependence as a desirable outcome of counseling. Yet there are many cultures where dependence is described as not only healthy but absolutely necessary. One example would be the Japanese concept of "*amae*." Doi (1974) described the Japanese concept of *amae* as technically referring to the relationship between a mother and her eldest son. While the son is young and dependent, he is prepared for the time when his mother will be old and dependent. Significantly, this concept of *amae* is widely used as the criterion for evaluating relationships between employer and employee, teacher and student, or many other relationships in society where dependence is considered a healthy and normal aspect of relationships. The counselor needs to consider a client's cultural perspective in determining the extent to which dependence might or might not be excessive. Because most counselors have been trained in a cultural context where dependence is devalued, it is even more important to consider the function that dependence might have in the client's cultural context.

A sixth assumption is that clients are helped more by formal counseling than by their natural support systems. Counselors need to endorse the potential effectiveness of family and peer support to a client. What happens more frequently is that counselors erode the natural support systems by substituting the "purchase of friendship" through professional counseling services in formal contexts. In many cultures, the noting of formal counseling is less preferred than nonformal or informal alternatives available to a client. The idea of telling intimate family secrets to a stranger is not allowed in many, if not most, of the world's cultures. These problems are dealt with inside the family or group context with little or no outside involvement. Part of you is with every other person you have supported or influenced and you, in turn, are surrounded by every person whose ideas have supported or been significant for you.

Wherever possible, the natural support systems surrounding a client should be mobilized as a valuable ally rather than as an assumed rival for the client's attention. If a client has to choose between the support systems and a counselor, there is a strong likelihood that the client will choose the support systems. Those natural support systems can be identified and mobilized in a multicultural counseling context. The health of the individual is tied in many ways to the health of the support units surrounding that individual. The counselor needs to include consideration of a client's natural support systems in an effective treatment plan for counseling.

A seventh assumption is that everyone depends on linear thinking to understand the world around them, where each cause has an effect and each effect is tied to a cause. This sort of linear thinking is most evident in the field of measurement. The use of measures for describing the goodness, badness, appropriateness, or inappropriateness of a construct are a necessity for good counseling. Tests in counseling require these measures, and any evaluation of counseling tends to be stated in measured degrees. How then can we adapt counseling to a cultural context where the cause and the effect are seen as two aspects of the same undifferentiated reality (as in Yin and Yang) with neither cause nor effect being separate from the other? Does light cause darkness? Does darkness cause light? Both are connected in a balance of complementarity, but neither causes the other.

Counseling has frequently erred in assuming that if a test, book, or concept is accurately translated in terms of its content, the translated tool will be effective and appropriate for most cultures. Not all person from all cultures are socialized to think in the same way. Consequently, it is important to change not only the content of counseling messages, but also the way of thinking underlying those messages. Although we spend a lot of time making sure that the content of our message is culturally appropriate, we spend less time adapting our implicit way of thinking behind the translated message.

The eighth assumption is that counselors need to change individuals to fit the system and not the system to fit the individual. Counselors spend a lot of energy on the importance of "adjustment," which assumes an absolute model to which we should adjust. We need to recognize when counseling should change the system to fit the individual in a more advocative mode, rather than always try to change the individual to protect the system. In many minority groups, counseling as a source of help has a bad reputation for taking the side of the status quo in forcing individuals to adjust or adapt to the institutions of society, even when we know that the client is right and the system is wrong.

It is important for counselors to differentiate between the best interests of the client and those of the surrounding social institutions. Frequently the counselor assumes that it is much more difficult to change the social institutions than to help the individual adapt to conditions "as they are," however unfair they may be. Counselors who do not at least ask the question about whether the best interests of the client are being served by existing social institutions—and whether those institutions can be changed at least in small ways—are failing in their professional obligation.

A ninth assumption is that history is not relevant for a proper understanding of contemporary events. Counselors are more likely to focus on the immediate events that created a crisis. If clients begin talking about their own history or the history of their "people," the counselor is likely to "turn off" and wait for the client to "catch up" to current events, which are held to have greater salience than past history. The client's perspective might require historical background knowledge that a client feels is relevant to the complete description of the client's problem from the client's point of view. In many cultures, a clear understanding of the historical context is necessary to understand the client's present behavior.

Counseling is a young profession in comparison with other professions in the world. Counselors usually lack a historical awareness of the ways in which people solved their psychological problems in the last thousands of years. Counselors frequently lack the patience for discovering a historical perspective in which the current situation may be transitional. Counselors sometimes are perceived to lack a respect for traditional, time-tested ways in which a particular culture has dealt with personal problems in preference for the latest trend or fad in counseling.

The tenth and last assumption is that we already know all of our culturally learned assumptions. In an era of diminishing resources, we need to recognize the dangers of a closed, biased, and culturally encapsulated system that promotes domination by an elitist group representing a special point of view. If we are unwilling or unable to challenge our assumptions, we are less likely to communicate effectively with persons from other cultures. Multicultural counseling is an attempt to integrate and coordinate our assumptions with contrasting assumptions of other persons from different cultures. In this way, culture complicates our lives as counselors, but it brings us closer to our client's culturally defined reality.

All counseling is, to a greater or lesser extent, multicultural. As we increase our contact with other countries and other cultures, we can expect to learn a great deal about ourselves. We can expect to challenge more of our unexamined assumptions about ourselves and the world about us. We can expect to move beyond the parochial concerns of our culturally limited perspective to look at the world around us in a new, more comprehensive perspective. The primary argument for multicultural awareness in counseling has less to do with the ethical imperative of how we should relate to others and more to do with the accuracy and effectiveness of counseling as an international professional activity.

2. A Test of Reasonable Opposites

We are moving toward a culture of the future that promises to be so different from our present lives that we hardly can imagine what it will be like. Furthermore, those who cannot adapt to that future culture will not survive. We are left with the alternative of learning adaptive skills through contact with cultures whose assumptions are different from our own. The means for learning those adaptive skills are through contact with different cultures, developing new ways of thinking, and challenging our unexamined assumptions.

Rothenberg's (1983) creativity research on the "janusian process" of cognition involved actively conceiving two or more opposites or antitheses at the same time. The Greek god Janus had two faces—one smiling and the other crying. In the janusian process, ideas or images are clarified and defined by opposite or antithetical concepts coexisting simultaneously. Janusian thinking is not illogical but a conscious and adaptive cognitive process. Carl Jung emphasized the reconciliation of opposites in self much in the same mode as Asian followers of Zen or the Tao tried to capture truth in a dialectical process. In science, the janusian process has been documented as important to the creative achievements of Einstein, Bohr, Watson, Darwin, Pasteur, and Fermi (Rothenberg, 1983). For example, Albert Einstein described as his "happiest thought," and "the key idea leading to his general theory of relativity," that a man falling from the roof of a house is both in motion and at rest simultaneously (Rothenberg, 1979).

Most of our educational emphasis is spent examining the rational and reasonable process of a single culturally learned viewpoint. I suggest we reexamine the starting point assumptions that determine the trajectory of those viewpoints. Many viewpoints, however similar, disagree because they have different starting points that lead them toward divergent assumptions. Looking at reasonable opposites will enlarge our repertoire of adaptive skills. A "test of reasonable opposites" provides a means to test those basic assumptions that frequently escape examination in our educational system.

The application of this test begins by identifying a basic but unexamined truth, such as the 10 assumptions discussed earlier, and the assumption(s) behind those truth statements. Second, it asks what the alternative policy positions are that would reverse those assumptions and provide a policy based on opposite or contrary assumptions. Finally, it compares the two statements and their assumptions to determine which alternative is more reasonable. In a surprisingly large number of instances, the opposite assumption seems at least as reasonable as, and sometimes even more so than, the original assumption. In applying the test of reasonable opposites, I have found: (a) that my thinking is usually so ambiguous that it is difficult to identify the opposite of what I say is true; (b) that once an opposite truth statement has been generated, it is often as reasonable as what I originally accepted; and (c) that the generation of reasonable opposites results in new and creative alternatives that otherwise might not have been discovered. Some examples of opposites might be: (a) Differences are important versus similarities are important; (b) counseling decreases pain versus counseling increases pain; and (c) you are right versus you are wrong.

The reasonable opposite provides a stimulating alternative to unexamined assumptions. There is an urgency for us to distinguish between multicultural disagreements (e.g., where the assumptions are different) and interpersonal conflict (e.g., where the assumptions are similar). By challenging our assumptions, we can develop adaptive skills for working with a wider range of different perspectives, and we can learn more about our own environment from other viewpoints. In the course of our social and professional evolution, these adaptive skills are likely to be very important. As an example, let us consider the assumption that a more complete "understanding" between two individuals will contribute to their communication, whereas "misunderstanding" is likely to damage the relationship. The reasonable opposite would be that a more complete understanding will be damaging, whereas misunderstanding might contribute to a more healthy relationship.

Pearce (1983) contended that a complete understanding is not only irrelevant and unexciting in a relationship, but may even be dangerous. The alternative is a kind of creative ambiguity that can deepen friendships, save marriages, improve businesses, and prevent wars. The theory of "coordinated management of meaning" (CMM) has 35 supporting studies to its credit. CMM boils down to this: How a listener interprets a speaker's remarks and acts on the interpretation is more important than whether the two understand each other. In short, good things *can* happen when there is misunderstanding among people, businesses, or nations. Pearce favored interpretation over understanding. People are getting along well despite and sometimes because of misunderstandings. If nations really understood one another accurately, there might be more war and turmoil than there is now. Relationships can sometimes thrive on misunderstandings. More understanding will not necessarily result in more harmony.

3. The Contrasting Assumptions of Non-Western Psychologies

Benesch and Ponterotto (1989) suggested that Asian clients rely more on intuition than reason in their world views. The "Eastern consciousness disciplines" assume that (a) ordinary consciousness is not the optimal state, (b) higher states of "multiple consciousness" exist, (c) people can attain higher states of consciousness through training, and (d) verbal communication about the higher states of consciousness is necessarily limited.

The separation of Asian and Western cultures sometimes obscures more than it illuminates (Nakamura, 1964). The common features of one hemisphere are either partly or imperfectly understood in the other hemisphere, or were conspicuous in a particular country at a particular time and then generalized to include the whole hemisphere. The assumptions underlying Asian psychological thinking relate to basic collective or corporate philosophical assumptions of the self in a context of human existence. In Asia there is less emphasis on individualism and more on a corporate identity, which balances aspects of the self. Likewise, there is a more positive interpretation of dependence and interdependencies within the unit, the family, and society. The family plays a particularly significant role as a model for defining the balance of roles for institutional social relationships of society. Many Asian cultures define the personality in relational terms, focusing on the relationship connections between individuals rather than the individuals themselves. The emphasis in these Asian systems is mainly on the structure of family, clan, class, and state through, which individuals relate to one another. However, Asian thinking is by no means unimodal.

Psychological explanation is not a Western invention. Ancient India developed a variety of personality theories, originally based on the gunas or attributes of the mind, dating back to Vedic literature of about 800–500 B.C. Each succeeding religion-philosophical system in India modified views of personality in its own way, generally emphasizing practical aspects of organizing, classifying, and understanding persons in relation to the family, society, and abstract values.

The development of psychological concepts in India went through a period that emphasized magic, in which people tried to understand nature, and a period that emphasized human concerns, as in Buddhism, in which inner harmony and psychic consciousness became the key to freedom. Awareness of suffering is a constant theme of Indian psychology, whereby the wise person escapes enslavement to selfishness by realizing the true nature of the universe.

Buddhism emphasizes the four noble truths and the eightfold path. The four noble truths are: (a) all life is subject to suffering, (b) desire to live is the cause of repeated existences, (c) the annihilation of desire gives release from suffering, and (d) the way of escape is through the eightfold path. The eightfold path is: (a) right belief, (b) right thought, (c) right speech, (d) right action, (e) right livelihood, (f) right effort, (g) right mindfulness, and (h) right concentration to escape from desire. These ideas spread throughout Asia to influence the understanding of personality in a variety of settings.

When Buddhism was imported to China around the first century B.C., it was modified to emphasize the social responsibility of Buddha's ethical teaching. The Chinese have been fairly characterized as valuing common sense and utilitarian ways of thinking. Even their philosophical teachings were based on practical subjects and included everyday examples of morality, politics, and a life-style that would result in successful living.

The indigenous Chinese view of personality developed from the teaching of Confucius (551–479 B.C.), emphasizing aspects of "characterological theory."

The basic aspects of this view emphasize the notions of face, filial piety, and proper conduct. The notion of face brings out an individual's felt moral worth, assessed according to his or her loyalty to his or her group rather than according to universal principles, with social deviance controlled more by public shaming than private guilt. Filial piety describes a compliant and submissive posture toward authority. Proper conduct (Li) defines the duty of persons and the necessity of observing proper forms of conduct for each social situation. The task of Chinese philosophy is to describe the "way" (Tao) to perfection of the personality along practical lines, synthesizing Confucian this-worldliness and Taoist other-worldliness to achieve sageness within and kingliness without.

Hsu (1985) described the concept of being a person (*jen*) in Chinese culture as involving a dynamic balance he called "psychosocial homeostasis." For every living human, being *jen* (personhood) is not a fixed entity. Like the human body, it is in a state of dynamic equilibrium. It is a matrix or a framework within which every human individual seeks to maintain a satisfactory level of psychic and interpersonal equilibrium, in the same sense that every physical organism tends to maintain a uniform and beneficial psychological stability within and between its parts.

Cheung (1986) went on to describe empirical studies of both normal and abnormal Chinese subjects that demonstrate multiple causal attributions and coping strategies for problem solving, suggesting an interactional paradigm. Psychological variables, somatic factors, and situational contexts all contribute to the Chinese understanding of the psychological. A systems model is more adequate to examine the multiple factors and to prescribe treatment. This interactional approach is similar to the biopsychological model of medicine, which is gaining popularity in Western medicine.

The Japanese, influenced by both India and China, adapted and expanded these models of balance and harmony through the uniquely Japanese perspective of Zen. Zen Buddhism believes that persons who are emancipated from the dualistic bondage of subjectivity and objectivity of mind and body are awakened to their own true nature, or the condition of *Satori* or enlightenment. In that state, the person is finely tuned to the reality both inside and outside. In his Zen center, Reynolds (1980) emphasized "phenomenological operationalism," where the uneasy mind is refocused and regulated.

Relationships in Japanese culture stress groups rather than persons. Whereas the basic social unit in the West is the individual, and groups of individuals create a society, Japanese society is more accurately understood as an aggregation of family units. Considerable importance is attached to esteem of the hierarchical order, with each person well defined in his or her role. Special attention is given to the family, clan, and nation as instrumental in defining loyalty through mutual exchange of obligation.

Role behavior becomes the means of self-realization for the modern Japanese. The individual is dedicated to and inseparable from his or her role, probably dating back to basic Confucian values embodied in the samurai elite of the 19th century. Carefully prescribed role relationships, beginning with the family, have significantly contributed to the stability of Japanese society despite rapid social change, at the cost of deemphasizing a sense of personal self. Achievement is not considered an individual phenomenon, but rather the result of cooperation, both collaterally and hierarchically, in the combined and collective efforts of individuals. DeVoss (1973) noted the "Internalized sanctions make it difficult to conceive of letting down one's family or one's social groups and occupational superiors. In turn, those in authority positions must take paternal care of those for whom they have responsibility" (p. 185). Horizontal relationships among equals are not emphasized in traditional Japanese culture. Social cohesion and social control is exercised through participation in organizations directed to community betterment. How the individual feels about participating is beside the point. One is expected to meet the social expectations of others as one subordinates oneself to social roles (DeVoss, 1973).

The Japanese self-consciously strive for higher goals to realize their ego ideal and are further motivated in this direction by a family-related, shame-oriented drive to be successful. The life-style is defined by attitudes toward work, illness, and death, whereby the person is duty bound to repay obligations. The ideals of self-denial are prominent in Japanese culture. The traditional Japanese family provides models through the father's omnipotence in the household and the mother's task to maintain harmony in the family. The individual reconciles tension by living in accord with prescribed roles within family and society. The source of conflict most likely to occur is between individual ambition and role responsibility.

Therefore, mental health depends on keeping these two opposing tendencies in balance, so that the individual can move freely from masochistic hard work in the daytime to narcissistic relaxation at home, without either tendency taking control. It is necessary for the individual to transcend these categories by balancing them without weakening either tendency.

4. The Role of Individualism in Counseling

Individualism is difficult to separate from collectivism because sometimes persons from individualistic cultures behave in "allocentric" ways to care for others as a means to express their individuality, whereas persons from collectivistic cultures may behave in "ideocentric" ways focusing on themselves as representatives of the group (Triandis, Brislin, & Hui, 1988).

Describing, understanding, and helping individuals has been a central theme in the concepts of "psychology" and "counseling" as an application of those concepts. However, the notion of the person is different across cultures. A Westernized description of the self is that of a separate, independent, and autonomous individual guided by traits, abilities, values, and motives that distinguish that individual from others. The contrasting notion of person in many non-Western cultures emphasizes relationships, connections, and interdependencies where that person is defined in a context and where the individual is not separated from the unit to which that individual belongs. Berry, Poortinga, Segall, and Dasen (1992) described the more individualistic cultures as more "idiocentric," emphasizing competition, self-confidence, and freedom, whereas collectivistic cultures are more "allocentric," emphasizing communal responsibility, social usefulness, and acceptance of authority. Collectivist cultures emphasize equality more than equity. However, the collectivist rules of justice only apply to "insiders," so that even more collectivist cultures treat outsiders the same as individualist cultures. It is possible to find individualism and collectivism in the same person at the same time, suggesting that individualism and collectivism may not be opposites but rather independent variables.

Christopher (1992) described the role of individualism in psychological well-being from a Western perspective. Individualism is described as a "disguised ideology" that has shaped the social sciences to uncritically adopt individualistic notions of the good life. Until the implicit individualism in the social sciences has been identified and made explicit, it will be difficult to transfer the theory and practice of counseling to cultures that are less accepting of individualism.

To understand the importance of individualism, we need to examine the role of "naturalism" as an implicit criterion. Citing the work of Taylor (1989), Christopher pointed out how naturalism assumes that people are ultimately explainable by the same natural scientific approaches for understanding the physical world that were developed during the Enlightenment. "However, naturalism not only involves an attempt to understand human beings as part of nature, but also demands that we abstain entirely from the use of subjective or anthropocentric categories in our account of the human" (Christopher, 1992, p.13). Secondary qualities of color, temperature, sound, and taste were treated as created sensations, whereas "mass" and "extension" were the only true characteristics of nature. However, the pretention to objectivity disguises its own implicit assumptions and biases in the physical and social sciences.

Lukes (1973) described the implicit values of individualism to include the dignity of the person, the priority for autonomy or self-direction, the need for privacy, and the goal of self-development. The notion of individuals as inherently worthy and dignified was based on a religious understanding of humans, and was later extended to the secular applications in the "natural rights" of man, growing out of the Enlightenment. The importance of autonomy disregards social commitments and obligations in favor of critical rational thought, growing out of the European Middle Ages. The importance of privacy resulted from turning inward for spiritual growth and insight. Self-development and realization of one's potential as a value grew out of the Renaissance, making the individual the focal point.

Lukes went on to describe the different varieties of individualism. (a) Methodological individualism suggests that explanations of social behavior are not accurate, or at least incomplete, unless they are grounded in facts and empirical data about individuals. (b) Political individualism defines the basis of authority in the purposes and uses of power by individuals. (c) Economic individualism is a justification of self-serving economic behaviors and their deregulation by outside authority. (d) Religious individualism refers to the direct connection between the individual and God without intermediaries. (e) Ethical individualism describes the individual as the criterion of moral evaluation and the basis of moral judgment. (f) Epistemological individualism presumes that knowledge is primarily a property of individuals.

Individualism is a viewpoint that has shaped modern Westernized life-styles in profoundly important ways. The heart of individualism is a metaphysical position of "the person as a disengaged or abstract self living in a disenchanted world" (Christopher, 1992, p. 105). Individualism presumes that the road to freedom requires that persons should be instrumental, rational, and expressive of themselves. Psychological well-being depends on individualistic indicators of health and illness. The uncritical acceptance of individualism has led to cultural bias in counseling that is captured by either objectivism on the one hand or relativistic subjectivism on the other hand.

Individualism has been closely linked to modernization, and individually held attitudes, values, motives, or dispositions have been considered a necessary precondition for modernization. Changes in the environment provide opportunities for modernization by individuals with the appropriate attitudes, values, and beliefs. Segall et al. (1990) concluded that "psychological research on modernization will focus on individual behavioral variables—treating them either as independent, mediating or dependent—that need to be measured" (p. 303)

Heilbronner (1975) pointed out the downside of Westernized values such as individualism. Civilization is threatened by (a) overpopulation, particularly in less industrialized countries; (b) the spread of nuclear weapons and methods of mass destruction to countries that have been exploited in the past; and (c) the demands of technological advancement on limited environmental resources. The Westernized life-style toward growth and development is spreading to Third World cultures that seek to overcome social problems through economic growth and materialistic consumption, and this has resulted in a less favorable climate of social satisfaction. Heilbronner sought the alternative to industrial destruction in preindustrial societies. Although science, technology, and industrialization have promoted material comforts, they have been less successful in promoting psychological well-being. The same individualistic cultural patterns that may have been adaptive at one stage of social development may require modification toward a more ecological perspective of preindustrial societies of our past, and perhaps postindustrial societies of our future as well.

5. The Power of Unintentional Racism

Counselors who presume that they are free of racism seriously underestimate the impact of their own socialization. In most cases, this racism emerges as an unintentional action by well-meaning, right-thinking, good-hearted, caring professionals who are probably no more or less free from cultural bias than other members of the general public. *Racism* is defined as a pattern of systematic behaviors resulting in the denial of opportunities or privileges to one social group by another. These behaviors are observable, measurable, verifiable, and predictable. Racism can refer to aversive behavior of individuals or of institutionalized social groups. Overt racism is intentional, where a particular group is judged inferior and/or undeserving. Covert racism is unintentional, where misinformation or wrong assumptions lead to inaccurate assessments or inappropriate treatments. Covert, unintentional racism is less likely to be changed because there is no awareness of dissonance between intention and action. The unintentional racist may behave in ways that are even contradictory to that person's underlying motives (Ridley, 1989).

Sedlacek and Brooks (1976) contended that most racism is unknowing or unintentional where people are unaware of the racist effects of their behavior. The key to changing the unintentional racist lies in examining basic underlying assumptions. Although these culturally learned basic underlying assumptions control our behavior, perceptions, understanding of rational behavior, and definition of *truth*, they usually remain unexamined. There are no courses in "Underlying Assumptions of Counseling," nor is this a frequent arena of research except perhaps in research on perception. There is rather the "assumption" that we all have the same understanding.

We depend on scientific objectivity to protect us from unintentional racism. However, in at least some cases, the very research on which we have depended to identify databased truth has contained implicit, unexamined assumptions that have continued this unintentional racism. In a recent review of human behavior in global perspective, Segall et al. (1990) pointed out the continuation of unexamined assumptions with regard to research on intelligence: "Much of the writing and thinking about race and intelligence has been sloppy, irrational, politically motivated, and extremely costly in human terms" (p. 100).

The controversy surrounding Jensen's (1969) research on intelligence and racial identity has demonstrated how both sides of the argument cite "scientific" evidence in support of their position. There are many other examples of research on intelligence in multiracial societies where one group has been politically and economically dominant and where the less powerful groups have been targets of discrimination justified on the basis of "racial differences" in intelligence. These attitudes toward culturally different groups can be traced to "scientific racism" (Guthrie, 1976; Williams, 1978) and Euro-American ethnocentricism in psychology (White, 1984). Sue (1981) described the "genetic deficiency" model, which promoted the idea that Whites are superior to Blacks and other non-White populations for biological reasons. These beliefs have been traced to the early scientific writings of Charles Darwin and Sir Frances Galton. The scientific arguments for racial discrimination persist particularly in the literature about culturally biased tests. Lifton's (1986) book *The Nazi Doctors* is overpowering in its documentation of how some of the most advanced and distinguished scientists of that time could be so profoundly misled by their unexamined assumptions about racial issues with disastrous consequences. Even good science can become bent by bad assumptions.

The scientific response to racism has tended to be simplistic. The Civil Rights Act of 1964 provides a good example of how powerful unintentional racism can be. Glazer (1975) took the position that when the government outlawed racial discrimination, racial minorities would be able to advance themselves as much as European immigrants had, so that each individual would be judged according to merit and be given equal opportunities. Takaki (1987) attacked that view for being simplistic. Merely prohibiting racial discrimination will not create equal opportunities in a society of unequal groups. "Structures of inequality such as poverty, inferior education, occupational stratification, and inner-city ghettos required the government to act affirmatively and to promote opportunities for racial minorities based on group rights. The ideas of individualism and meritocracy actually reinforced the reality of racial inequality, for they in effect blamed minorities themselves for their impoverished conditions" (Takaki, 1987, p. 11).

Science has provided reliable and valid data to help solve many of the problems in the modern world. We have come to depend on science to solve all of our problems because science has come to represent values of objectivity, fairness, and truth. However, the scientific method can only be as objective, fair, and truthful as the original underlying assumptions defining a particular area of scientific inquiry. The weakness of science is not in its methods, but rather in the assumptions—both examined and unexamined—of the scientists using and applying those methods.

There is a great deal of controversy surrounding the use of the construct "race." Helms (1990) and others emphasized the importance of race and racial identity as meaningful constructs. Others (Atkinson, Morten, & Sue, 1993) argued against the continued use of *race* as a category because of its pseudoscientific associations with a biological classification that has been discredited by anthropological and other biological sciences. Miles (1989) gave a concise history of racism as an idea. He also provided a critical analysis of the controversies surrounding the topic of racism. Miles' book made a strong case for the usefulness of racism as a political concept.

Miles acknowledged that the term *racism* is discredited as a scientific/biological term and is negatively loaded as a term of political abuse. It is this political implication of the term *racism* that gives the construct of "race" a meaning. First of all, Miles took a historical view of the concept going back to the 15th and 16th centuries, when it applied primarily to differences between Europeans and Muslims. Second, Miles also linked the concept to "the capitalist mode of production," bringing in the close relationship between racism and socioeconomic factors. Third, Miles brought in the "Western" world context of racism as a philosophical construct of cultural beliefs. These three factors provide the context in which racism is best understood.

The concept of racism is frequently used as an ideology to categorize people and for the attribution of meaning. There is a similarity between racism, nationalism, and sexism in this regard as negative forces in modern society. Racism brutalizes and dehumanizes both its object and those who articulate it. Therefore, it is a problem for the total social context where it is articulated and where it promotes exclusionary practices. Racism has come to represent a pervasive force of exploitation by one group against another group where the protection of self-interest becomes more important than fairness, equity, justice, and truth.

According to Miles (1989), there are several factors that are important to a historical understanding of racism toward the less powerful outsiders by the more powerful insiders. First, representations of the outsiders implies both including those who are like us and excluding those who are not like us, in which there is an implied superiority/inferiority relationship. Exclusion and inclusion are the two sides of racism. Second, racism has not been limited to Black–White relationships or even the colonial context, but has been widely applied elsewhere. Third, racist representations of the outsider change along with the changing social, economic, or political conditions, with attention to class differences. Fourth, physical features such as skin color or other somatic characteristics are often used to characterize the outsider, although racism does not require these characteristics. Fifth, scientific discourse, if based on the assumptions of representational inclusion/exclusion, may be used to legitimize those earlier representations.

The concept of racism has broadened as we have become more aware of its complexity in recent years. Ridley (1989) pointed out some underlying assumptions about modern racism that demonstrate its pervasiveness. First, racism is reflected in behavior—in what the person does rather than how that person feels or thinks—although attitudes are important in motivating people to behave differently. Second, racist acts can be performed by prejudiced as well as nonprejudiced persons. There is no causal relationship in which racism depends on prejudice as its antecedent. Well-intentioned but misinformed persons can still behave in racist ways. Third, racism is not the sole responsibility of any single ethnic group. Anyone can be racist. Fourth, the criteria for judging an act as racist lie in the consequences rather than the causes of the behavior. Consciousness raising is not enough to eliminate racism, and will not prevent racist acts by itself. Fifth, racism is perpetuated by the power or powerlessness of groups with respect to one another.

Miles (1989) linked racism to the process of seeing history in racial terms, where the powerful are separated from the powerless and where those in power are presumed to have the right or even the responsibility to exclude the powerless from consideration. As an ideology, it is necessary to acknowledge the complexity of racism, avoiding simplistic applications to historical events. As a political and economic force, it is always essential to view racism with regard to its consequences through including some and excluding others' access to power. Racism may often include contradictory and multidimensional ideas in an unthinking and unexamined justification for action.

It is extremely important for counselors to understand how a term such as *racism* is being used in the literature and by their clients. Racism does not need to be intentional. There are several ways in which unintentional racism can interfere with counseling. Ridley (1989) identified several examples in his analysis of racism process variables.

First, the counselor might contend that all clients are treated equally, regardless of color. Color blindness is sometimes a rationalization for a counselor who needs to feel impartial, who is uncomfortable discussing ethnic/racial issues, who is insecure about his or her own views about race, or who has several unresolved issues regarding race. The error is to abstract the minority client from the client's specific cultural context, whereas abstracting the counselor from the counselor's cultural context as well. As a consequence, deviations from this abstract normal become pathological. The counselor is likely to apply a "self-reference criterion" in judging others according to what the counselor would say, do, or feel under the same conditions.

Second, the counselor might become "color conscious"—assuming that all of a client's problems derive from the client's cultural background. The assumption is that each culture has developed an inevitable and irreversible pattern that is its destiny. Terms such as *culturally deprived*, *underprivileged*, and even *minority* may result from color consciousness. The counselor may experience guilt about the treatment of oppressed minorities and feel a need to atone for that guilt, whereas he or she may overlook instances of real psychopathology independent of the client's cultural background.

Third, the client may exhibit cultural transference. A client works through emotions and experiences by transferring feelings from his or her background experiences to the counselor. If a client has had positive or negative experiences with people from the counselor's cultural group, he or she will likely transfer those positive or negative feelings to the counselor. The therapist may fail to recognize a client's positive or negative behavior as a transference phenomenon, and will therefore be less likely to respond appropriately.

Fourth, the counselor might exhibit cultural countertransference. This refers to a counselor being influenced by previous positive or negative experiences with people from the client's culture. Consequently, the counselor's assessment of a culturally different client might be distorted by irrational projections; the counselor might focus more on his or her own projections than the client's actual problem.

Fifth, the counselor might misinterpret cultural ambivalence. Cross-cultural therapy is complicated by power and control needs by both the counselor and the client. A counselor might respond in either a condescending or paternalistic manner to reinforce learned helplessness and client passivity. A more dependent counselor might respond to cultural ambivalence with guilt feelings and might easily be manipulated by a perceptive client. As a result, the focus of counseling becomes counselor-centered rather than client-centered.

Sixth, pseudotransference may occur when a culturally different client responds defensively to the counselor's unintentional racism, which is then interpreted by the naive counselor as pathology. In fact, the client's reactions may be based on accurate and real assessments of the counselor's own unexamined racism. Such defensiveness might be in response to stereotyped attitudes of the counselor, whether positive or negative, toward the client as a product of a particular cultural background.

Seventh, the counselor may misinterpret client nondisclosure. Different cultures teach and encourage different levels of self-disclosure as appropriate. If the client is to benefit from therapy, it may be necessary to disregard culturally learned patterns of nondisclosure to outsiders from other cultures. However, if the client chooses to self-disclose, this behavior might also be misunderstood as culturally inappropriate.

There are many changes occurring that will increase the urgency of changing culture-bound counselors who are unintentional racists. The increased proportion of minorities in the U.S. population will require much more attention to culturally different perspectives in counseling. Likewise, the Immigration Act of 1990 will dramatically increase the numbers of legal immigrants from foreign countries from about 500,000 a year to more than 700,000 a year. The social, political, and economic world order is also changing so that the United States occupies a less powerful, independent position in relation to other countries internationally.

Finally, the diverse variety of special interest groups that are beginning to define their separate cultural identities will each require special attention. The culture-bound counselor's competence will come under attack not merely for immoral behavior, but—in some ways more seriously—for inaccurate assessment of the situation. The unintentional racist will require special and remedial attention to fit the multicultural reality of the modern world.

5. Conclusion

We are at the starting point in developing multicultural awareness as a criterion for counseling. Only those who are able to escape being caught up in the web of their own assumptions and maintain a balanced perspective will be able to communicate effectively with other cultures. The dangers of cultural encapsulation and the dogma of increasingly technique-oriented definitions of *counseling* have been frequently mentioned in the rhetoric of professional associations in the social services as criteria for accreditation. To escape from what Wrenn (1962, 1985) called cultural encapsulation counselors need to challenge the cultural bias of their own untested criteria. To leave our assumptions untested or, worse yet, to be unaware of our culturally learned assumptions is not consistent with the standards of good and appropriate counseling.

CHAPTER 4

Asking the Right Questions Is the First Stage of Awareness

Major objective:

1. To understand and identify culturally learned assumptions.

Secondary objectives:

1. To demonstrate the importance of challenging implicit culturally learned assumptions.
2. To identify barriers to understanding culturally learned assumptions.
3. To present strategies for identifying and changing culturally learned assumptions.

Our basic assumptions determine how we see the world, and each of us sees the world more or less differently. Patterns of assumptions construct a framework we call "culture" within the person. Culture is not external to the person. The first stage of training, awareness, identifies the trainee's internalized assumptions or cultural patterns. With this awareness, the trainee should be able to begin asking the right questions, which is the first step in the task of developing a multicultural awareness.

Several guidelines are important to consider in organizing the awareness stage of a training program. Each trainee comes in with a separate agenda. It is important to help trainees identify their own agendas and then build on those agendas or revise them to fit the needs of the unit. A frequent mistake in training is when the trainer imposes his or her own agenda while ignoring the trainees' perceived needs. One way to build on the trainees' implicit or explicit agenda is to draw data and examples from the participants. In that way, the training is based less on abstractions and is more immediately relevant to the persons being trained. If the awareness component can teach participants something about themselves that they did not already know in relation to their own multicultural needs, values, or assumptions, the participants will be more receptive to the knowledge and skill-training components. It is also important to allow every opportunity for trainees to demonstrate their own pretraining skills for teaching one another. Once they have had an opportunity to teach, they will be more receptive to being taught.

Awareness training needs to balance lectures or information with experiential exercises that apply information in practical ways. The exercises need to be kept short (5–10 minutes), with clearly defined objectives to hold the trainees' attention. Preview the training plan at each stage to indicate where you are going next. Each group will have several "gatekeepers" who will shape the group's reaction to the training. Identify gatekeepers early and attend to their advice so they become invested in the program's success and legitimacy. It is important not to move on to the next training agenda without debriefing participants to make sure none is confused about the exercise objectives or unintentionally offended. Finally, keep a backup plan in mind for unexpected opportunities or problems that emerge.

1. Challenging Culturally Learned Assumptions

We do not give up our prevailing assumptions easily. We have a tendency to see evidence that supports our assumptions more clearly than evidence that challenges those assumptions. For that reason, it is important to develop training approaches that guide multicultural learning and development in a structured way. The various approaches to training need to provide enough "safety" so that trainees are willing and able to consider changing their prevailing assumptions about other cultures, but also enough "challenge" so that trainees accept the necessity to learn new assumptions. The intellectual approach, teaching about a culture's style of living and social patterns in a formal lecture classroom setting, is perhaps the most traditional training approach. Adaptations of the intellectual or "university" approach have focused on cognitive skills and factual information needed to adjust to an unfamiliar culture.

However, knowing the right response to a situation does not guarantee the facility or the inclination to use it. The advantage of an intellectual approach is its inclusion of factual background in describing another culture accurately in its similarity and dissimilarity to more familiar cultures. The disadvantages arise when the cognitive or intellectual aspects of adjustment are emphasized to the exclusion of other approaches.

The self-awareness approach emphasizes learning about your own cultural bias before you enter into another culture. You have to understand your own values before you can adjust to the value systems of another culture. Persons understand their appropriate roles in another culture through contrasts between familiar and unfamiliar assumptions. Self-awareness is a necessary preliminary step to any intercultural training approach, although self-awareness does not deal directly with the other culture. In learning about other cultures, we learn a great deal about ourselves. Self-awareness provides a secure understanding of our own priorities and value assumptions, but self-awareness is only the beginning of the training process.

The culture awareness approach is focused on the cultural setting. The "culture assimilator" is a technique presenting a paragraph-length situation requiring a decision and several responses, one being more culturally appropriate than the others. The participant is trained to identify the best of several alternative responses to the situation. Examples are situation or context specific, and participants have to select from alternative explanations. Thus, participants learn to "assimilate" into the unfamiliar culture by learning to anticipate both the alternative responses and the characteristics of a favored response. The advantage of a culture assimilator is that it combines several elements of culture learning in a measure of intercultural competency. The disadvantages lie in its oversimplification of both the limited alternatives and the uniform appropriateness of one alternative response in a complex cultural setting.

The process awareness approach looks at people's behavior. Behavior modification combines elements of other training approaches. The emphasis is on specific behaviors appropriate to a specific situation in a specific foreign culture to increase the positive effects and reduce the negative effects of desired outcomes. If trainees learn the skills necessary to increase comfort and foster positive experiences, they also will be able to decrease stress, anxiety, or negative experiences. In a simulation of a series of potentially stressful situations, the trainee can rehearse an attitude and behavioral response that will help to perceive the situation in a positive perspective. The advantage of behavior modification is that it bridges the differences between familiar back-home and unfamiliar foreign situations, which helps the trainee to develop specific adaptive attitudes and behaviors. The disadvantage is its narrow focus and the difficulty of anticipating complex stressful situations in a foreign culture.

The laboratory approach looks at experiences in controlled settings. Experiential training approaches depend on direct contact between the trainees and persons from the foreign culture. Such an approach might take place at a simulated Southeast Asian village in Hawaii, such as the one that was designed for Peace Corps training, or in an "intercultural communication workshop" where foreign students and local residents compare their impressions, attitudes, and insights. Experiential approaches depend on the simulated or real multicultural experiences within a structured environment to produce culture learning. The emphasis is on emotional rather than rational aspects of multicultural adjustment. Experiential training distinguishes the direct "experience" of another culture from indirect "discussions" about the other culture. The advantages of experiential training are in providing an authentic and realistic setting to learn culture-specific multicultural skills. The disadvantages relate to the need for a skilled facilitator to interpret the experience and the need for access to persons from the foreign culture.

Multicultural training is far from a precise science, but it continues to build on the hope that past mistakes need not be repeated and the knowledge that failure of multicultural contacts are always enormously expensive and often tragic. Although existing methods are vulnerable to criticism, continuing attempts to identify alternatives for intercultural awareness are becoming more critically important than ever in our global village.

In training for increased multicultural understanding it is necessary to generate experience-based learning about oneself in an active, rather than a passive, role. Improving one's effectiveness in multicultural counseling involves much more than learning a new language of terms and concepts about cultural similarities and differences. As yet, there is no objective measure of cultural differences. Students must first recognize their own style of behavior, attitudes, and underlying assumptions. Unless students become participants in the multicultural communications process, they will not be able to benefit from the experiences of multicultural contact.

Trainees are placed in situations similar or analogous to those they might encounter in the host culture to rehearse their own responses to the problems they might expect to encounter in the host culture. Trainees then can explore alternative solutions to those problems and discover the consequences of each alternative. The unfamiliar situation also forces trainees to examine their own feelings and reactions to the problem situations as well as their personal values, beliefs, attitudes, assumptions, and expectations related to multicultural experience. After becoming more thoroughly acquainted with the other culture, trainees can begin to integrate and conceptualize learning, generalizing from the training experience to the anticipated living and working situation in the host culture. Each person begins to recognize the kinds of information needed to solve new problems or the skills that must be acquired to be effective. In the host country, trainees become better able to utilize available resources to meet those needs and continue their multicultural education. Also, by taking advantage of spontaneous learning opportunities as they arise, trainees gain practice in applying skills and knowledge.

Earlier research pointed out the weakness of a university-based classroom for training persons in multicultural communications. In the experience-based learning model, the trainee learns the skills of empathetic understanding of others' feelings directly through making decisions and communicating. The participant learns how to make independent decisions based on incomplete, unreliable, and often conflicting information. The participant learns to become involved and committed by staying in emotional contact with the target culture. The participant learns to accept and understand the value systems of others, allowing participants to shape and influence their own personal behavior. Finally, each participant learns to follow the problem-solving process through a specific and appropriate action. The experience-based model involves learning directly from one's social environment through observation and questioning by turning every situation into an opportunity for learning. The participant learns to define as well as to solve problems in a context where the facts are less relevant than the person's perceptions of those facts. The criteria of success are not external or even measurable but more frequently evidenced in the intangible relationship established with the target audience.

2. Barriers to Changing Culturally Learned Assumptions

Once counselors are trained and begin to apply their training, they confront barriers that must be crossed skillfully. Training does not eliminate barriers. Some of our messages, particularly those across cultures, are accidental and are not intended to be sent. Other messages that are directed toward others are deliberate and are communicated with a specific intention on the part of the sender. Training can improve and increase intentional communication across cultures. There are several obvious barriers to accurate communication across cultures and that protect culturally learned assumptions from change (Barna, 1991). None of these patterns is a barrier for "insiders," but they often become barriers for "outsiders."

Decreasing the Barrier of Assumed Similarity

First, assumed similarity becomes a barrier by diminishing the importance of differences in a cross-cultural encounter. The real differences may be less obvious but extremely important to accurate communication. There are ways to escape from assuming similarity. The "self-reference criterion" says, "Do unto others as you would have them do unto you." What if they do not want done unto them like you do?

- Do your homework on the culture you intend to visit regarding both similarities and differences with your own culture.
- Do not presume that people who "look" alike or who "speak the same language" will not be significantly different.

69

- Check out your assumptions by indirect observation or direct questions whenever possible.

Decreasing the Language Barrier

There is the obvious barrier of language differences. Language is much more than learning new sound symbols. Knowing a little of a foreign language only allows visitors to make fluent fools of themselves if they are unaware of the implicit meanings behind the sound symbols. Some ways that may help decrease multicultural communication barriers are following:

- Learn the language.
- Find someone who can speak the language.
- Ask for clarification if you are not sure what was said.

Decreasing the Nonverbal Communication Barrier

Third, nonverbal communications such as gestures, posture, tone of voice, and timing often control what we say. It is difficult to recognize unspoken codes that come so automatically that they may not even be deliberate in our own more familiar culture but communicate a definite feeling or attitude nonetheless.

- Do not assume you understand any nonverbal communication unless you are familiar with the culture.
- If the nonverbal communication is insulting in your culture, do not take it personally.
- Develop an awareness of your own nonverbal communication that might be insulting in certain cultures.

Decreasing the Preconceptions and Stereotypes Barrier

The fourth barrier, preconceptions and stereotypes, consists of overgeneralized beliefs that provide structure in any ambiguous contact. You see or hear pretty much what you want to or expect to see or hear, screening out many contradictory impressions. When you first become slightly aware of another culture, those half-formed stereotypes are most likely to betray communications. The stereotype has a tendency to become realized through a "self-fulfilling prophecy" of the communicator.

- Make every effort to increase awareness of your own preconceptions and stereotypes of cultures you encounter.
- With this awareness, reinterpret the behavior of people from another culture from their cultural perspective.

- Be willing to test, adapt, and change your perceptions to fit your new experiences.

Decreasing the Evaluation Barrier

A fifth barrier is the tendency to evaluate the content of communication received from others by an approving or disapproving judgment. "Everyone seems to speak with an accent except those people who talk like myself." Premature evaluation frequently interferes with accepting and understanding other persons from their point of view.

- Maintain objectivity.
- Recognize that you cannot change a person's culture overnight.
- Do not judge someone from another culture by your own cultural values until you have come to know the people and their cultural values.

Decreasing the Stress Barrier

A sixth barrier is the typically high level of anxiety that goes along with the multicultural contact where the visitor is dealing with unfamiliar experiences. Multicultural situations are often ambiguous and result in stress because you are not sure what others expect of you or what you can expect of them.

- As multicultural barriers are reduced, you can expect the level of stress to diminish.

Decreasing the Organizational Constraints Barrier

A seventh barrier relates to the "organizational constraints" that may control what you do even when you know they are inequitable. Organizations shape your communications in ways that primarily protect the organization's interests.

- Identify the authority/responsibility/reporting relationships reflected in the formal organization chart.
- Look for patterns of personal interaction that seem to deviate from the formal organization as your informal communication channels.
- Recognize that an organization does not exist apart from people; check and confirm the limits of formal and informal personal influence.
- Clarify your role, knowledge, and experience with the other person to the extent that you maintain the integrity and loyalties demanded by your position.

Changing assumptions and crossing barriers to multicultural understanding can best be accomplished through distinct structured training approaches. The rest of this chapter describes and explains 15 such approaches that you may find useful in changing assumptions or crossing barriers.

Several brief exercises that have been helpful for multicultural awareness training are described next. Each exercise needs to be matched carefully with the specific needs of a training situation. The awareness exercises serve both to identify the questions that participants are already asking and to teach them some of the alternative questions they should be asking to complement what they know.

3. Strategies to Identify and Challenge Assumptions

The following structured exercises demonstrate practical approaches to identify and challenge culturally learned assumptions in a training program. There are many additional training strategies available in the literature, or a creative trainer can generate original approaches to capture implicit and unrecognized culturally learned assumptions.

The Truth Statement

We often focus on the process of training without looking at the basic assumptions that are implicit in our training content. Generate a "truth statement" related to an obvious and widely accepted truth that most or all of the group are likely to accept, and modify it through discussion until everyone agrees to its truthfulness. When everyone has written down the statement, ask them all to write a second statement explaining why their first statement is true. When everyone has completed a second statement, ask them to write a third statement explaining why the second statement is true. When everyone has completed a third statement, ask them to write a fourth statement explaining why the third statement is true. You may choose to go on to a fifth and sixth statement, but probably by this time most participants have reached the point where they're saying, "I don't know or even care why it is true. It's just true!" Most in the group are probably frustrated and irritated, and some may be even hostile toward the trainer.

Discuss: (a) how hard it is to follow the chain of implicit assumptions underlying statements we accept as truthful; (b) how we get angry when pushed back to those assumptions in an argument or discussion; and (c) how frequently the implicit underlying assumptions go unexamined. Often participants say something like: "Why are we wasting our time talking about something so obviously true? Now, let's get on with the training and stop wasting time." You may want to discuss how group members believed in the same beginning truth statement for entirely different reasons.

THE TRUTH STATEMENT AWARENESS EXERCISE

Participant Objectives:
1. To identify a statement believed to be true.
2. To identify the chain of evidence proving the statement true.
3. To identify the basic assumption behind the evidence.

Learning Objective:
1. Truth is based on culturally learned assumptions.

The Label Exercise

How do you discover when another person's perception of you may differ from your own perception of yourself? Organize participants into small groups of five to eight persons. Attach a gummed label of *positive* adjectives or nouns to the forehead or back of each group member and ask the group to discuss any topic relevant to the program. Interact with each participant as if the adjectives or nouns on his or her forehead or back label were true for each of the other participants, with all participants considering each other's label as real and truthful for a 5- to 10-minute interaction.

Each participant will know which labels are on the foreheads of the others in the group, but will not know his or her *own* label. The labels may be typed up beforehand, or you may ask each participant to write an appropriate label, making sure that no participant gets his or her own label for the discussion. When the participants have successfully identified the labels on their foreheads or backs, they can remove the labels. The objective is to provide clues to another person about the label on his or her forehead through behavior toward that person without directly giving away his or her identity. Can you accurately interpret how others perceive you based on what they say or do to you?

Can participants successfully guess their labels or accurately interpret cues from others in the group? When all participants have guessed their labels, discuss the function of actual labels by which others perceive and evaluate us. If some participants have not guessed their labels within 5 to 10 minutes, ask them to remove their labels anyway and begin the discussion. The emphasis is on the wide diversity of perceived identity labels that we attach to one another.

THE LABEL AWARENESS EXERCISE

Participant Objectives:
1. To provide feedback to others appropriate to their assigned label.
2. To analyze feedback from others appropriate to one's own label.
3. To identify one's own label accurately based on feedback.

Learning Objective:
1. Each of us wears a culturally assigned label in the perception of others.

Stereotypes Awareness

Distribute one or more note cards to each participant. Write an incomplete sentence stem on the blackboard relevant to the training program such as, "Most refugees will say that Americans are...." Ask participants to complete the sentence with one or two words on their note card. An associate will gather the note cards and code the responses while the trainer discusses stereotypes and generalizations. Typically, the responses emphasize wealth, affluence, or money as the preferred perceptions.

When the note cards are tabulated, they probably will illustrate how most participants responded in approximately the same way, demonstrating the opinions that are "known" to be true even prior to discussion. The stereotypes discussed after this exercise are not abstractions but concrete examples from the participants.

STEREOTYPES AWARENESS EXERCISE

Participant Objectives:
1. To display a consistent and uniform stereotype to others.
2. To analyze stereotypes displayed by others.
3. To examine the basis of stereotypes.

Learning Objective:
1. Culturally learned perceptions may be more important than reality in controlling our behavior.

Outside Experts

Sometimes it is difficult for outside experts to understand information provided by a host culture. Patterns of response that are obvious and consistent from the host culture's point of view may seem frustrating, inconsistent, uncooperative, and even hostile to the outside expert who does not know the host culture's rules.

Request volunteers from the group to leave the room briefly and return as an "outside expert team" invited into the host culture to identify the group's problem and to explore solutions. In a large group, you may select a separate team for every 8 or 10 participants to work simultaneously.

While the volunteers are outside the room, instruct the remaining participants on the three rules of their host culture:

1. They may respond only by a "yes" or "no" to any question. All questions by the outside experts must be questions that can be answered "yes" or "no."
2. Men may respond only to men and women only to women. Female participants may ignore all questions by male experts and male participants may ignore all questions by female experts.
3. If the expert is smiling when asking a question, the same-gender participant may say "yes," but if the expert is not smiling when asking a question, the same-gender participant may say "no."

The experts return and are instructed about the first rule—that all their questions must be answered "yes" or "no"—to give them a clue about the host culture's rules and to reduce frustration. The experts are encouraged to work individually and to roam the room asking as many participants "yes/no" questions as possible, speaking loudly enough so that other participants can hear as data are gathered. After about 10 minutes, the experts report back to the group on the nature of the host culture's problem with suggestions for solutions.

Typically the experts have generated an elegant interpretation of their data based on the yes/no responses. When the experts have shared their observations, you thank the participants, lead a round of applause for their contribution, and then reveal the other two cultural rules. The discussion may emphasize the importance of understanding a culture's rules before collecting data. Participants learn to recognize that the inconsistency may be by the outside expert (sometimes smiling, sometimes not) as well as by the host culture people, and that what one person says may differ from what the other person hears. Discussion should emphasize the process of entering the host culture as an outside expert.

In debriefing participants, these frequently observed patterns might be helpful:

- The experts frequently disregard nonverbals such as gender or smiling, which profoundly shape their data.
- The experts frequently experience the host culture as inconsistent when actually it was the expert who was inconsistent, sometimes smiling and sometimes not smiling.
- The experts frequently describe the host culture in negative terms ("I wouldn't want to spend summer vacation there!") when in fact the host culture was trying to be hospitable within the limits of its rules.
- The data gathered by the experts tell more about the expert's priorities than about the host culture.

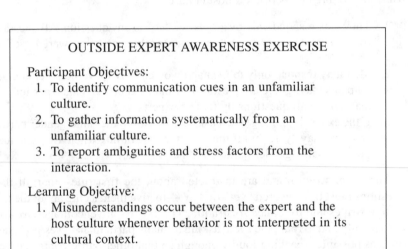

OUTSIDE EXPERT AWARENESS EXERCISE

Participant Objectives:
1. To identify communication cues in an unfamiliar culture.
2. To gather information systematically from an unfamiliar culture.
3. To report ambiguities and stress factors from the interaction.

Learning Objective:
1. Misunderstandings occur between the expert and the host culture whenever behavior is not interpreted in its cultural context.

Drawing a House

We are culturally conditioned to respond in predetermined ways to different situations. Ask participants to select a partner as culturally different from themselves as possible. Distribute one page of paper and one pen to every team of two persons. Ask each two-person team to hold on to the same pen or pencil and, with both persons holding the same pen at the same time, to draw a house on the paper. Instruct the teams partners not to talk with one another while doing the task.

After 2 or 3 minutes, ask them to stop and collect the house drawings. Show each drawing in turn to the group, and encourage participants to talk about or present their "house" to the group, discussing any special problems or surprises that came up during the task. Then lead a discussion on how we are culturally conditioned to respond by emphasizing relationship (e.g., accommodating our partners) or task (e.g., drawing a "good" house). Likewise, we may be culturally conditioned to favor the role of leader (who controlled the pencil?) or follower (who facilitated the leader?).

The cultural patterns of real-life responses are of course situationally specific for each cultural group, and in real life no single extreme (leader–follower, task–relationship) will apply uniformly to any one cultural group. The discussion should focus on examples of how two cultures might not share the same culturally conditioned expectations in the same situation. In some cases, cultural differences will be facilitative and preferred, as in a work team where one member favors the leader role and the other favors the follower role. In other cases, cultural differences will present problems, as in a work team where one member favors relationships and the other favors task accomplishment.

DRAW A HOUSE AWARENESS EXERCISE

Participant Objectives:
  1. To demonstrate situational leader–follower patterns.
  2. To demonstrate situational relationship–task patterns.
  3. To report patterns of personal culture.

Learning Objective:
  1. Cultural differences are displayed in situational patterns of behavior.

Nested Emotions

Sometimes it is difficult to interpret what someone from another culture is feeling. Our emotional response to a situation is usually mixed, emphasizing conflicting feelings. Interview a particularly articulate participant from a contrasting culture on an emotionally loaded, simulated role-play situation for about 3 minutes. After the interview, distribute a rating sheet listing 10 or more emotions such as love, happiness, fear, anger, contempt, mirth, surprise, determination, or disgust. Beside each emotion, provide a semantic differential from the number "1" (least) to the number "10" (most), asking participants to describe the degree of emotional feeling they thought the interviewee was feeling while in the role of the person being interviewed. Ask the interviewee also to complete the semantic differential, indicating how he or she was actually feeling while in the role of the person being interviewed.

When everyone has completed their semantic differentials, ask the interviewee to (a) read the number indicating a degree of feeling he or she checked for each item and (b) explain the reasons for that choice while the participants check the accuracy of their perceptions about what the interviewee was feeling. The discussion that follows might emphasize clues to identify nested emotions for the interviewee's culture and highlight emotions that are particularly difficult for an outsider to detect.

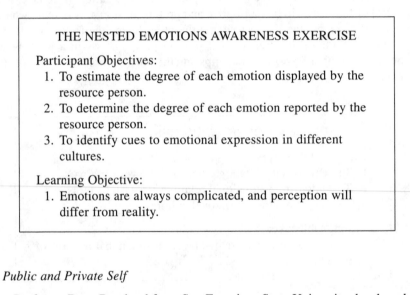

THE NESTED EMOTIONS AWARENESS EXERCISE

Participant Objectives:
1. To estimate the degree of each emotion displayed by the resource person.
2. To determine the degree of each emotion reported by the resource person.
3. To identify cues to emotional expression in different cultures.

Learning Objective:
1. Emotions are always complicated, and perception will differ from reality.

Public and Private Self

Professor Dean Barnlund from San Francisco State University developed a list of topics based on the work by Sidney Jourard. These topics may be public to some persons and private to others. Frequently, we assume that topics we consider public also will be considered public by others, and hence we unintentionally violate the other person's privacy. The list of items, available from Barnlund, includes five items from each of the areas of (a) attitudes and opinions, (b) tastes and interests, (c) work or studies, (d) money, (e) personality, and (f) body. The trainer may wish to generate a new list appropriate to the specific training program. The more extensive original list of public and private items can be found in Jourard's (1964) book *The Transparent Self*. Figure 3 shows Barnlund's modified list.

FIGURE 3

Categories of Public and Private Self-Disclosure

Objective

To compare different roles for public disclosure of private information appropriate to visitor and host culture residents.

Instructions

Please mark each of the following topics as:

Private: if it is comfortable to discuss only with self and intimates.

Public: if it is comfortable to discuss with casual friends, acquaintances, or strangers.

	PUBLIC	PRIVATE
ATTITUDES AND OPINIONS:		
1. What I think and feel about my religion; my personal religious views	_____	_____
2. My views on Communism	_____	_____
3. My views on racial integration	_____	_____
4. My views on sexual morality	_____	_____
5. The things I regard as desirable for a person to be	_____	_____
TASTES AND INTERESTS:		
1. My favorite foods; my food dislikes	_____	_____
2. My likes and dislikes in music	_____	_____
3. My favorite reading matter	_____	_____
4. The kinds of movies and TV programs I like best	_____	_____
5. The kind of party or social gathering I like best; the kind that bores me	_____	_____
WORK OR STUDIES:		
1. What I feel are my shortcomings that prevent me from getting ahead	_____	_____
2. What I feel are my special strong points for work	_____	_____
3. My goals and ambitions in my work	_____	_____
4. How I feel about my career; whether I'm satisfied with it	_____	_____
5. How I really feel about the people I work for or with	_____	_____

continued

FIGURE 3 *continued*
Categories of Public and Private Self-Disclosure

	PUBLIC	PRIVATE
MONEY:		
1. How much money I make at work		
2. Whether I owe money; if so, how much	_____	_____
3. My total financial worth	_____	_____
4. My most pressing need for money right now	_____	_____
5. How I budget my money	_____	_____
PERSONALITY:		
1. Aspects of my personality I dislike	_____	_____
2. Feelings I have trouble expressing or controlling	_____	_____
3. Facts of my present sex life	_____	_____
4. Things I feel ashamed or guilty about	_____	_____
5. Things that make me feel proud	_____	_____
BODY:		
1. My feelings about my face	_____	_____
2. How I wish I looked	_____	_____
3. My feelings about parts of my body	_____	_____
4. My past illnesses and treatment	_____	_____
5. Feelings about my sexual adequacy	_____	_____
TOTAL PRIVATE TOPICS		_____

Note. From personal communication, D. Barnlund, 1988, San Francisco State University. Reprinted with permission.

Ask each participant to review the list (in written or verbal form) and indicate whether the topic is private (e.g., comfortable to discuss only with self and intimate friends) or public (e.g., comfortable to discuss with casual friends, acquaintances, or strangers).

When everyone has identified the number of public items, tabulate the number of participants who had public items in six or more categories (30–25; 24–

20; 19–15; 14–10; 9–5; 4–0). You will probably discover a bell-shaped distribution of scores on public and private levels among group members. You may then discuss the effect of respecting one another's privacy in working together, even though that level may be different from your own.

PUBLIC AND PRIVATE SELF-AWARENESS EXERCISE

Participant Objectives:
1. To demonstrate clearly learned and differentiated levels of privacy in a group.
2. To assess one's personal level of privacy relative to the group.
3. To examine the basis of public and private information in different cultures.

Learning Objective:
1. What is public for one person may be private for another.

Critical Incidents

The effectiveness of a training program usually is determined by its relevance to solving specific practical problems of a participant. Problem situations can become valuable training tools. A critical incident occurs in a brief (5- to 6-minute) period of time, requires a decision to be made, and has serious consequences if a wrong decision is made, but it does not clearly show which decision is the right one ahead of time. For this training situation, the incident should involve persons from culturally different backgrounds. Collect examples of problem situations or decisions that (a) have no easy answers, (b) project serious consequences, and (c) occur with some frequency.

You might divide participants into problem-solving groups to discuss the cultural element and perceived conflict within each situation, along with an intervention plan for dealing with the situation.

You also might ask individuals to respond to a situation (a) as they would *like* to respond, (b) as they think they *should* or are *expected* to respond, and (c) as they actually *would* respond in real life. By distinguishing between these three levels of response choices, the situation might open up a discussion on response alternatives that participants face in real life.

CRITICAL INCIDENTS AWARENESS EXERCISE

Participant Objectives:
1. To identify culturally appropriate responses to a situation.
2. To identify personally preferred responses to a situation.
3. To examine the influence of cultural norms
   in responding to a situation.

Learning Objective:
1. Situations are defined by both personal and cultural
   considerations.

What You Said, Felt, and Meant in a Tape Recorder Exercise

We tend to confuse messages about what others actually said, what they felt while they were saying it, and what they meant or intended by a statement. Cultural differences tend to confuse the accurate communication of messages even further. By separating these three functions, we may be better able to analyze the messages we receive and be more articulate about the messages we send.

Organize participants into two-person dyads, with one person designed as the "speaker" and the second person as the "listener." The speaker will speak for 1 minute about his or her culture, saying as much as possible within that 1-minute time period. The listener will then repeat back everything the speaker said, felt, and meant about his or her culture. The listener will have 1 minute to complete that task. Then the listener and speaker will discuss for 1 minute how complete and comprehensive the listener had been in repeating back what the speaker had said, felt, and meant. The speaker and listener may then exchange roles and begin the 3-minute process all over again in their different roles.

TAPE RECORDER AWARENESS EXERCISE

Participant Objectives:
1. To attend accurately to the factual information being
   conveyed.
2. To articulate clearly the facts and inferences being conveyed.
3. To interpret the meaning and feelings being conveyed.

Learning Objective:
1. What someone says may be different from what he or
   she means.

Implicit and Explicit Cultural Messages

There are explicit and implicit levels of communication across cultures. Participants are matched into culturally similar two-person teams where both members are likely to understand the other's point of view. Each team contains one speaker and one "alter ego." The alter ego is instructed to say out loud what the speaker is thinking but not saying.

Two teams work together to plan a script that contains two levels of the conversation between culturally different persons: one explicit and one implicit. The four-person group then presents a role play to the larger group where two persons from culturally different backgrounds carry on a discussion while, after each statement, the alter ego for the speaker says out loud what the speaker is probably thinking but not saying directly. The exercise is useful for learning to interpret the mixed messages we send and receive in multicultural communication and articulate the interval dialogue of culturally different clients.

IMPLICIT AND EXPLICIT CULTURAL MESSAGES

Participant Objectives:
1. To express accurately what someone from a similar culture is thinking but not saying.
2. To interpret the implicit messages accurately.
3. To incorporate both explicit and implicit messages in an appropriate response.

Learning Objective:
1. What someone says may be different from what he or she means.

Decision Making

Sometimes the decisions made by persons from another culture do not seem logical to those outside that cultural context. Bring an articulate and authentic "resource person" into the training session from a particular culture. Ask the resource person to describe to the group one difficult decision he or she has had to make where the person's cultural values were an important factor. Ask the resource person not to disclose the actual decision that was made, but to provide background material leading up to a final decision. When each participant has had a chance to ask questions and learn the appropriate background information, ask each group member to predict the resource person's actual decision and to provide the reason for making such a decision.

When all participants have completed their prediction and rationale, ask the resource person to disclose the actual decision and the reason for making it. The resource person's presentation could be prerecorded on videotape and used for many sessions. The objective of this exercise is to understand the decision alternatives from the resource person's cultural perspective, rather than from each participant's own self-reference criteria.

DECISION-MAKING AWARENESS EXERCISE

Participant Objectives:
1. To articulate the logic leading up to decision making in another culture.
2. To identify the decision outcome by a culturally different person.
3. To match culturally appropriate outcomes with logical decision-making processes.

Learning Objective:
1. What seems logical in one culture may not seem logical in other cultures.

Drawing Your Culture

Sometimes our verbal facility in describing our culture betrays us by abstracting the less rational and more emotional aspects of our cultural influences. By drawing the symbols that describe what our culture means, it is possible to escape from the preconceived format we usually use to describe our identity.

Divide the group into units of about three to five persons sitting in a circle. If possible, arrange for the group to sit around a table. Provide each individual with a sheet of paper that may be ordinary typing paper or newsprint, depending on the space available. Also provide each individual with a pen or pencil. If possible, provide participants with pens and pencils of different colors or felt tip markers if the paper is large enough.

Ask each individual to spend about 5 to 10 minutes drawing his or her culture. Participants may draw pictures of events in their lives that have influenced them in their culture. They may also draw symbols that are particularly meaningful in their culture. They may draw any combination of designs, doodles, or lines that have meaning to them in terms of their culture. However, they may not draw or write any *words* on their paper.

At the end of the predetermined time limit, ask the participants to stop drawing. Then ask each participant to present his or her drawing, with explanations of what the symbols or drawings mean, to the other members of the small unit. Each member of the unit should be instructed to spend about the same amount of time, about 5 minutes, describing and explaining the drawing to unit members so that each person has the same opportunity and all units complete their explanations at about the same time.

When all members of all units have completed their explanations to the other members of their unit, you may ask each unit to report back to the larger group on any particularly useful insights they discovered during the exercise. This exercise is useful for articulating some of the nonverbal, symbolic, or less rational and more emotional aspects of our culture that are often difficult to describe in words.

DRAWING YOUR CULTURE

Participant Objectives:
1. To draw the figures or symbols important to their cultural identity.
2. To explain or express the figures or symbols they have drawn to other members of a small group.
3. To listen and understand the figures or symbols other members of a small group have identified as important to their cultural identity.

Learning Objective:
1. Our cultural identity contains nonverbal, nonrational, and symbolic elements that are difficult to express using language.

Being Normal and Being Abnormal

We are used to thinking of the construct "normal" both as the way *most* people are and/or the way most people *should* become. Therefore, we help persons adapt to the measures of normal so that they can become well adjusted.

In the space provided, indicate (a) the way in which you are "abnormal" for each of your reference groups, (b) the ways that your being abnormal or "different from most" is a positive quality you want to keep, and (c) the ways that your being abnormal or "different from most" is a negative quality that interferes with your life in some ways.

Your Ethnicity:
   Positive
   Negative
Your Nationality:
   Positive
   Negative
Your Religion:
   Positive
   Negative
Your Language:
   Positive
   Negative
Your Age:
   Positive
   Negative
Your Gender:
   Positive
   Negative
Your Place of Residence:
   Positive
   Negative
Your Social Status Level:
   Positive
   Negative
Your Economic Status Level:
   Positive
   Negative
Your Educational Status Level:
   Positive
   Negative
Your Formal Affiliations:
   Positive
   Negative
Your Informal Affiliations:
   Positive
   Negative

When all participants have completed identifying positive and negative aspects of their being atypical as members in their reference group, ask them to select a partner they know well and trust to compare and discuss each other's list of positive and negative consequences of their reference group memberships.

BEING NORMAL AND BEING ABNORMAL

Participant Objectives:
1. To identify how each participant is unique and different from other typical reference group members.
2. To identify positive aspects of their uniqueness.
3. To identify negative aspects of their uniqueness.

Learning Objective:
1. Being different from others in your reference group has both positive and negative consequences.

Identifying the Self-Reference Criterion

We often see what we expect to see. We look at others and imagine how we would feel if we were in that situation. We presume that others must be feeling what we would have been feeling. This self-reference criterion becomes troublesome when others do not see or experience events in the same way that we do. It is difficult to suspend judgment according to the self-reference criterion and to perceive the situation from the other person's point of view.

This exercise helps you identify the extent to which your judgments are influenced by your own self-reference criterion. A number of different subjects are listed next, along with a 7-point scale to evaluate that topic. Indicate how you think your culturally different partner would respond toward that topic in a favorable or unfavorable direction.

Example:

Chocolate
Unfavorable   1   2   3   4   5   6   7   Favorable

The check mark at 7 indicates that you believe your partner reacts very favorably toward chocolate.

Now place a check mark for each of the following items showing how you believe your culturally different partner would respond toward that item.

1. University Education
   Unfavorable   1   2   3   4   5   6   7   Favorable
2. Public Welfare
   Unfavorable   1   2   3   4   5   6   7   Favorable
3. Gun Control
   Unfavorable   1   2   3   4   5   6   7   Favorable

4. Right to Life
   Unfavorable   1   2   3   4   5   6   7   Favorable
5. Making Friends with Strangers
   Unfavorable   1   2   3   4   5   6   7   Favorable
6. Having Children
   Unfavorable   1   2   3   4   5   6   7   Favorable
7. Watching Television
   Unfavorable   1   2   3   4   5   6   7   Favorable
8. Drug and Alcohol Abuse
   Unfavorable   1   2   3   4   5   6   7   Favorable
9. The President of the United States
   Unfavorable   1   2   3   4   5   6   7   Favorable
10. The Future
    Unfavorable   1   2   3   4   5   6   7   Favorable

Additional categories can be added with a more specific reference to the task, population, or process of your target audience. The categories should be selected so that (a) they are safe enough to express a difference of opinion between partners without serious consequences, but also (b) that they are controversial enough to stimulate a difference of opinion between partners.

When both persons have completed their estimation of what their partner would score for each topic, have them compare papers and check each topic for accuracy. Encourage them to discuss reasons for inaccuracy in their estimations.

IDENTIFYING THE SELF-REFERENCE CRITERION

Participant Objectives:
1. To estimate the extent to which a culturally different partner will respond unfavorably to a topic.
2. To estimate the extent to which a culturally different partner will respond positively to a topic.
3. To check out the accuracy of one's perception about how a culturally different partner will respond.

Learning Objective:
1. Our culturally different partners may respond differently from how we expect on controversial topics.

Values Auction

The objective of this exercise is to identify the individual and collective priorities of a group, indicated by the amount of each individual's limited resources that are allocated to a particular goal compared with the amount the group is willing to allocate in the final purchase of that goal.

Distribute $10,000 to each participant in $100 and $500 bills of play money. The amount may be $100,000 allocated in $1,000 and $5,000 bills of play money if desired. Each participant should be given the same amount of play money.

Distribute a Values Auction worksheet indicating the items to be auctioned. Participants are asked to indicate a budget of how much of their personal limited resources they are willing to allocate to each topic. This serves as a budget guideline for each participant after the bidding starts. When each item is sold, each participant indicates the highest amount they bid on the item and the amount for which the item finally sold.

Values Auction Worksheet

Items for Sale:	Budget Bid	Final Bid
A satisfying and fulfilling marriage		
Freedom to do what you want		
A chance to direct national destiny		
The love and admiration of friends		
Travel and tickets to any cultural or athletic event		
Complete self-confidence with a positive outlook on life		
A happy family relationship		
Recognition as the most attractive person in the world		
A long life free of illness		
A complete library for your private use		
A satisfying religious faith		
A month's vacation with nothing to do but enjoy yourself		
Lifetime financial security		
A lovely home in a beautiful setting		
A world without prejudice		
The elimination of sickness and poverty		
International fame and popularity		
An understanding of the meaning of life		

Items for Sale: Budget Bid   Final Bid

A world without graft, lying, or cheating
Freedom within your work setting
A really good love relationship
Success in your chosen profession

When the auction has been completed, the facilitator can lead the group in a discussion of those items for which the bids were high and those for which the bids were low. To what extent do these bids reveal the value priorities for the group? For the individuals in the group? Did everyone want the same items or did they have different wants? Were any participants surprised by what happened?

THE VALUES AUCTION

Participant Objectives:
1. To allocate limited resources, indicated by budgeted bid, across a range of values.
2. To make bids in competition with other group members indicating the relative value of each value.
3. To identify values most highly esteemed by group members as indicated by the allocation of limited resources.

Learning Objective:
1. The values people say they believe in may be different from the values toward which they allocate their limited resources.

---

4. Conclusion

These brief examples have been used in a variety of multicultural training programs to motivate participants toward knowledge and skill development. The exercises each depend on an appropriate training context where the purpose of the exercise is followed up by the trainer. By creating an appropriate context, the trainer may facilitate learning indirectly as the participants exchange ideas with one another. Sometimes the unintended outcomes of meaningful interactions may be more important than anticipated, and frequently the "surprises" that come up during training provide the most exciting opportunities to a skilled trainer. Exercises are not a substitute for a trainer's skill, and these suggestions are offered in the hope that they may supplement the trainer's own detailed planning of a carefully prepared multicultural training program.

We direct more accidental or unintended messages toward people from other cultures than toward persons from our own culture. Persons who share the same cultural background are in a better position to interpret what is said and what is not said in the terms intended by the sender, whereas persons from another culture may grossly misinterpret a simple gesture, expression, or implied attitude owing to a different cultural viewpoint. Hints, clues, understatements, and appropriate omissions are some of the more subtle tools of communication that present barriers to multicultural communication.

Although we are not able to eliminate all accidental messages without seriously reducing the spontaneity of normal communication, accidental messages are likely to complicate and frustrate communication when they become excessive. As a measure of multicultural awareness, we might establish the goal that accidental communication be no more frequently directed to culturally different persons than to culturally similar persons. Through training, we are likely to challenge our culturally learned assumptions, and learn to communicate more accurately, meaningfully, and intentionally.

Unfortunately, there is seldom any opportunity to confirm whether the message sent and message received fit with one another. More often two persons assume they know what the other is saying without feeling any need to double-check their interpretations. As the sender and receiver become more familiar with one another's culture, they are more likely to be accurate in their communication. The goal of multicultural training is to facilitate feedback skills that minimize accidental communication and maximize intentional communication among persons from different cultures, thereby reducing barriers of communication.

PART II

Knowlege of Multicultural Information

CHAPTER 5

Developing a Cultural Identity

Major objective:

1. To describe the process of developing a cultural identity.

Secondary objectives:

1. To demonstrate culture shock as a change-promoting process in identity formation.
2. To describe the importance of power relationships in racism and prejudice.
3. To describe alternative models of racial/ethnic identity development.

Identity is developed in a cultural context. Belonging to a cultural group means accepting the beliefs and symbols of that group as having meaning and importance in a profoundly personal sense. Identity includes personal elements such as one's name, social elements such as one's family, and cultural referents such as one's ethnicity. This combined description of identity has also been referred to as personality. Tapp (1980) provided a comprehensive description of personality development from a multicultural viewpoint. As we become more aware of how ethnographic, demographic, status, and affiliation variables have shaped our lives, we become more "intentional" in knowing our own multicultural identity. We become more aware of our own cultural identity through contact with persons from different cultures.

Contrasting cultural dimensions separates groups of individuals from one another. We can look at those differences on three levels: (a) the international level, (b) the ethnic level, and c) the social role level.

At the international level, cultural factors such as country and its role in world affairs, national allegiance, language, and upbringing serve to separate people from one another. At the ethnic level, ethnic background separates groups often within the same country. Groups labeled as *Black*, *Chicano*, *Native American*, *Asian-American*, and *White* are distinct from one another as well as from a loosely defined dominant American culture. At the social role level, groups or individuals such as administrators, housewives, hardhats, or club members may define themselves as sharing the same culturally subjective viewpoint. Culture shock describes the process of crossing these boundaries.

1. Culture Shock

Culture shock is a profoundly personal encounter with persons from a different culture (Pedersen, in press,b). The experience of culture shock is not the same for any two persons or for the same person at two points in time. Oberg (1958) introduced the concept "culture shock" to describe anxiety resulting from losing one's sense of when and how to "do the right thing." This adjustment process involves a nonspecific state of uncertainty, where the persons do not know what others expect of them or what they can expect of the others with emotional, psychological, behavioral, cognitive, and physiological consequences.

The most frequently cited indicators of culture shock include the absence of familiar cues about how to behave, the reinterpretation of familiar values about what is good, an emotional disorientation ranging from anxiety to uncontrollable rage, a nostalgic idealization of how things used to be, a sense of helplessness in the new setting, and a feeling that the discomfort will never go away. Variations on the culture shock label with similar characteristics have included culture fatigue, language shock, role shock, and pervasive ambiguity. Any new situation, such as a new job, divorce, graduation, being fired, being arrested, cancer, or radical change, involves some adjustment of role and identity that might result in culture shock.

The culture shock experience (Figure 4) has been classified into five stages or categories (Adler, 1975), such as (a) initial contact, (b) disintegration of the old familiar cues, (c) reintegration of new cues, (d) new identity formation, and (e) biculturalism. Each stage is described in terms of its perceptions, emotional range, behaviors, and interpretations. These stages have been described as a "U curve" or a "W curve" when the person returns "home," going from higher to lower to higher stages of personal adjustment.

The "U-shaped" adjustment curve associated with culture shock describes a process similar to the stages in developing cultural identity to be discussed later in this chapter.

The first stage of initial contact has been called the "tourist" or "honeymoon" stage because the visitor experiences this new experience as exciting and intriguing, and is living in a kind of fantasy about the new experience. The person has not really "left home" yet in terms of the person's real identity.

FIGURE 4
The Five Stages of Culture Shock

Stage	Perception	Emotional Range	Behavior	Interpretation
Contact	Differences are intriguing Perceptions are screened and selected	Excitement Stimulation Euphoria Playfulness Discovery	Curiosity Interest Assured Impressionistic Depression Withdrawal	The individual is insulated by his or her own culture. Differences as well as similarities provide rationalization for continuing confirmation of status, role, and identity.
Disintegration	Differences are impactful, contrasted Cultural reality cannot be screened out	Confusion Disorientation Loss Apathy Isolation Loneliness Inadequacy	Depression Withdrawal	Cultural differences begin to intrude. Growing awareness of being different leads to loss of self-esteem. Individual experiences loss of cultural support ties and misreads new cultural cues.
Reintegration	Differences are rejected	Anger Rage Nervousness Anxiety Frustration	Rebellion Suspicion Rejection Hostility Exclusive Opinionated	Rejection of second culture causes preoccupation with likes and dislikes; differences are projected. Negative behavior, however, is a form of self-assertion and growing self-esteem.

(continued)

FIGURE 4 (continued)
The Five Stages of Culture Shock

Stage	Perception	Emotional Range	Behavior	Interpretation
Autonomy	Differences and similarities are legitimized	Self-assured Relaxed Warm Empathic	Assured Controlled Independent "Old hand" Confident	The individual is socially and linguistically capable of negotiating most new and different situations; he or she is assured of ability to survive new experiences.
Independence	Differences and similarities are valued and significant	Trust Humor Love Full range of previous emotions	Expressive Creative Actualizing	Social, psychological, and cultural differences are accepted and enjoyed. The individual is capable of exercising choice and responsibility and is able to create meaning for situations.

(From *Counseling American Minorities* (4th ed.) by D. R. Atkinson, G. Morten, and D. W. Sue, 1993, Dubuque, IA: Wm. C. Brown. Copyright 1993 by Wm. C. Brown. Reprinted with permission.)

The second stage begins when the full impact of differences hits the person in ways that can no longer be ignored. The person experiences loneliness and responds with depression or self-blame and withdrawal. Being "different" leads to many failures in the new setting and a feeling of helplessness.

The third stage begins with anger and fighting back "against" the others in this new setting. Self-blame turns into hostility, rejection, and attacks against the new setting to protect the person's self-esteem and redirect the blame for failure.

The fourth stage begins when both similarities and differences are recognized, and the person becomes more self-assured. The person can see both strengths and weaknesses in the new setting that demonstrate what should be done, even though the person cannot yet figure out how to do it.

The fifth stage ideally leads toward a bicultural or multicultural identity that includes competence in both the old and new settings. The person can see what needs to be done and is developing the skill to respond appropriately.

The U-shaped adjustment curve, or the W-shaped adjustment curve, describes both entry and reentry as duplicating the same process. This shape begins Stage 1 in the upper left, Stage 2 along the left side, Stage 3 at the bottom, Stage 4 along the right side, and Stage 5 at the upper right showing change from high to low to high adjustment over time.

Church (1982) discussed 11 empirical studies in support of the U-curve hypothesis. These data support the general hypothesis through the first three stages in an inverted "J curve," but do not support a full recovery to the fully functioning levels the person experienced back home. Five other studies that Church cited did not confirm the U-curve hypothesis. Regardless of whether the lack of proof relates to inadequate measures of change or that the U curve is an invalid construct, the U curve continues to flourish as a convenient description of the developmental process.

Furnham and Bochner (1986) discussed some problems with the U-curve hypothesis. First, there are many dependent variables to consider such as depression, loneliness, homesickness, and other attitudes. Second, the definition of a U shape is uneven because different persons start out at different levels of original adjustment adequacy and then change at different rates. Third, research on interpersonal aspects of culture shock seems more promising than the intrapsychic aspects. In any case, the smooth, linear process of adaptation suggested by a U curve oversimplifies the erratic and elusive reality. We do not know enough about how the stages relate to each other in terms of their relative importance, the order of occurrence, the groups most vulnerable, and the progression of change (Furnham, 1988).

The early research on culture shock compared it to a disease that resulted in disability and that could be cured with the right treatment. Culture shock was described as a "stress reaction" resulting from disorientation regarding values, norms, and expectations resulting from change and adaptation and a "deficit" of resources for an appropriate response. Gudykunst and Hammer (1988) emphasized uncertainty reduction as an essential deficit resulting in culture shock. "The reduction of uncertainty and anxiety is a function of stereotypes, favorable contact, shared networks, intergroup attitudes, cultural identity, cultural similarity, second language competence, and knowledge of the host culture" (p. 132). Stephen and Stephen (1992) linked culture shock to fear of negative psychological consequences such as loss of control or frustration, negative behavioral consequences through exploitation or derogation, negative evaluations or stereotyping by out-group members, and negative evaluations or rejection by in-group members for having contact with out-groups.

Other recent research on culture shock has emphasized the "growth" or "educational" model. The experience of acculturative stress is not entirely negative, but may include a positive and creative force to stimulate, motivate, and enhance long-term change. People develop skills and abilities through culture shock that may not otherwise be available. Acculturative stress (Berry et al., 1992) is not necessarily a negative process. Kealey (1988) found that many persons who were successful abroad had experienced intense culture shock. Culture shock is a learning experience that leads to greater self-awareness and personal growth. This educational/developmental approach to culture shock is beginning to replace the disease/deficit descriptions of culture shock. On the one hand, there is the possibility of relatively harmonious change through culture shock and acculturation, whereas on the other hand, culture shock can result in severe psychological conflict.

Furnham and Bochner (1986) highlighted the potentially positive consequences of culture shock, advocating a skill-learning response to the culture shock experience. These skills may include language learning, turn taking in conversation, learning rules of communication, knowing the protocol of politeness, identifying communication styles, and learning appropriate nonverbal behaviors. Learning appropriate skills enhances multicultural competence and increases the likelihood of success in the host culture. These skills include: (a) knowing the rules for interpersonal communication; (b) accommodating the effect of biological factors, demographic characteristics, and geopolitical conditions; and (c) understanding the characteristics of their own culture from the host culture viewpoint. Culture shock may be viewed as a specialized form of learning and educational growth, combining a social skills model with a culture-learning model to increase the potentially positive consequence of multicultural contact.

The culture shock model has a broad application to many crises situations (Coffman, 1978; Coffman & Harris, 1984). Adapting to different roles as in divorce, loss of employment, or institutionalization is functionally equivalent to entering a foreign culture. Coffman pointed out how the culture shock model applies to elderly mental patients who were moved from one ward to another, or persons going through career changes, divorce, widowhood, retirement, or disability. The greater the perceived differences between the old and the new environment, the greater is the culture shock. When the new situation requires different and unfamiliar responses to familiar stimuli, habitual responses need to be unlearned as well, causing more severe culture shock. The culture shock model offers a promising approach to understanding adjustment difficulties generally as one model of social change.

There are many positive aspects in learning to adjust to other cultures through culture shock. All learning involves change and movement from one frame of reference to another. Culture shock is related to exploring a new cultural landscape in every learning opportunity. The individual goes through a highly personal experience of special significance that results in learning new, previously unfamiliar self-identities. Change is provocative. The individual is forced into sometimes painful self-examination and introspection, with the consequences of frustration, anxiety, and personal pain. The individual is confronted with new relationships as an outsider looking in. The individual learns to try out new tentative attitudes through trial and error until the right responses are discovered. As a result, however, the individual has learned about self, the home culture, and new identities in the host culture. By comparing the familiar and the unfamiliar, the individual learns to grow toward multicultural perspectives and develop alternative futures from which to choose. The frustrations lead to self-understanding and personal development. Likewise, the related phenomena of role shock, culture fatigue, and future shock present the same opportunities and difficulties to each individual experimenting with new ideas.

Coffman and Harris (1984) described culture shock as having six identifying features: (a) cue problems, (b) value discrepancies, (c) an emotional core, (d) a set of typical symptoms, (e) adjustment mechanisms, and (f) a pattern of emergence over time. When the cues or messages we receive in another culture are confusing, it is usually because familiar cues we have learned to depend on are missing, important cues are there but not recognized as important, or the same cue has a different meaning in the new culture. Many of the problems in culture shock involve learning to deal with new cues. Familiar values define *good, desirable, beautiful,* and *valuable.* Each culture values its own behaviors, attitudes, and ideas. Although the visitor does not need to discard familiar values, it is necessary to recognize alternative value systems in order to adapt to a new cultural system.

Cultural shock has an emotional core and produces a heightened emotional awareness of the new and unfamiliar surroundings, whether as a sudden "shock" or as a gradual "fatigue" that occurs over a period of time. The emotional effect of this experience may include anxiety, depression, or even hostility ranging from mild uneasiness to the "white furies" of unreasonable and uncontrolled rage.

The specific symptoms of culture shock focus either on dissatisfaction with the host country or idealization of the home country. The host culture is criticized as being peculiar, irrational, inefficient, and unfriendly. The visitor is likely to fear being taken advantage of, being laughed at or talked about, and not being accepted, and thus wants to spend more time around people from his or her home culture. The visitor might develop a glazed, vacant, or absent-minded look nicknamed the "tropical stare," or withdraw for long periods by sleeping or being otherwise inactive. Minor annoyances in the host culture become exaggerated, and the few remaining links with the home culture, such as "mail from home," become extraordinarily important.

Strategies for adjustment that worked in the home culture might not work for the visitor in a new host culture. The visitor may need to spend a greater amount of energy making adjustments and learning new strategies. Direct confrontation and openness might facilitate adjustment in the home culture. Defensive strategies might range from hostile stereotyping and scapegoating of the host culture to "going native" and rejecting the visitor's own home culture.

Culture shock is likely to last over the visitor's entire stay in the unfamiliar culture, reappear in a variety of forms, and not be limited to an initial adjustment. As familiar cues are replaced by unfamiliar cues, the visitor experiences a genuine identity crisis, requiring either that the former identity be disowned or that multiple identities for each of the several cultures encountered be created and maintained. In either case, the visitor is required to reintegrate, confront, and challenge the basic underlying assumptions of his or her personality.

Coffman went on to make suggestions for visitors experiencing or anticipating culture shock. First, the visitor needs to recognize that transition problems are usual and normal in the stress of adjusting to a strange new setting. The visitor can be helped to recognize, understand, and accept the effects of adjustments in the context of a host culture support system.

Second, the maintenance of personal integrity and self-esteem becomes a primary goal. The visitor often experiences a loss of status in the new culture where the language, customs, and procedures are strange or unfamiliar. The visitor needs reassurance and support to maintain a healthy self-image.

Third, time must be allowed for the adjustment to take place without pressure or urgency. Persons adjust at their own rate, and they recognize that their reconciliation with the host culture, although painful, enhances their future effectiveness.

Fourth, recognizing the patterns of adjustment helps the visitor make progress in developing new skills and insights. Depression and a sense of failure are recognized as a stage of the adjustment process and not as a permanent feature of the new experience.

Fifth, labeling the symptoms of culture shock helps the visitor interpret emotional responses to stress in the adjustment process.

Sixth, being well adjusted at home does not ensure an easy adjustment in a foreign culture. In some cases, visitors who are uncomfortable "back home" may find it easy to adjust to a foreign culture. In extreme cases of maladjustment, visitors are more likely to carry their "back-home" problems with them into the new culture. With existing measures, it is difficult to predict a hard or easy adjustment for most individuals.

Seventh, although culture shock cannot be prevented, preparation for transition can ease the stress of adjustment. Preparation might include language study, learning about the host culture, simulating situations to be encountered, and spending time with nationals from the host culture. In all instances, the development of a support system is essential to helping the visitor reconstruct an appropriate identity or role in the new culture.

In reviewing the literature about culture shock, a recurring theme is the opportunity for learning, the process or stages of adjustment, the identifying features, and suggestions for minimizing its negative effects in a subjective reevaluation of individual identity. The key to understanding and controlling the effect of culture shock lies within the visitor as well as in the manipulation of the environment.

Ruben and Kealey (1970) found that in at least some cases sojourners from the Canadian International Development Agency who had undergone intensive culture shock during transition abroad were ultimately more productive than those who had experienced little or no culture shock. Perhaps those who are most aware of their own subjective perceptions experience more shock. For whatever reason, culture shock teaches lessons that perhaps cannot be learned in any other way, and in that respect culture shock contributes to developing a multicultural identity. Considerable research has been done on international or intercultural adjustment, but thus far there are few if any widely accepted guidelines or measures.

2. Racism, Prejudice, and Power

Although theories of cultural or ethnic identity development disagree about the highest or final stage of identity development, they generally agree that the lowest stage is where people are captured by racism and prejudice. The most frequently encountered examples of racism and prejudice are displayed by what

White (1984) called a "Euro-American ethnocentricity." According to this perspective, the criteria for normal behavior, personal beauty, and competence are based on characteristics associated with a dominant culture in the European and later Euro-American traditions.

Liberation movements for women, minorities, the handicapped, the aged, and other special populations in the 1960s and 1970s began to accept the idea that judging all populations by a narrow standard was racist and dominated by prejudice. Special populations began to develop their own separate criteria for group identity. White (1984) developed a seven-dimension psychology of Blackness. Jones and Korchin (1982) described research about how psychology is understood in the Third World, with Khatib and Nobles (1977) describing African peoples, Tong (1971) describing the Chinese, and Martinez (1977) describing the LaRaza psychology of Hispanics and others. McGoldrick, Pearce, and Giordano (1982) began developing criteria for "White" ethnic groups as culturally defined populations also at about this same time. A wide range of psychologies classified specific groups of "Third World minorities," ethno-cultural groups, and specific special populations according to different and separate characteristics.

Racism is generally defined as "prejudice" plus the power to enforce that prejudice on other people. Ponterotto and Pedersen (1993) described racism as increasing rather than decreasing in sociocultural–political settings. Prejudice needs to be studied and wherever possible prevented from exploiting power. Ponterotto and Pedersen described strategies and procedures for preventing prejudice. Most of these strategies focus on levels of power.

Pinderhughes (1984) examined the feelings and behaviors related to differences in power across ethnic and racial groups in an insightful discussion of treatment interventions. She described the feelings of the more powerful as experiencing: comfort, gratification, luck, safety, security, pleasure, happiness, superiority, masterfulness, entitlement, hopefulness, high esteem, anger toward noncompliant people, fear of anger by less powerful groups, guilt about injustices, and fear of losing power. She described the feelings of less powerful persons by comparison as experiencing: less comfort and gratification, anxiety, frustration, vulnerability, pain, depression, deprivation, incompetence, inferiority, exhaustion, being trapped, hopelessness, helplessness, low self-esteem, fear of abandonment, and loneliness.

Likewise, Pinderhuges (1984) contrasted the behaviors of the more powerful with those of the less powerful. She described the behaviors of more powerful people as: impacting the system, creating opportunity, taking responsibility, exerting leadership, blaming the less powerful, devaluing pain and suffering, distrusting others, maintaining control, justifying power, displaying paranoia, isolating the less powerful, dominating others, displaying rigidity, blaming the victim, and justifying aggression. She described the contrasting behaviors of less powerful persons as: lacking opportunity or ability to change the system, lacking access to responsibility and leadership, attributing positive attributes to people in power, distrusting and guarding against the powerful groups, denying powerlessness, displaying paranoia in a passive dependency, isolating and avoiding the more powerful groups, being passive aggressive, being rigid to control the effects of powerlessness, striking out aggressively, and identifying with the aggressor.

Access to power is a recurring theme in studying multicultural issues. Taylor and Moghaddam (1987) described theories of intergroup relations that attempt to explain prejudice and racism between more powerful and less powerful groups.

First, there is the "realistic conflict theory," which assumes that people working toward shared goals develop a sense of group identity. Conflict between groups arises when there is competition for scarce resources. Intergroup cooperation emerges when there are superordinate goals requiring groups to combine their resources. People are guided by self-interest.

Second, there is the "social identity theory," where people make social comparisons between their own group and other groups to determine their social identity. Sometimes this process leads to a negative social identity and dissatisfaction leading to changes of the relationships between groups toward a more just and fair balance. Sometimes it is not possible to identify with the group of first choice.

Third, there is the "equity theory," where people strive for justice in their relationships and avoid injustice. A relationship is judged "just" when the ratio of one group's inputs and outcomes are equal to those of other groups. When that ratio is unequal, psychological distress is experienced by both groups, requiring the restoration of justice. This perspective favors advantaged groups and tends to be simplistic.

Fourth, there is the "relative deprivation theory," where discontent results from comparison with "better off" groups. People believe that they can attain and deserve a better situation than they have. The basis of social comparisons is almost always biased in favor of the more powerful groups.

Fifth, there is the "elite theory," where talented individuals move up into the elite and those with less talent move down. If this circulation of talent is not allowed, the governing elite is overthrown. This explanation polarizes society into powerful and powerless categories.

The differentiation of culturally defined groups in terms of their own separate identity (Black, Asian American, Hispanic, Native American) and the increased awareness of each person's multicultural identity are further reflected in the range of labels indicating or implying powerful or powerless characteristics. The importance of developing a multicultural identity is clearly documented in these socioeconomic and political trends of our times. As a first step in developing a multicultural identity, it is therefore important to clarify how some of the most frequently used cultural terms might be used (Atkinson et al., 1993). The words used to describe and explain multiculturalism have taken on very special meanings.

The term *race* or *racial* has been used to differentiate groups, even though it more accurately refers to biological differences of physical characteristics or genetic origin that might differentiate one group of people from another. The social sciences have generally recognized differences between Caucasoid, Mongoloid, and Negroid races, which satisfies the biological requirements of differentiation and genetic relationship but does not justify or explain differences in social behavior where similar patterns cut randomly across racial lines.

The term *ethnic* is derived from the social or cultural heritage a group shares that relates to customs, language, religion, and habits passed on from one generation to the next. For example, Jews are not appropriately described as a race but might more appropriately be an ethnic group.

The term *culture* is again different, where members of the same racial or ethnic group might still be culturally different from one another. There are perhaps thousands of definitions of *culture* in the literature, but generally they agree that it is a shared pattern of learned behavior that is transmitted to others in the group. Not only may different ethnic groups in a single racial group have different cultures, but within a single ethnic group there may also be different cultures.

A fairly recent controversy is whether age, life-style, socioeconomic status, gender role, and other such affiliations should be referred to as "culturally" different from one another. On the one hand, these groups fit many if not most of the definitions of culture; but on the other hand, they detract from the precision of culture as a concept. The development of value typologies where culturally different groups can be identified according to their "subjective culture" suggests patterns of values that are or are not shared with one another. The concept of subjective culture has given an appropriately flexible measure for the degree of cultural similarity in contrast to a polarized "us or them" division of insiders from outsiders.

Within each individual there is still another level of analysis that differentiates members of the same culture. Each individual has to cope with culturally different roles, particularly when visiting a foreign culture. We can cope with our conflicting cultural roles because (a) we rank them in terms of the importance of each role for our own identity, (b) most identities apply only in certain contexts and are constantly changing, and (c) these rankings and identities are constantly changing. The roles we value most highly define our "primary" identities, which we have either learned since childhood or been converted to as adults. Therefore, all interpersonal role relationships are, to some extent, multicultural (Brislin & Pedersen, 1976).

In the relationships between cultures, one group often tends to dominate the other. A variety of terms such as *culturally deprived* or *culturally disadvantaged* have emerged to identify the less dominant culture, or minority, group. In usage at least, these terms have tended to take on a pejorative meaning that is frequently offensive to the less powerful or more exploited group. More neutral terms such as *culturally different* or *culturally separate* have been used to avoid the offensive connotations, but these terms have also been less than satisfactory. The political implications of the unequal distribution of power among groups of people have tended to complicate our descriptions of how culturally different groups relate to one another. In our contact with cultural groups other than our own, it is important to be aware of the political as well as the social implications of power.

On a global scale, the phenomenon of nationalism and the rediscovery of indigenous values present a full range of possibilities in defining identity through social relationships. Within each social group we see differentiation into clusters of shared identity whose members become increasingly dependent on one another while asserting their independence from other clusters. As we get more complex in defining the many people of different cultures, we encounter a variety of ways that cultural diversity is accommodated in different social systems. The visitor to a foreign culture needs to recognize the various ways that a host culture accommodates culturally different persons, both to understand multicultural differences in the host culture and to understand his or her role as a stranger in that culture.

Alternative cultures are often described in patronizing stereotypes as irrelevant or dangerous. Culturally encapsulated individuals are able to evade alternative realities by creating an artificial world around themselves. Isolation requires cultivation of insensitivity to cultural variations among individuals and loyalty to a singular unchanging notion of truth. Different cultural values are excluded, and the world is typically divided into polarized categories of political confrontation. Those who are brought up to depend on one authority, one theory, and one truth become trapped in their way of thinking, believing that their's is the universal and the only way. They become trapped in an inflexible structure that resists adaptation to alternatives. They are unable to see the world as others see it, trapped by the boundaries of their own parochial belief system (Maruyama, 1992).

Pluralism refers to groups that share a similar cultural identity across groups, with each group having its own rich and poor, powerful and weak, old and young. Pluralism is the preferred mode for developing a multicultural identity. We may best look at pluralism by contrast with the other alternatives. Assimilation would be less desirable in a culture that tolerates a wide range of differences among its people. Integration in a pluralistic society tends to occur through a series of shifting alliances on a more unequal rather than an equal basis. Isolation in a pluralistic society would be dangerous and likely to result in conflict between cultural groups for limited resources through a series of internal conflicts.

Research on the "contact hypothesis" suggests how different cultural groups can relate to one another successfully in a pluralistic society by creating "favorable" conditions for multicultural contact and avoiding "unfavorable" conditions (Amir, 1969; Miller & Brewer, 1984). Favorable conditions that tend to reduce intergroup conflict exist when: (a) there is equal-status contact between members, (b) the contact is between members of a majority group and the higher status members of a minority, (c) the social climate promotes favorable contact, (d) the contact is intimate rather than casual, (e) the contact is pleasant or rewarding, and (f) the members of both groups interact in functionally important activities while developing shared goals.

Unfavorable conditions that increase the likelihood of intergroup conflict occur when: (a) contact produces competition, (b) contact is unpleasant and involuntary, (c) one's group's prestige is lowered as a result of the contact, (d) frustrations lead to scapegoating, and (e) moral or ethical standards are violated.

Spontaneous intergroup contact does not occur under favorable conditions, but is much more likely to occur under unfavorable conditions, resulting in conflict between cultural groups. It is important to examine the balance of power for intergroup contact and to provide favorable conditions to promote a harmonious multicultural identity.

3. Racial/Ethnic Identity Development Models

Erikson's stages of identity development theory apply less accurately to minority groups than to the dominant Euro-American culture. The early development of typologies for describing stages of identity development for Blacks (Cross, 1971; Thomas, 1971), Asian Americans (Sue & Sue, 1972), and Hispanics (Szapocznik, Kurtines, & Fernandez 1980) stimulated research in a wide range of ethnic identity stage-based models.

The process of identity development is essentially linked to cultural factors. Sue (1977) described a two-dimensional model matching locus of control with locus of responsibility. His model is divided into four cells. The first cell matching internal control and internal responsibility describes dominant culture values and is achievement-oriented. The second cell matching internal control and external responsibility is where people have the power to change if given the chance, but where the typical response is to attack the system and challenge the value of counseling. The third cell matching external control and internal responsibility is similar to the role of oppressed minorities, where self-hatred and marginality are problems. The fourth cell matching external control and external responsibility is where the system is blamed for any and all failures and where people need to learn appropriate coping skills.

Kitano (1989) provided a model, also divided into four cells, that looks at the two dimensions of assimilation and ethnic identity. The first cell is described by a high level of assimilation but a low level of ethnic identity where people lump themselves together as "Americans" without differentiation. The second cell is described by a high level of assimilation and a high level of ethnic identity where people are bicultural or multicultural in their orientation. The third cell is described by a high level of ethnic identity and a low level of assimilation (e.g., new immigrants or traditional, isolated, or separatist cultural groups). The fourth cell is described by a low level of assimilation and a low level of ethnic identity as well (e.g., dropouts or persons alienated from society at all levels).

Thomas (1971) provided a six-stage model of "Negromachy" to cut through the confusion of Black ethnic identity development as a process. His first stage was one of withdrawal. His second stage was one where individuals testify to what they believed. His third stage involved processing information on or about the Black heritage. His fourth stage involved actively working through Black subgroups. His fifth and final stage was "transcendental," where each of us is a member of humanity in a membership that goes beyond groups. It is significant that Thomas' model moves in a divergent direction from a narrow to a broad focus.

Writing independently at about the same time on the topic of Black ethnic identity, Cross (1971) came up with a four-stage model. His first stage was a preencounter, where the world is described as "anti-Black." His second stage involved an encounter that validated the person's Blackness. His third stage involved immersion and a deliberate rejection of non-Black values. His fourth stage emphasized internalization to sharply define a secure sense of Black identity. Cross' early descriptions were "convergent," moving from a broad to a narrow focus in identity development. Cross (1991) later expanded his earlier design to move from a broad focus to a narrow convergent focus midway in the identity development process and then toward a broader "divergent" focus at the highest stages.

Jackson (1975) also had a Black identity development model with four stages. The first stage emphasized passive acceptance of things as they are. The second stage emphasized active resistance to the way things are. The third stage involved "redirection" to find new ways and to make changes. The fourth stage was internalization of identity by taking the best elements of all previous stages. Marcia (1980) based his research on Erikson's stages of crisis in ego identity formation, incorporating stages of identity diffusion, foreclosed identity, and finally an achieved identity. Delworth (1989) built on Marcia's work to focus on gender-related aspects of identity development. Relationships form a central aspect of identity development for women. Ponterotto and Pedersen (1993) discussed still other examples of stage-graded models of identity development.

Most stage development models suggest that individuals experience three to five phases or stages of cultural identification. First, there is an identification with the dominant culture in a preencounter, conformity, or traditional stage. Second, there is an awakening to the impact of racism in a transitional encounter or dissonant stage. Third, there is an identification with one's own ethnic group. Fourth, there is an internalization and integration of both cultures. The literature on Nigrescence, or Black racial identity, has led the research literature about ethnic identity development formation.

In the best known stage model, Helms (1985) characterized stage-based identity development models as putting the responsibility for adaptation on the minority individual rather than society, which tends to blame the victim. The research on ethnic identity development models has described an alternative framework. Standard identity development models do not account for the adaptation process in change and assume that identity develops in a linear, continuous process. Helms' five assumptions about minority development models summarize the extensive literature on development of an identity by minority peoples. These five assumptions pervade the literature on developing a minority identity.

1. Minority groups develop modal personality patterns in response to White racism.
2. Some styles of identity resolution are healthier than others.
3. Cultural identity development involves shifts in attitudes involving cognitive, affective and conative components.
4. Styles of identity resolution are distinguishable and can be assessed.
5. Intracultural and intercultural interactions are influenced by the manner of cultural identification of the participants. (From *Black and White Racial Identity: Theory, Research and Practice* (p. 30) by J. E. Helms, 1990, Westport, CT: Greenwood Press. Copyright 1990 by Greenwood Press. Reprinted by permission.)

Helms (1984, 1990) has been a leader in researching the various minority identity models. In her own cognitive development model, she traces the development of racial consciousness from historical and sociocultural information, through skill building and cognitive/affective self-awareness, and finally to cultural emersion. Helms (1990) summarized the literature on Nigrescence theories of identity development. Most theories defined the process of moving from less healthy White-defined stages of identity to more healthy self-defined racial transcendence, even though the labels of different stages were different for each theory. Helms also pointed out the similarity of content in how stages were described by Akbar (1979), Banks (1981), Cross (1971), Dizzard (1970), Gay (1984), Gibbs (1974), Jackson (1975), Milliones (1980), Thomas (1971), Toldson and Pasteur (1975), and Vontress (1971), even though each researcher worked independently, reacting to racism and prejudice in society. Helms (1990) summarized the stages regarding Nigrescence identity development (see Table 1).

Helm's work in ethnic and racial identity development has resulted in many research studies. Helms (1984) and Parham and Helms (1981) demonstrated that counselors must be particularly aware of their own stage of multicultural development and respect their clients' stages as well. Parham and Helms found that Black students in the preencounter stage preferred White counselors, whereas those in the other three stages of the paradigm had varying degrees of preference for a Black counselor.

Helms (1990) described each stage as a world view used to organize information about self and society related to the person's maturation level. The first Preencounter stage is divided into an "active form," where the person deliberately idealizes Whiteness or denigrates Blacks, or a "passive form," where the Black is assimilated into White society. The second Encounter stage deals with the Black who is confronted by racial affronts and indignities and is searching for his or her own Black identity. The third Immersion stage is where the Black withdraws into a stereotyped Black perspective that is internally defined. The fourth stage of Emersion is when the Black develops a nonstereotyped Black perspective. The fifth stage of Internalization moves toward a positive, internalized perspective of Black identity. The sixth stage involves Commitment to that positive internalized perspective. Helms's adaptation of these models in her Racial Attitudes Identity Scale (RAIS) summarizes these perspectives into the four stages of Preencounter, Encounter, Immersion/Emersion, and Internalization (see Table 1).

Smith (1991) developed a model of ethnic identity development around conflicts experienced in a pluralistic society. These conflicts include:

1. Ethnic awareness versus ethnic unawareness;
2. Ethnic self-identification versus nonethnic self-identification;
3. Self-hatred versus self-acceptance;
4. Self-acceptance versus other-group acceptance;
5. Other-group rejection versus self-acceptance;

TABLE 1

Summary of General Characteristics of the Black Racial Identity Stages

Stages	General Theme	Emotional Themes Identity	Identity Components		
			Personal Group Orientation	Reference Identity	Ascribed
Preencounter					
Active	Idealization of Whiteness	Anxiety, Poor self-esteem	Negative	White/Euro-American White American	
Passive	Denigration of Blackness	Defensiveness	Idealized positive	White/Euro-none non-American Black)	
Encounter					
Events	Consciousness of race	Bitterness, hurt, anger	Positive	White/Euro-American	None
Experience		Euphoria	Transitional	Black	Black
Immersion/Emersion	Idealization of Blackness, denigration of Whiteness	Rage, self-destructiveness, impulsivity	None	Black	Black
			Positive euphoric	Black	Black
Internalization	Self-transcendence	Positive, controlled, calm, secure	Bicultural	Black	Black
Commitment		Activistic	Positive	Pluralistic	Black/African

Note. From *Handbook of Cross-Cultural Counseling and Therapy* (p. 30) by J.E. Helms, 1990, Westport, CT: Greenwood Press. Copyright 1990 by Greenwood Press. Reprinted by permission.

6. Other-group rejection versus self-rejection;
7. Ethnic identity integration versus ethnic identity fragmentation or diffusion; and
8. Ethnocentrism versus allocentrism.

These conflicts are experienced as phases in identity development that must be resolved for development to occur. The salient conflicts go through four phases or stages.

- Phase 1: Preoccupation with self or the preservation of ethnic self-identity. During this phase, contact with other groups may be either positive or negative, but it is usually negative. The person preserves ethnic identity with ego defense mechanisms or by identifying with the aggressor.
- Phase 2: Preoccupation with the ethnic conflict and the salient ethnic outer-boundary group. During this phase, the person is preoccupied with seeking refuge or safety in his or her own community. Anger, guilt, or remorse are typical of this period.
- Phase 3: Resolution of conflict. During this phase, there is an attempt to go beyond the experiences of previous stages so that the heightened awareness or tensions become less salient. The person searches for a solution to the conflicts of previous stages.
- Phase 4: Integration. During this phase, the person integrates previous experiences toward a comprehensive ethnic identity. If the person is unsuccessful in integrating the previous experiences in a positive resolution, the result is confusion regarding ethnic identity.

Smith (1991) went beyond conceptualizations of ethnic identity as a response to ethnic or racial oppression and offered 18 propositions regarding ethnic identity development within the context of minority/majority status:

1. Developing ethnic identity means making one's ethnic membership salient.
2. Developing an ethnic reference group means depending on that group for one's social identity.
3. Individuals identify with different ethnic reference groups.
4. Each ethnic group has signs and symbols indicating allegiance and membership.
5. Persons construct a social order based on "we" and "they" relationships.
6. Ethnic identity is different for majority than for minority group members.
7. The status of one's ethnic group determines whether one's identity is positive or negative.

8. Positive self-esteem results from accepting one's ethnic membership group as a positive reference group.
9. Minority status is a source of stress for ethnic minorities.
10. Ethnic minorities differ in their psychological accommodation of the majority.
11. In pluralistic societies members of minority and majority groups share one another's salient conflicts.
12. In pluralistic societies members of minority and majority groups experience the same patterns of conflict.
13. Members of majority and minority groups know the psychological dynamics of their salient conflicts.
14. Persons experiencing salient conflicts go through the four phases.
15. Individuals use defense mechanisms when their ethnic identifications are conflicted.
16. A complete ethnic identity requires resolution of salient conflicts.
17. Both race and ethnicity influence an individual's ethnic identity.
18. One's career development depends on maintaining salient reference group perspectives of ethnic identity.

Recent research on ethnic identity development has emphasized salience as a primary concept. Cross (1991) modified his earlier (Cross, 1971) views on Black ethnic identity development summarized by Helms earlier in this chapter.

The first stage of Preencounter is a resocializing experience describing how assimilated as well as deracinated, deculturalized, or miseducated Black adults are transformed. Persons at this stage are distinguished by their value orientation, historical perspective, and world view where race has limited personal or negative personal salience.

The second stage of Encounter is where the person's old identity seeks to defend itself against change. Something significant happens to challenge the old identity as a kind of "culture shock." The issues of ethnic identity become personal salient and highly emotional.

The third stage of Immersion Shill Emersion is a "transition period," where the old perspective is demolished and a new frame of salient reference is put in place. The person is immersed in a new world of Black culture to which the person is dedicated and loyal. Emersion is the process of emerging from the emotionality and sometimes oversimplifications of the Immersion period. This stage is very powerful and traumatic, sometimes resulting in regression, fixation, or dropping out of involvement with Black issues.

The fourth stage of Internalization is the working out of problems from the transition period. A thoughtful and considered salience occurs, ranging from nationalism to bicultural or multicultural perspectives. Racial identity concerns are now matched to other identity concerns such as religious, gender, career, class, and role in a reduction of dissonance and a reconstitution of personality.

The fifth stage of Internalization-Commitment represents the long-term translation of Black identity into a comprehensive life plan or commitment. It may be necessary to recycle through the previous four stages from time to time or issue to issue as the person and situation change. Nigrescence does not result in a single ideological stance such as Black nationalism or Afrocentrism, but is more broadly focused on the wide range of potentially salient identities resulting from the first four stages.

Cross (1971) described his earlier theory of Nigrescence as a pyramid moving convergently from the broad foundation of preencounter to the apex of internalization. Cross described his more recent theory of Nigrescence as more of an "hourglass" shape converging in the transition period of Stage 3 and then moving to a broad focus in Stage 4.

Kim (1981) described an Asian-American Identity Development Model, where conflict is resolved in a five-stage progress from a negative self-concept and identify confusion to a positive self-concept and positive identification with Asian Americans.

The first stage of Ethnic Awareness occurs when the person becomes aware of ethnocultural origins, often through family members or relatives.

The second stage of White Identification is often linked to the time when children begin attending school. A sense of being different tends to alienate Asian children from their own ethnic background.

The third stage of Awakening to Social Political Consciousness is where the Asian American recognizes his or her minority group membership. The reassessment of White values and attitudes, although traumatic, leads to a more positive self-concept.

The fourth stage of Redirection to Asian-American Consciousness is where the person develops a sense of pride and active participation in developing his or her role within his or her Asian-American identity.

The fifth stage of Incorporation results in a secure balance of a person's various identities as potentially salient under different conditions.

Arce (1981) also presented a model of Chicano Identity whose transitional phases of (a) Forced Identification, (b) Internal Quest, (c) Acceptance, and (d) Internalized Ethnic Identity closely resemble the stages in other theories of ethnic/racial identity development.

The Minority Identity Development Model combines elements of the previous models in a comprehensive framework. This model, presented by Atkinson, Morten, and Sue (1983), describes development in five stages.

1. Conformity: preference for values of the dominant culture to those of their own culture group.
2. Dissonance: confusion and conflict toward dominant cultural system and their own group's cultural system.
3. Resistance and immersion: active rejection of dominant society and acceptance of their own cultural group's traditions and customs.
4. Introspection: questioning the value of both minority culture and dominant culture.
5. Synergetic articulation and awareness: developing a cultural identity that selects elements from both the dominant and minority cultural group values (see Table 2).

The theories of racial/ethnic identity development provide a structure for looking at identity development in other populations as well. Recent research on White identity development has applied the patterns and theories of minority identity development to the majority populations. Ponterotto and Pedersen (1993) reviewed the most prominent theories of White identity development.

Ponterotto and Pedersen described the work of Phinney (1989, 1990) linking ethnic/racial identity development to more broadly based theories of identity development. Ethnic/racial identity is seen as an important component of self-concept, especially for adolescents. The primary issues of (a) stereotypes and prejudice toward their group and (b) contrasting value systems require the person to make choices. Those who successfully resolve these two issues develop an "achieved" ethnic identity, whereas those who fail to resolve the issues develop a "diffused" or "foreclosed" identity. Borrowing from Tajfel (1978), Berry and Kim (1988) described the alternative outcomes of ethnic identity conflicts as: (a) alienation or marginalization from their own cultural group, (b) assimilation into the dominant culture, (c) withdrawal or separation from the dominant culture, or (d) integration or biculturalism where both their own ethnic identity and their connection with other social groups are potentially salient.

Phiney's (1990) model of ethnic identity has three stages to track the process of exploring ethnic group issues, which provide still another alternative framework.

The initial stage of Ethnic Identity Diffusion or Foreclosure involves persons accepting the values and attitudes of a dominant culture. Persons at this stage do not necessarily prefer the dominant group perspective, but the issue has little personal salience for them.

The second stage of Identity Search and Moratorium involves exploration of ethnic identity issues, often as the result of an encounter experience or personal crisis.

TABLE 2
Summary of Minority Identity Development Model

Stages of Minority Development Model	Attitude Toward Self	Attitude Toward Others of the Same Minority	Attitude Toward Others of a Different Minority	Attitude Toward Dominant Group
Stage 1: Conformity	Self-depreciating	Group depreciating	Discriminatory	Group appreciating
Stage 2: Dissonance	Conflict between self-depreciating and appreciating	Conflict between group depreciating and group appreciating	Conflict between dominant-held views of minority hierarchy and feelings of shared experience	Conflict between group appreciating and group depreciating
Stage 3: Resistance and Immersion	Self-appreciating	Group appreciating	Conflict between feelings of empathy for other minority experiences and feelings of culture centrism	Group depreciating
Stage 4: Introspection	Concern with basis of self-appreciation	Concern with nature of unequivocal appreciation	Concern with ethnocentric basis for judging others	Concern with the basis of group depreciation
Stage 5: Synergetic Articulation and Awareness	Self-appreciating	Group appreciating	Group appreciating	Selective appreciation

Note. From *Counseling American Minorities: A Cross-Cultural Perspective* (2nd ed., p. 198) by D.R. Atkinson, G. Morten, and D.W. Sue, 1983, Dubuque, IA: Wm. C. Brown. Copyright 1983 by Wm. C. Brown Publishers. Adapted by permission.

The third stage of Ethnic Identity Achievement is where racial/ethnic identity issues have become salient and the person becomes more accepting of his or her new ethnic identity in a healthy bicultural or multicultural identity.

Hardiman (1982) examined race and gender issues in the context of social identity theory in a five-stage White identity model. Social identity includes conscious or unconscious membership that contributes to a person's conception of him or herself. Hardiman looked at gender, occupation, religion, and White racial identity as contributing to that self-perception.

The first stage of Hardiman's model is No Social Consciousness, where the person does not recognize or accept the restrictions of any particular social role and presumes to act spontaneously/independently.

The second stage is Acceptance, where the person is suddenly aware of his or her social role and profoundly changed to conform with that role.

The third stage of Resistance results in critical analysis of restrictions imposed by the social role, resulting in rebellion and some rejection of social pressure to conform from others who share the same social role.

The fourth stage of Redefinition involves adapting the rules of the person's social role to fit the circumstances, and rediscovering the importance of that social role in this new personalized context.

The fifth stage of Internalization integrates insights from the previous four stages into this newly defined social role or identity.

Hardiman (1982) developed her White racial identity theory on the autobiographies of four White women and two White men. In Stage 1, the individuals operated naively from their own needs, extending from birth to about age 4 or 5. Stage 2 was a transition period emphasizing acceptance and role learning that extended into adult years. Stage 3 involved resistance to the "myths" they had learned and an emotionally painful reaction toward their own "Whiteness." In Stage 4, the individuals redefined their identities in a more positive direction, acknowledging both strengths and limitations. In Stage 5, the individuals internalized and established the new identities as their own.

Helms (1984) also developed a White identity model with six stages and two phases. During the first phase, which she called Abandonment of Racism, the first three stages occur. The first stage of Contact involves initial limited contacts between Whites and Blacks or other racially defined groups, in which they realize that Blacks and Whites are treated differently. The second stage of Disintegration is where the White acknowledges and understands the benefits of being White while feeling guilty for enjoying these benefits. The third stage of Reintegration involves accepting a belief in White superiority where the guilt and self-blame of previous stages turn into anger and aggressiveness.

During the second phase of Defining a Nonracist White Identity, the White person enters Stage 4 of Pseudoindependence, where responsibility for racism is acknowledged and an alternative nonracist identity is sought. The fifth stage of Immersion/Emersion involves the hard work of developing a new identity and gathering accurate information. The sixth stage of Autonomy describes an end goal of openness and flexibility through self-actualization.

Ponterotto's (1988) four-stage model of racial consciousness was developed with White counselor trainees in mind. Ponterotto relied on Helms' earlier work applied to graduate students studying multicultural counseling. The first stage of Ponterotto's model was Preexposure, where the White students had little awareness or interest in multicultural issues and were quite comfortable with the status quo. The second stage of Exposure involved confrontation with multicultural issues, often through taking a course on multiculturalism. The students became aware of racism and were motivated by guilt and anger to make changes. The third stage of Zealot-Defensive was where the students became pro-minority and anti-White in their attempt to make things right. The fourth stage of Integration was where the students processed their anger and guilt feelings toward a more balanced perspective. Ponterotto and Pedersen (1993) identified a variety of tests for measuring White identity development. It is important to synthesize the various measures of racial/ethnic/cultural identity development and to recognize the importance of cultural factors for identity development among all populations.

4. Conclusion

Theories of identity development from Erikson (1968), Horney (1967), and others have long established the importance of the sociocultural context in identity formation. Until recently, the measures of identity have been defined by the dominant culture with other minority populations having to either adapt to those dominant culture characteristics or suffer the consequences. The research on racial/ethnic/cultural stages of identity development have made a significant contribution to research on identity development generally. Although there are many differences across the various research models studying racial/ethnic/cultural identity development, the general patterns apply across the various models.

First, there is a clear differentiation between lower and higher levels of development regarding the person's identity. This development is usually related to intentional/unintentional, conscious/unconscious, or articulate/inarticulate aspects. In some cases, the lower levels of development correlate with measures of illness or personal inadequacy, whereas higher levels of development correlate with healthy, competent functioning.

Second, it is clear that culture relates to the process of personal identity development in profoundly meaningful ways. *Culture*, broadly defined, describes the significant experiences that lead the person to defined roles. It should be clear to the reader that measures of identity development that disregard cultural aspects are likely to be inaccurate and inadequate.

Third, identity development indicates a process similar to "culture shock," in which individuals are confronted by themselves and by others who are different from themselves. This culture shock process is where much of the learning takes place that results in identity development.

Minority populations, and particularly Black minority authors from at least the last 200 years in the United States, began the process of reflecting on culture and identity issues in social, political, and economic situations. In most cases, these persons were not psychologists, although the implications of their ideas were certainly psychological. As we examine racial/ethnic/cultural identity development as a process, it is important to recognize these ideas as having a history that goes far beyond the last several decades.

CHAPTER 6

The Patterns of Cultural Systems

Major objective:

1. To become aware of cultural patterns and relationships between individuals and groups.

Secondary objectives:

1. To separate objective facts from subjective inferences.
2. To describe culture as objective values to be discovered.
3. To describe culture as a construction of explanations based on experiences.
4. To describe a personal cultural orientation through the Cultural Grid.

Culture is complex but not chaotic. We understand cultural systems through understanding patterns of cultural systems. These patterns are defined by personalized assumptions, attitudes, and opinions of individuals. Culture is composed of the internalized perspectives shared by persons at a particular time and place. Cultural systems are the networks of relationships between individuals and groups who share the same perspectives.

I have discussed the importance of awareness to identify underlying assumptions and how those assumptions control behaviors through culturally learned expectations and values. I have demonstrated how two persons who are guided by different culturally learned assumptions might disagree without one necessarily being right and the other necessarily being wrong. When two individuals or groups do not share the same culturally learned assumptions, the likelihood for misunderstanding and conflict is high.

There is a new field of "cultural psychology," which combines anthropology and ethnopsychology, that is especially strong among cognitive scientists focused on cultural patterns.

The basic idea is that our representations of reality (including social and psychological reality) become part of the realities they represent; and many casual processes are constraining precisely because of our representations of them and involvement with them. A central goal of cultural psychology is to examine the way people make personal use of their customary practices, traditional institutions, symbolic and material resources, and inherited conceptions of things to construct a world that makes sense and to constitute a life space in which they can feel at home. (Stigler, Shweder, & Herdt, 1990, p. vii)

This chapter explores the implications of cultural psychology.

1. Separating Fact from Inference

The importance of culturally learned assumptions becomes most clear in the separation of fact from inference. Two individuals from different cultures may think that the basis of their differences is "factual" when in actual fact it is "inferred." A statement of fact is defined as objective reality that can be verified and confirmed through the testimony of a neutral witness. However, a statement of inference is a conclusion that goes beyond objective facts or verifiable events that can be observed. Through inferences, people attribute motives, expectations, attitudes, or values to others. Brislin (1993) pointed out: "If people make attributions that eventually prove incorrect, they may behave in ways that are also incorrect before they find out that their attributions are wrong. Put another way, people might find themselves in a puzzling intercultural encounter. They make an attribution, follow up their thinking with seemingly appropriate behaviors, and only later discover that both the attribution and behaviors were faulty" (p. 44).

Statements of fact are (a) based on direct observation or experience, (b) confined exclusively to what was directly observed, (c) limited to the particular event observed, (d) subsequent and not prior to observation, and (e) essential for attaining agreement between individuals or groups.

Statements of inference are (a) made before, during, or after the situation or event; (b) generalized beyond what was directly observed; (c) not limited to the particular situation; (d) based on some degree of probability; and (e) ones that frequently result in honest disagreement between individuals or groups.

Select an article from the newspaper involving conflict between persons from different cultural perspectives and ask yourself the following questions to separate facts from inferences in that article:

1. Which cultural identities (broadly defined) are mentioned specifically in the article?
2. Which cultural identities are implied or inferred in the article?

3. What objective and observable/verifiable facts do you know about the participant's behavior?
4. What inferences are you likely to make about each participant's behavior?
5. Can you describe the events described in that article from the separate and distinct viewpoint of each participant?

In debriefing your results, consider the cultural patterns in your thinking. There are two different and contrasting perspectives regarding how cultural patterns are derived. One perspective suggests that cultural patterns are "discovered" and that cultural values describe the person's "disposition" to display specific behaviors. In this perspective, cultural values are treated much like traits in trait-factor theory. The advantages of a dispositional perspective of culture are that it (a) provides clearly defined categories to describe a person's culture, (b) helps to explain the historical origin of cultures, and (c) provides a relatively uncomplicated focus for one's cultural identity. The disadvantages of a dispositional perspective of culture are that it (a) encourages simplistic interpretations of culture, (b) is hard to prove dispositions, and (c) disregards the constantly changing characteristics of culture.

An alternative perspective suggests that cultural patterns are constructed by the individual according to the time, place, and circumstances of "experiences." Constructivism has been more popular in the European literature than in the United States, but it seems to be gaining popularity in the United States as well. The advantages of a constructivist perspective of culture are that it (a) allows for complexity by incorporating situational factors, (b) allows for individualized and personalized profiles of culture, and (c) is dynamic and adapts to the constantly changing environment. The disadvantages of a constructivist perspective of culture are that it (a) eludes precise measurement and nomothetic analysis, (b) requires constant redefinition according to circumstances, and (c) complicates the separation of individual from cultural differences.

2. Discovering Dispositional Values

Cultural systems are the structures people use to organize their experiences and to explain the experiences of others. These systems are divided into objective and subjective cultures (Triandis, 1980). Objective culture includes verifiable information such as names, ethnicity, gender, age, education, kinship relationships, economic background, and occupation, to name a few of the more obvious. These indicators of culture are objective because they can be verified by independent observers. Subjective culture is more difficult to verify and includes feelings, beliefs, conceptions, judgments, hopes, intentions, expectations, values, and meanings. Subjective culture is inferred rather than observed directly. Both objective and subjective cultures are important but must be distinguished to prevent the confusion of mistaking inferences for factual information.

Values are more often products of a person's subjective culture. Attempts to treat values as objective verifiable facts have not been very successful. Values define the boundaries of cultural systems, and therefore are very important for communicating with culturally different persons. A cultural value does not require external proof or outside verification to be accepted as true. Groups depend on similar values to communicate with one another and explain their identity, as was demonstrated earlier. Values become a yardstick for groups to include or exclude individuals from the group. Groups with different value systems experience conflict or disagreement because they experience the same events differently. Each group begins from different assumptions and therefore makes different inferences. Examples of conflict between Arabs and Jews in the Middle East, of nationalities in Eastern Europe, or of ethnic groups in the United States demonstrate clearly the conflict resulting from groups that presume different beliefs or values.

The value differences may result from different national affiliations, different ethnic identities, or different social roles. At the level of nations, the people are separated by their country's role in world affairs, languages, and political loyalties. At the ethnic level, the people are separated by competing with one another for the same pool of limited national resources, with some ethnic groups having more power than others. People who are separated by their social roles as administrators, housewives, hard hats, or other special interest groups use exclusion to build their membership's visibility and to enhance their own solidarity.

The problem with differentiating cultural systems solely by their values is that cultures are more complicated and dynamic than traditional value perspectives seem to suggest. The description of cultures by their values suggests that culture is a trait or "disposition" to do one thing and not do another. Values presume a constancy over time, place, and person that denies the very dynamic nature of culture. People who value "kindness" may act unkindly. People who value "fairness" may act unfairly. This variability applies to people who presume to share the same cultural values and priorities. These people act differently from one another even though they maintain the same cultural disposition according to their values. The more clearly defined and absolute these cultural categories are, the more likely they are to bend the data to fit their own rigid framework of standard typologies, mixing fact with inference. Value typologies are convenient but simplistic definitions of culture.

The best known value typology was designed by Kluckhohn and Strodtbeck (1961) (Table 3).

TABLE 3
Kohl's Interpretation of the Kluckhohn–Strodtbeck Model

Orientation	Range		
Human Nature	Most people can't be trusted.	There are both evil people and good people, and you have to check people out to find out which they are.	Most people are basically pretty good at heart.
Person–Nature	Life is largely determined by external forces, such as God, fate, or genetics. A person can't surpass the conditions life has set.	People should, in every way, live in complete harmony with nature.	Our challenge is to conquer and control nature. Everything from air conditioning to cloning new cells has resulted from having met this challenge.
Time	People should learn from history and attempt to emulate the glorious ages of the past.	The present moment is everything. Let's make the most of it. Don't worry about tomorrow; enjoy today.	Planning and goal setting make it possible for people to accomplish miracles. A little sacrifice today will bring a better tomorrow.
Activity	It's enough to just "be." It's not necessary to accomplish great things in life to feel your life has been worthwhile.	The main purpose for having been placed on this earth is for our own inner development.	If people work hard and apply themselves fully, their efforts will be rewarded.

(Continued)

125

TABLE 3 *continued*
Kohl's Interpretation of the Kluckhohn–Strodtbeck Model

Orientation	Range		
Social	Some people are born to lead others. There are "leaders" and there are "followers" in this world.	Whenever I have a serious problem, I like to get the advice of my family or close friends in how best to solve it.	All people should have equal rights, and all should have complete control over their own destinies.

Note. From *Survival Kit for Overseas Living* (pp. 84–85) by L.R. Kohls, 1979, Chicago: Intercultural Network, SYSTRAN. Copyright 1979 by Intercultural Press. Adapted by permission.

People are not evaluated in terms of what they do. A frequently quoted English language expression is: "If you don't know what to do, at least *do* something." An equivalent common Chinese expression is: "If you don't know what to do, at least *don't do* anything." A task-oriented person is likely to be uncomfortable in a culture that values relationship building more than task accomplishment.

Finally, under the Kluckhohn–Strodtbeck Model, attitudes toward social relations likewise are assumed to be different from one group to another. The power structure in hierarchical cultures is authoritarian—from the role of the father in a family to the ruler in the state. In other cultures, equality is emphasized and each individual group member is allotted equal power. In a third alternative, the group as a unit is expected to manage power and to control its own members.

Carter (1991) provided a review of counseling research on the Kluckhohn–Strodtbeck Model of value orientations. Carter pointed out that understanding a culture's values is essential for understanding the uniqueness of that culture as well as for defining similarities for appropriate interaction across cultures. The Kluckhohn–Strodtbeck Model has a long history of use across disciplines in the social sciences, resulting in measures of cultural difference, frameworks for comparing cultures, development of culturally sensitive treatments, measuring counselor effectiveness, identifying cultural preferences, and organizing cultural information. The presumption is that mismatches of cultural values inhibit the delivery of psychological services and complicate the communication process.

Carter recognized the limitations of the Kluckhohn–Strodtbeck approach for studying within-group and between-group patterns of cultural similarity and difference. However, he was persuasive in documenting how studying historical and cultural values helps counselors understand racial and ethnic inequalities across culturally different people. Values are useful for learning about one's self as a starting point for learning about culturally different alternatives. Values provide a framework for organizing historical knowledge about cultures as long as the value labels are not confused with the more complicated cultural realities and inferred values are not treated as objective fact.

Cultural values have stimulated a great deal of research relevant to counseling. Stewart (1972) developed a list of value perspectives for "American" and "Contrast-American" organized around the Kluckhohn–Strodtbeck categories to demonstrate cultural differences. This Contrast-American simulation has been useful in establishing cultural differences. Ibrahim (1991) developed a measure of "world view" as a mediating variable in counseling and development interventions. Her work on this world view measure is based on the Kluckhohn–Strodtbeck framework of human nature, social relationships, nature, time orientation, and activity orientation. Carter and Helms (1987) developed a measure of White racial identity attitudes and cultural values; Szapocznik, Scopetta, Arannadle, and Kurtines (1980) developed a measure of Cuban values; and Trimble (1976) measured aspects of Native-American Indian cultures all from the Kluckhohn–Strodtbeck framework. Sue and Sue (1990) described the Kluckhohn–Strodtbeck framework as "one of the most useful frameworks for understanding differences among individuals and groups" (p. 138). Kluckhohn and Strodtbeck's Value Orientation Framework has made a significant contribution toward the discovery of cultural values in different cultures.

3. The Construction of Cultural Patterns

Constructivism challenges the realist and objectivist versions of science. Neimeyer (1993) described the boundaries of constructivist assessment. This viewpoint is based on the premise that we do not have direct access to a singular, stable, and fully knowable external reality. All of our thinking is culturally embedded, interpersonally forged, and necessarily limited. According to the constructivist perspective, emphasis is placed on personal meaning, the influence of relationships on creating meaning, and the subjective nature of knowledge, judging methods more according to their viable utility than the independent validity. This approach assumes that people are actively oriented toward a meaningful understanding of life, that they are denied direct access to any external reality, and that they are continuously developing or changing. McNamee and Gergen (1992) provided a theoretical basis for social construction in counseling and therapy, pointing out the implications for client–counselor relationships and for the practice of counseling.

A study of the constructionist perspective begins with an examination of the "self." The European and American psychological literature describes self as self-contained, self-reliant, independent, standing out in a group, egocentric, a centralized equilibrium structure, selfish, a distinctive whole set contrastively against other such wholes, and rationalistic (Hermans, Kempen, & Van Loon, 1992). In a world context, this Euro-American perspective is fairly exotic and ethnocentric. A diological view of the self goes beyond the limits of rationalism and individualism to the "stories" and dialogues people have told about themselves to understand where they fit in the world. The self is constructed by defining its social connections and plurality of relationships. "The embodied nature of the self contrasts with conceptions of the self found in mainstream psychology, which are based on the assumption of a disembodied or rationalistic mind" (Hermans et al., 1992, p. 23).

Hermans et al. (1992) described how a person "constructs" his or her own theory of self in a sociocultural context. In their definition, the *self* is "diological" and transcends the boundaries of both individualism and rationalism. They traced the history of the constructionist perspective back to Italian philosopher Giambattista Vico, German philosopher Vaihinger, and American psychologist George Kelly (Mahoney, 1988). Vico credited human nature with a creative force of "ingenium" by which people change the physical world and create history by constructing relationships. Vaihinger identified the importance of "fiction" as a scientific instrument for going beyond the "hypothesis" of reality as we experience it toward constructing a higher development of thought. Kelly's notion of personal constructs contended that understanding depends on the alternative interpretations available to us. Kelly's constructs are the criteria by which some things are seen to be alike and others to be different in a way that challenges objective reality (Hermans et al., 1992).

If we describe the world as objective, we assume that people's different perceptions of the world are, to a greater or lesser extent, inaccurate. It assumes that our differing beliefs and perceptions about the world are not relevant. We describe the world independent of its context, and our experiences are judged by absolute measures of logical rationalism. However, our experiences describe a subjective world of imagination and reality that is defined by metaphors (Lakoff & Johnson, 1980). Reality is not the discovery of absolute truth, but an understanding of the complex and dynamic relationships between events. Life is a "narrative" of interacting stories in which there are many roles (Bruner, 1986; Sarbin, 1986) that locate the self in a cultural context. The dialogical description of self describes the construction of culture in a personal context—not as an abstraction but as a product of our experienced relationships (Howard, 1991).

Steenbarger (1991) applied the contextualist theme of a divergent reality to counseling and development as an alternative to linear, stage-based, convergent hierarchies. Steenbarger identified three problems regarding the linear development "growth" models: (a) In their emphasis on linearity, stage-based models cannot account for the complexity of human development. Change is rarely unidirectional but more often multidirectional. (b) In their emphasis on invariant sequences of structural unfolding, stage-based models cannot account for important situational influences in the developmental process. Growth occurs through interactions with the environment rather than through the independent unfolding of intrapersonal aspects. (c) In an attempt to reduce development to uniform sequences, stage-based theories assume troublesome value premises. The objective norms implied by a fixed uniformity are in conflict with a multicultural and culturally diverse reality around us. The alternative is to view development in a context of person–situation relationships.

According to social role theory, the self is a social construction from roles that have been internalized through interactions with others, as described by the work of Goffman, Mead, Sarbin, and Allen (cited in Steenbarger, 1991). The person is not unfolding from a unitary core so much as constantly "becoming" while changing the salience of alternative selves or roles. As the sociocultural context changes, so the salient self also changes to accommodate and adapt. In this context, counseling is the process by which a person constructs and deconstructs reality.

The life-span approach to development is also contextual in emphasizing the multidirectionality of life plans and psychosocial adaptation. The emphasis is not on traits or behaviors but on the "goodness of fit" between person and environment. Throughout one's life span, one develops by responding to crises in a dialectical and continuously changing trajectory, as described by Steenbarger (1991) and the research he cited.

Claiborn and Lichtenberg (1989) reviewed the literature on interactional counseling where the individual is seen in a sociocultural context. As the person interacts with the environment, change is reciprocal through a multidirectional rather than a unidirectional process in a cause–effect relationship. Each event is both cause and effect according to this interactional view. Role definitions are negotiated in a dialogue or conversation with others. The counselor participates in this dialogue and becomes part of the client's new environment; he or she changes that environment by introducing new—and hopefully more constructive—roles for the client.

Hofstede (1980, 1986, 1991) provided an example of constructed patterns of similarities and differences among subjects from more than 55 different nations around the world. The resulting data were factor analyzed into four dimensions. The first dimension was distributed from High to Low Power Distance measures. The second dimension was distributed from Weak to Strong Uncertainty Avoidance measures. The third dimension was distributed from Individualist to Collectivist perspectives. The fourth dimension was distributed from Masculine to Feminine perspectives. These constructs were used to describe patterns of similarity and differences in the distribution of responses across countries.

The four dimensions describe how patterns of thinking, feeling, and acting were constructed differently by different populations throughout the life span. Hofstede (1991) described these patterns as "mental programs" that provide "software" for the mind to function. Each person reacts to the social environment in different ways by constructing a perception of reality that is functional. Hofstede equated this mental software with culture as "the collective programming of the mind which distinguishes the members of one group or category of people from another" (p. 5). Culture is distinguished from the universally shared characteristics of human nature on the one hand and from the uniquely individualized characteristics of personality on the other. Culture is programmed both in response to the universal characteristics of human nature and the specialized perspectives of personality.

According to Hofstede, cultural differences are manifested in four ways. First, symbols of words, gestures, pictures, or objects express cultural meaning to the individual. Second, heroes provide role models for the individual's behavior. Third, rituals demonstrate collective activities that are socially essential for persons within that culture. Fourth, values express a broad range of tendencies and preferences that have a functional purpose within each culture.

The four cultural dimensions in Hofstede's model describe patterns of preference. Although the dimensions were derived from patterns of how people constructed their culture, once they are abstracted the cultural patterns may function as typologies that describe ideal and alternative perspectives or types. However, real cases almost never correspond to a single ideal type. The cases are complex and much more multidimensional than any one type would suggest. The artificiality of these four types does present an opportunity, however. Pedersen and Ivey (in press) developed four synthetic cultures for generating four contrasting styles of applying microcounseling skills in a "culture-centered" approach to counseling. Each of the four synthetic cultures represents one "type," with Alpha representing high power distance, Beta representing strong uncertainty avoidance, Gamma representing strong individualism, and Delta representing strong masculinity. Because none of

TABLE 4
Differences in Teacher/Student and Student/Student Interaction Related to the Individualism Versus Collectivism Dimension

Collectivist Societies	Individualist Societies
• Positive association in society with whatever is rooted in tradition	• Positive association in society with whatever is "new"
• The young should learn; adults cannot accept student role	• One is never too old to learn; "permanent education"
• Students expect to learn how to do	• Students expect to learn how to learn
• Individual students will only speak up in class when called on personally by the teacher	• Individual students will speak up in class in response to a general invitation by the teacher
• Individuals will only speak up in small groups	• Individuals will speak up in large groups
• Large classes split socially into smaller, cohesive subgroups based on particularist criteria (e.g., ethnic affiliation)	• Subgroups in class vary from one situation to the next based on universalist criteria (e.g., the task "at hand")
• Formal harmony in learning situations should be maintained at all times (T-groups are taboo)	• Confrontation in learning situations can be salutary; conflicts can be brought into the open
• Neither the teacher nor any student should ever be made to lose face	• Face-consciousness is weak
• Education is a way of gaining prestige in one's social environment and of joining a higher status group ("a ticket to a ride")	• Education is a way of improving one's economic worth and self-respect based on ability and competence
• Diploma certificates are important and displayed on walls	• Diploma certificates have little symbolic value
• Acquiring certificates, even through illegal means (cheating, corruption), is more important than acquiring competence	• Acquiring competence is more important than acquiring certificates
• Teachers are expected to give preferential treatment to students (e.g., based on ethnic affiliation or recommendation by an influential person)	• Teachers are expected to be strictly impartial

Note. From "Cultural Differences in Teaching and Learning" by G. Hofstede, 1986, *International Journal of Intercultural Relations, 10*(3), pp. 312–314. Copyright 1986 by Pergamon Press. Reprinted by permission.

TABLE 5

Differences in Teacher/Student and Student/Student Interaction Related to the Power Distance Dimension

Small Power Distance Societies	Large Power Distance Societies
• Stress on impersonal "truth" that can in principle be obtained from any competent person • A teacher should respect the independence of his or her students • Student-centered education (premium on initiative) • Teacher expects students to initiate communication • Teacher expects students to find their own paths • Students may speak up spontaneously in class • Students allowed to contradict or criticize teacher • Effectiveness of learning related to amount of two-way communication in class • Outside class, teachers are treated as equals • In teacher/student conflicts, parents are expected to side with the student • Younger teachers are more liked than older teachers	• Stress on personal "wisdom" that is transferred in the relationship with a particular teacher (guru) • A teacher merits the respect of his or her students • Teacher-centered education (premium on order) • Students expect teacher to initiate communication • Students expect teacher to outline paths to follow • Students speak up in class only when invited by the teacher • Teacher is never contradicted nor publicly criticized • Effectiveness of learning related to excellence of the teacher • Respect for teachers is also shown outside class • In teacher/student conflicts, parents are expected to side with the teacher • Older teachers are more respected than younger teachers

these synthetic cultures occurs in the real world, they become a safe setting to practice multicultural counseling skills and increase the counselor's repertoire of cultural styles.

The practical implications of each cultural tendency were indicated by Hofstede (1986) as they might apply to the educational setting (Table 4).

In contasting the collectivist societies with the individualist societies, I am examining the differences between the United States and Third World countries. Individualism has an important function in the theory and practice of counseling as I have already indicated and continue to document in later

TABLE 6

Differences in Teacher/Student and Student/Student Interaction Related to the Uncertainty Avoidance Dimension

Weak Uncertainty Avoidance Societies	*Strong Uncertainty Avoidance Societies*
• Students feel comfortable in unstructured learning situations; vague objectives, broad assignments, no timetables	• Students feel comfortable in structured learning situations; precise objectives, detailed assignments, strict timetables
• Teachers are allowed to say "I don't know"	• Teachers are expected to have all the answers
• A good teacher uses plain language	• A good teacher uses academic language
• Students are rewarded for innovative approaches to problem solving	• Students are rewarded for accuracy in problem solving
• Teachers are expected to suppress emotions (and so are students)	• Teachers are allowed to behave emotionally (and so are students)
• Teachers interpret intellectual disagreement as a stimulating exercise	• Teachers interpret intellectual disagreement as personal disloyalty
• Teachers seek parents' ideas	• Teachers consider themselves experts who cannot learn anything from lay parents, and parents agree

chapters. It is useful to identify the specific ways in which a collectivistic and contrasting perspective may construct a quite different reality in which to live.

In contrasting small power distance societies with large power distance societies, it is useful to consider the importance of power relationships in counseling across cultures (Table 5). I have already identified the importance of power relationships across cultures. It is important to recognize that an equal distribution of power is preferred in some but not all cultures and that other cultures are quite comfortable with an unequal distribution of power.

In contrasting weak uncertainty avoidance societies with alternatives (Table 6), it is important to recognize that some cultures appreciate and function well in a highly structured setting, whereas others require more spontaneity. The counselor needs to function differently in these two contrasting cultural settings applying more or less structure appropriately.

In contrasting the societies displaying characteristics more traditionally associated with a feminine role from those societies traditionally associated with a masculine role (Table 7), it is important to suspend value judgments. This dimension is perhaps the most controversial of the four dimensions, and to the extent that one extreme seems more natural the opposite extreme may seem less appropriate.

TABLE 7
Differences in Teacher/Student and Student/Student Interaction Related to the Masculinity Versus Femininity Dimension

Feminine Societies	Masculine Societies
• Teachers avoid openly praising students	• Teachers openly praise good students
• Teachers use average student as the norm	• Teachers use best students as the norm
• System rewards students' social adaptation	• System rewards students' academic performance
• A student's failure in school is a relatively minor accident	• A student's failure in school is a severe blow to his or her self-image and may lead to suicide in extreme cases
• Students admire friendliness in teachers	• Students admire brilliance in teachers
• Students practice mutual solidarity	• Students compete with each other in class
• Students try to behave modestly	• Students try to make themselves visible
• Corporal punishment severely rejected	• Corporal punishment occasionally considered salutary
• Students choose academic subjects in view of intrinsic interest	• Students choose academic subjects in view of career opportunities
• Male students may choose traditionally feminine academic subjects	• Male students avoid traditionally feminine academic subjects

In reviewing Tables 4–7, it is apparent how the culture for each group was constructed as a functional response to the situation and relationships between persons in those situations. Although no individual nor group can fairly be labeled by one or another extreme on the four dimensions, individuals construct their own identities about self and cultural relationships incorporating responses similar to these lists of preferences.

4. A Personal–Cultural Orientation

Rather than labeling persons according to their culture, it might be more functional to understand the ways that different cultural influences lead individuals to behave in a particular way through constructing a "personal–cultural orientation" toward the situation or event. Accuracy in assessment and interpretation requires that we understand each person's behavior in the sociocultural context where that behavior occurred. Behaviors are frequently interpreted and changed without regard to the sociocultural context, resulting in misattribution and inaccurate data. Perhaps the most important reason for understanding a person's cultural context is to facilitate accuracy in the assessment and interpretation of a person's behavior. The Cultural Grid is an attempt to demonstrate how a personal–cultural orientation is constructed.

Hines and Pedersen (1980) developed the Cultural Grid to: (a) help identify and describe the cultural aspects of a situation, (b) help form hypotheses about cultural differences, and (c) explain how to train people for culturally appropriate interactions. The Cultural Grid is an open-ended model that matches social system variables with patterns of behavior, expectation, and value in a personal–cultural orientation to each event (Pedersen & Pedersen, 1985).

The Cultural Grid provides a means to describe and understand a person's behavior in the light of learned expectations and values. This more complicated approach to culture takes a broad and comprehensive perspective of culture beyond the traditional limits of fixed categories or dimensions. The Cultural Grid makes it easier to separate cultural from personal variables by identifying patterns of similarities and differences in the attributions or expectations attached to an action or behavior.

The 3 x 4 categories of the Cultural Grid, as shown in Table 8, assume that culture is so dynamic and complex that it changes even for each individual from one situation to another. Rather than describe a person's "culture" in the abstract, it seeks to identify an individual's personal–cultural orientation in a particular situation through attention to his or her behavior and its meaning.

A multicultural identity is complex (incorporating a great many cultures at the same time) and dynamic (in that only a few cultures are salient at any one point in time). The Cultural Grid presents a synthesis of the personal and social system variables that contribute to a multicultural identity. The Cultural Grid also provides guidelines for integrating your own multicultural identity with the identity of others through managing culturally learned behaviors and expectations.

TABLE 8
The Intrapersonal Cultural Grid

Social System Variables	Behavior	Expectation	Values
Ethnographic nationality ethnicity religion language			
Demographic age gender affectional orientation physical abilities			
Status social economic political educational			
Affiliation formal (like family or career) informal (like a shared idea or value)			

The Cultural Grid is based on the notion that culture is "within the person." The Grid provides a framework for integrating the cognitive variables of behavior, expectations, and value with the social system variables that have shaped the cultural identity for a single individual. The elements of the Cultural Grid are also useful for understanding the relationship between two or more individuals. The following examples demonstrate applications of the Cultural Grid to the relationship of two or more persons.

A person's behavior by itself does not communicate a clear message or intention. Only when that behavior is analyzed within a context of the person's salient social system variables does the person's intended message become clear. The context is best described by what is called "expectation." Expectation is a cognitive variable that includes behavior-outcome and stimulus-outcome expectancies and guides an individual's choices: "If this...(behavior) then that...(expectation)." The social system variables are essential to both persons in a relationship for understanding one another's anticipated outcome. The skill of extrapolating expectations from social system variables improves with practice.

After having examined your own and the other person's most salient social system variables, it should be possible for you to identify both your own and the other person's expectations for anticipated outcome such as "friendship," "trust," or "harmony." By applying the Cultural Grid to relationships, it is possible to understand and modify each person's behavior so that an appropriate step is taken toward a mutually valuable anticipated "win-win" outcome.

Every counseling relationship contains a multicultural perspective to a greater or lesser extent. The Cultural Grid serves to:

- classify cultural perspectives in a complex yet dynamic framework without reducing culture to static and fixed dimensions;
- differentiate between personal and cultural perspectives in an event;
- link culturally learned behaviors with the culturally learned expectations and values behind those behaviors; and
- link culturally learned behaviors, expectations, and values with the appropriate social system contexts in which those responses were learned.

Behaviors do not easily reveal the learned expectations, consequences, or meanings that are intended through that behavior. Similar behaviors may have different meanings, and different behaviors may have the same meanings. It is important to interpret behaviors accurately in terms of the intended expectations, consequences, and meanings attached to those behaviors. If two people are accurate in their interpretations of each other's behavior, they do not always need to agree. The two people may agree to disagree and work together in harmony nonetheless.

This framework becomes useful in understanding a person's personal–cultural orientation to behave in expected or unexpected ways when confronted with problems. The Intrapersonal Cultural Grid becomes a useful tool of analysis through following a series of four steps—going from the particular and concrete to the more general and abstract.

First, identify and separate a particular behavior in yourself or someone else. The behavior should include a particular action, decision, or thought. Define that behavior narrowly enough so that it becomes specific. For example, analyze the behavior of reading this book.

Second, identify the expectations behind this behavior: "If I do this...then *that* will happen." What do you expect to happen as a result of that behavior? When you decided to read this book, you probably had several expectations in mind. You may have expected to learn new ideas, fulfill a requirement, catch up on the literature, or prepare to work in a multicultural setting. There are many expectations, both explicit and implicit, attached to each behavior.

Third, identify the values behind each expectation. Some examples of values might include learning, change, relevance, competence, responsibility, to name just a few of the values that might justify the explanations that explain your behavior of reading this book.

Fourth, ask yourself from where those values came. Who taught you those values? This may require you to analyze the thousands of social system variables from ethnographic, demographic, status, and affiliations that continue to be meaningful to you. Your personal–cultural orientation toward the decision to read this book was constructed out of the expectations and values taught to you by salient social system variables in your life.

The Intrapersonal Cultural Grid provides a framework for analyzing the way in which a personal–cultural orientation is constructed within the individual, and how to understand a person's behavior from within that person's cultural context.

The Interpersonal Cultural Grid (Figure 5) is an attempt to apply the same basic idea to the relationship between persons or groups by separating behaviors from expectations.

The Interpersonal Cultural Grid includes four quadrants. Each quadrant explains one large or small part of a relationship between two individuals or groups. Salience may change from one quadrant to the other as the relationship changes.

In the first quadrant, two individuals have similar behaviors and similar positive expectations. There is a high level of accuracy in both individuals' interpretations of one another's behavior and the positive shared expectations behind that behavior. This aspect of the relationship is congruent and probably harmonious. Both persons are smiling, and both persons expect friendship.

FIGURE 5
The Interpersonal Cultural Grid

Behavior

		Same	Different
	Same or Positive	I	II
Expectation			
	Different or Negative	III	IV

In the second quadrant, two individuals have different behaviors but share the same positive expectations. There is a high level of agreement in that both persons expect trust and friendliness, but there is a low level of accuracy because each person perceives and incorrectly interprets the other's behavior as different and probably hostile. This quadrant is characteristic of multicultural conflict where each person is applying a self-reference criterion to interpret the other person's behavior. The conditions described in Quadrant 2 are very unstable and, unless the shared positive expectations are quickly made explicit, the salience is likely to change toward Quadrant 3. It is important for at least one of the two persons to capture the conflict in this second quadrant, where the persons may agree to disagree or adapt to one another without feeling threatened because they both have shared positive expectations.

In the third quadrant, the two persons have the same behaviors but now they have different expectations, and at least one of them probably has a negative expectation for the relationship. The similar behaviors give the appearance of harmony and agreement, but the hidden different or negative expectations may destroy the relationship. One person may continue to expect trust and friendliness, whereas the other person is now negatively distrustful and unfriendly even though they are both presenting smiling and glad-handing behaviors. If these two persons discover that the reason for their conflict is a difference of expectation, they may be able to return to Quadrant 2 and reverse the escalating conflict between them. If the difference in expectations is ignored or undiscovered, the conflict eventually moves to the fourth quadrant.

The fourth quadrant is where the two people have different and/or negative expectations and they stop pretending to behave in congruent ways. The two persons are "at war" with one another and may not want to increase harmony in their relationship any longer. This relationship is likely to result in hostile disengagement. It is very difficult to retrieve conflict from this fourth quadrant because one or both parties has stopped trying to mediate or reduce the conflict.

Although the behaviors are relatively easy to identify as congruent/similar or incongruent/dissimilar, it is much more difficult to identify the expectations accurately. Rubin, Kim, and Peretz (1990) discussed the difficulties in accurately identifying another person's expectations. First, multicultural conflict might be based on misattributions and misperceptions, but both parties respond to their perception of reality, whether true or not. Second, there is usually a lack of reliable or complete information about what others expect, resulting in partisan or self-serving expectations by both parties. Third, both culturally different parties typically have stereotyped expectations about one another rather than accurate data. Fourth, any perceived inaccuracy or inappropriateness in assessing the other person's expectations may destroy the relationship. Fifth, selective perception, attributional distortion, and self-fulfilling prophecies might increase rather than decrease conflict.

Smiling is an ambiguous behavior. It may imply trust and friendliness or it may not. The smile may be interpreted accurately or it may not. Outside of its learned context, the smile has no fixed meaning. The example of smiling provides a means to apply the four types of interaction to distinguish among ideal, multicultural, personal, and hostile alternatives.

Now, let us consider how the Cultural Grid describes two alternative sequences of events between an employer and employee over a 5-week period. In the first example, the importance of expectation behind each behavior is not considered. You can see the relationship disintegrate as the participants move toward increasingly hostile perspectives. In the second example, the importance of the expectation behind each behavior is considered. You can see that the participants have maintained the relationship between the more workable Type I and Type II perspectives.

EXAMPLE 1:

A young employee is having difficulty working with his older employer from a different country, but neither is skilled in attending to the other's cultural identity.

First Week

The employer and employee behave quite differently, with the employee being friendly and informal and the employer being formal and professionally cool toward others.

The different behaviors suggest at face value that the employer and employee have different expectations for what constitutes "appropriate" behavior. However, in this case, both intend friendliness. (Type II)

Second Week

The differences between this employer and employee have continued to persist and have now become a source of irritation and conflict between them. As the different behavior patterns persist, both people may well conclude that they do not share the same expectations for efficiency or effectiveness in the work place or perhaps even for liking one another as persons. (Type III or Type IV)

Third Week

The employee considered modifying his behavior to become more formal because he needed the job, but he felt like he was being dishonest in compromising his own ideals. The employer considered modifying his behavior to become less formal because he needed the employee, but he felt like that would not be fair to his other employees nor to his concept of how the office should be run. One or the other partner may compromise his beliefs and change his behavior to fit the other's, but even if their behaviors become similar their expectations for why they are behaving as they are will become even more divergent. Compromise by either person would likely result in personal as well as professional dislike and animosity. (Type III)

Fourth Week

Both the employer and employee finally give up, saying they have tried everything humanly possible to make the situation work. As a result, the employee either leaves or is fired. This total conflict situation occurs when both behaviors and expectations are now so totally different or negative that there is little motivation to work toward harmony. (Type IV)

Fifth Week

Both employer and employee conclude that there is a low level of agreement between them. Neither person is aware that there is also a low level of accuracy in his communication with the other. (Type IV)

EXAMPLE 2:

In an alternative scenario, the young employee is having difficulty working with his older employer from a different country, but both are skilled in attending to cultural variables of interaction.

First Week

Although the employer and employee behave quite differently, they examine the reason or expectation for each other's behavior from the other person's viewpoint. The different behaviors are understood as different expressions of the same shared expectation for "excellence." (Type II)

Second Week

Because both the employer and employee share the same expectation, they are able to interpret one another's behavior accurately and focus on the expectation they both share rather than on their differences. (Type II)

Third Week

Because they have the same expectations, the employer and employee may modify their behaviors toward the other without feeling like they are compromising their principles. They may also agree to disagree and maintain their contrasting behavior style now that they know what the other's behavior means. (Type II or Type I)

Fourth Week

Both partners are likely to move toward a more harmonious situation where the similarity of expectations results in more similar behaviors, with both employer and employee modifying their behaviors somewhat to fit the other. Ultimately, both expectations and behaviors are likely to become more similar and harmonious. (Type II or Type I)

Fifth Week

By examining the cultural expectations and values behind each other's behavior, both employer and employee are now able to accurately assess the other's expectation. At this point, it is easier to decide if the two people are similar enough in their behaviors and expectations to work together and to tolerate the other's different behavior. (Type II or Type I)

The open-ended range of personal and social system categories indicated by the Cultural Grid provides a conceptual road map for the counselor or interviewer to interpret a person's behavior accurately in the context of learned expectations. For example, a counselor might be interviewing a Black, teenaged, wealthy, highly educated student on a personal problem. The student refers back to each of these indicated social system variables as salient to the problem during the half-hour interview. However, the counselor is so fixated on the fact that the student is in a wheelchair and is paraplegic that the counselor treats the student's handicap as the single most salient aspect of the student's culture during the whole interview. The actual problem had little or nothing to do with the student's handicap, and the counselor's assessment was inaccurate.

The introduction of a personal–cultural orientation construct provides the means to resolve a dilemma in multicultural counseling. On the one hand, data suggest that patterns of both group and individual similarities and differences must be accounted for in multicultural contact. On the other hand, attempts to describe patterns of similarities and differences through fixed dimensions or categories result in stereotyping. Although fixed data about cultures may be predictive in the form of aggregate trends in large groups that are more or less homogeneous, they are less predictive for individuals within those cultures (Atkinson, Staso, & Hosford, 1978). An accurate assessment of another person's personal–cultural orientation is complex and dynamic, but is important to counselors and interviewers.

The Cultural Grid is a useful tool for analyzing multicultural situations. It provides practical assistance in managing the complexity of culture. The Grid is also useful for analyzing case studies:

- The Cultural Grid provides a framework to portray a perspective that confirms the personal and cultural orientation for each situation.
- Personal–cultural orientations can be compared across time or people to demonstrate how the same behavior can be explained by different expectations or values in different cultural settings.
- The dynamic and changing priorities of social system variables are matched with personal/cognitive variables for each time and place.
- A comprehensive description of culture includes demographic, status, and affiliation as well as ethnographic cultural variables in the range of analysis.
- The close relationship between culturally learned behaviors and culturally different expectations or values behind similar behaviors is clearly distinguished.

I have introduced two different approaches for interpreting cultural systems. The Kluckhohn-Strodtbeck approach is the more conventional and traditional basis for defining culture. I also introduced a constructivist perspective. In an attempt to build on these perspectives of culture, I considered an alternative approach in the Cultural Grid, which describes culture as complex and dynamic. When multicultural conflict is not appropriately understood and accounted for, it may quickly evolve into interpersonal conflict where differences in behavior produce differences in expectation and value. The Cultural Grid suggests one framework for assessing the range of complex variables that determine behavior and reflect expectations or values in each event for each individual. By combining both the personal and systems aspects of a person's cultural identity in the Cultural Grid, it is possible to take "snapshots" of how a person's culture influences each behavior in specific, rather than general, ways.

The practical advantage of the Cultural Grid is that it increases a person's accurate assessment of another person's behavior in the context of the latter's culture. Without reference to these expectations and values, one is unable to interpret accurately any behavior outside its cultural context.

The matching of cultural with personal data provides a framework for understanding how culture works both in the aggregate and the individual instance. This understanding of culture is an important foundation for developing basic multicultural skills in subsequent chapters.

The Cultural Grid has a practical use in managing cultural conflict. In each application, the same series of steps for applying the Cultural Grid are followed:

Step 1: Identify the relevant social system variables (about 10 or 12) in the person or persons being considered;

Step 2: Identify the behaviors displayed or presented by the person or persons being considered;

Step 3: Identify the expectations that probably would be attached to the behavior for each of the social systems if that system were salient;

Step 4: Identify the social systems variable that is most likely to be salient for the person or persons being considered at the time the behavior was displayed; and

Step 5: Explore the possibility that the expectation for the most likely salient social systems variable is the interpretation intended by the person or persons.

Usually there are many different expectations attached to each behavior. If you begin by emphasizing those expectations that are shared by two persons, you are more likely to move toward a Type I (ideal) or Type II (multicultural) relationship with a higher potential for harmony and positive outcomes.

5. Conclusion

When the judge asked Willy Sutton why he robbed banks, he responded, "Why judge, because that's where the money is!" In the same way, we might say that cultural patterns are important because that is where the power is. By looking at the separation of fact from inference, discovered values from constructed cultures, and the Cultural Grid framework, this chapter has attempted to identify why cultural patterns are so important for understanding all behaviors. This chapter has described several alternative ways that cultural patterns have been used to interpret behavior as well as the advantages and disadvantages of each. In each explanation, it seems clear that culture is not an external force but an internalized perspective of reality as we know it.

If culture is indeed within the person, then developing a multicultural identity becomes an essential part of personal development. We need to go beyond the obvious labels used to describe individual and collective cultural identities. We need to recognize the principle of culture shock in all processes of adapting our identity to each new context. We need to understand the process of developing an identity as a complex but not chaotic series of stages or categories. Finally, we need to see our multicultural identity as a synthesis of the many cultures in our lives. This synthesis is both complex and dynamic, shaping both our expectations and our behaviors. We construct our own cultural identity.

As we continue to develop our multicultural awareness, knowledge, and skill, a clear and accurate perception of our own multicultural identity becomes an essential element. Our ability to shape and influence our environment, bring about desired changes, and find harmony with others depend on knowing ourselves and our cultures.

CHAPTER 7

Review of the Research on Multicultural Counseling

Major objective:

1. To identify the empirical research foundation of multicultural counseling theory and practice.

Secondary objectives:

1. To review the historical development of research on multicultural counseling.
2. To review the research on counseling minorities.
3. To review international research on counseling.
4. To review conceptual and theoretical perspectives of multicultural counseling.
5. To review multicultural counseling from the counselor's viewpoint.
6. To review multicultural counseling from the client's viewpoint.

Multicultural counseling objectives presume that each counselor, client, presenting problem, and counseling environment is shaped by many different interacting culturally defined relationships. From this perspective, all counseling is to some extent multicultural. Counseling theories and strategies that ignore culture are not likely to be either appropriate or accurate because they do not interpret the client's behavior in his or her cultural context.

The cultural context includes both similarities and differences. In a sense, the multicultural counselor must become "cross-eyed," emphasizing both the differences and the similarities between people. If cultural differences are overemphasized, the results are stereotypes and exclusionary practice. If cultural similarities are overemphasized, the result is an imposition of control by the dominant culture.

1. The Historical Perspective

Because culture is complex and dynamic, the research on multicultural counseling has frequently been flawed. Ponterotto and Casas (1991) pointed out 10 weaknesses of the research: (a) There is no unified conceptual framework, (b) the counselor–client process factor is overemphasized and psychological factors are underemphasized, (c) too much research is based on analogues and simulations rather than real-world interactions, (d) intracultural or within-group differences are too frequently disregarded, (e) there is an overdependence on samples of convenience, (f) there is continued reliance on culturally biased measures, (g) the subject's cultural background is inadequately described, (h) the limits of generalizability are not typically indicated, (i) there is inadequate input from minorities, and (j) there is a failure of responsibility to feed back results to the minority subjects. This chapter seeks to guide the reader toward examples of excellent research on multicultural counseling already widely and conveniently available elsewhere.

By viewing counseling and therapy in their multicultural context, several points become apparent: (a) Counseling functions have spread rapidly to become a complex social industry on a worldwide basis; (b) counseling as we know it is a label for one of the many alternatives for intervention to influence a person's mental health; (c) counseling as the preferred alternative is based on assumptions generic to a very small portion of the world's people; and (d) a multiculturally appropriate application in counseling is necessarily responsive to the social context (Lefley & Pedersen, 1986; Pedersen, 1985).

The historical spread of counseling has been documented in a wide range of cultures. Although mental health problems are similar across cultures, the labels have changed from one culture to another over time. What has changed is the complex classification of the environments where counseling is being applied, and the categories of problems, illness, difficulty, or crisis. A specialized counseling industry has developed to meet this need. The number of consumers as well as the number of providers is rising in proportion to the increasingly liberal definition of *appropriate* criteria for entering counseling and therapy (Favazza & Oman, 1977; Triandis, 1985). Although the labels of counseling might be new, the functions of how help is provided are probably not new. Torrey (1986) made a strong case that "witch doctors" and psychiatrists use the same techniques. Multicultural counseling in the domestic context has been characterized by the political and economic interaction of special interest and minority groups throughout the country (Sue & Sue, 1990).

The domestic context of multicultural relations has been characterized by political influence and socioeconomic impact. Ironically, the basis of dissatisfaction was written into the idealist promises of the Declaration of Independence. As a nation, we have experienced a social revolution that has idealized a state of equality among races, genders, generations, and peoples. We have been taught that only those who make use of their opportunities and develop special skills can be assured of their fair share. The concept of equality is thereby diluted to a "numbers game," granting us the equal right to become unequal, as perceived by the minorities, through competing with one another (Dreikurs, 1972). Bryne (1977) pointed out how the perception of equality has politicized the delivery of counseling services in our domestic social context. Likewise, Aubrey (1977) pointed out the trend in counseling to emphasize normal developmental concerns of individuals to the exclusion of a special group's concerns in the name of "equality."

With the civil rights movement of the 1950s, the militancy of minorities for change gained momentum. With the growth of the community mental health movement of the 1960s, mental health care became the right of all citizens, not just the wealthy or middle-class dominant majority (Atkinson et al., 1983; LeVine & Padilla, 1980). The issues of feminism and popular dissent nurtured by the anti-Vietnam War movement fostered a climate of discontent where protest was accepted and in some cases even demanded. The stigma of discrimination became synonymous with any attempt to treat groups differently. However, Sue (1981) suggested that minority groups may not be asking for equal treatment as much as for equal access to power. Differential treatment is not necessarily discriminatory or preferential. Multiculturally skilled counseling is almost necessarily and inevitably differential across cultures in providing an appropriate counseling service for each group.

With increased publications on minority group counseling in the late 1970s and 1980s, a great deal of confusion has occurred in the use of terms like *race, ethnicity, culture,* and *minority* (Atkinson et al., 1993). The term *race* technically refers to biological differences, whereas *ethnicity* rightly refers to group classifications as was discussed earlier in chapter 2. People of the same ethnic group within the same race might still be culturally different. Other terms such as *culturally deprived* or *culturally disadvantaged,* and even the more modern *culturally different* and *culturally distinct,* were created to explain why a minority group is out of step with the majority population. Minorities, then, are groups of people singled out for unequal and different treatment and who regard themselves as objects of discrimination (Atkinson et al., 1993).

2. The Minority Perspective

The most complete annotated bibliography on "Treatment Considerations with Culturally Diverse Populations" has been compiled by Chang et al. (1992) at the California School of Professional Psychology, Berkeley, Alameda. This annotated bibliography on Native Americans (30 pages), Asians and Asian Americans (90 pages), African Americans (146 pages), and Hispanic/Latinos (84 pages) provides the most comprehensive review of the minority perspective in the contemporary counseling literature. This chapter does not seek to summarize those sources.

There are several excellent resources for reviewing the literature on counseling minorities. Sue and Sue (1990) emphasized the political sensitivity of counselors working with culturally different clients, and Pedersen, Draguns, Lonner, and Trimble (1989) compiled an edited version of different and cultural perspectives. Culture-specific counseling techniques have been highlighted by Pedersen et al. for providing culturally sensitive, relevant, and appropriate services to minority clients. Multicultural counseling guidelines were organized by Sue and Sue into those with: (a) appropriate process and appropriate goals, (b) appropriate process and inappropriate goals, (c) inappropriate process and appropriate goals, and (d) inappropriate process and inappropriate goals.

Atkinson et al. (1993) focused on counseling American minorities to help establish the necessary and sufficient conditions for working with culturally different clients and the within-group diversity among minority groups as well. They documented the failure to meet mental health needs of minorities, the consequences of unmet needs, and the underutilization of mental counseling services that are available, and they identified specific barriers to counseling minorities.

Locke (1992) provided a comprehensive model for culture-specific counseling. Locke's model focuses on increasing the counselor's self-awareness of his or her own cultural heritage, beginning with the individual and then moving to family, community, culture, and global influences for a comprehensive awareness of cultural diversity in and among nine minority groups. Lee and Richardson (1991) also provided an excellent review of counseling ethnic and racial minorities by emphasizing the cultural dynamics of 13 specific cultural groups. Ramirez (1991) developed a "multicultural orientation" for counseling that includes: (a) striving for self-actualization, (b) adaptability to different environments, (c) designing innovative solutions to problems, (d) achieving social justice, and (e) getting the most out of life. Ramirez emphasized the importance of "cognitive and cultural flex." Vargas and Koss-Chioino (1992) edited an excellent review of family counseling among minority groups. Cheatham and Stewart (1990) edited an interdisciplinary approach to counseling Black families that emphasizes both conceptualizations and implications of counseling.

Throughout the literature about counseling minorities, the primary issue involves the consequences of contact between groups or cultures where one group is perceived as more powerful than the other. To a great extent, the literature about the minority perspective has to do with the access to power. This aspect is of fundamental concern whenever a majority culture and a minority culture group come into contact.

The "contact hypothesis" mentioned earlier tests the assumption that just bringing people from different groups together will result in more positive intergroup relations. Amir (1969), Miller and Brewer (1984), and others reviewed the literature from social psychology on the contract hypothesis and drew three basic conclusions. First, when groups come together under favorable conditions, the intergroup contact does result in more positive relationships. Second, when groups come together under unfavorable conditions, the intergroup contact results in an increase of negative relationships and disharmony. Third, spontaneous intergroup contact is more likely to occur under unfavorable conditions than under favorable conditions. These unfavorable conditions are most easily illustrated in the relationships between dominant and minority groups. Atkinson et al. (1993) included the condition of being oppressed as an important defining characteristic of any minority group. This might be the case even when the group is not a numerical "minority," as in the literature about women as a minority group. Therefore, the literature on minority relations reflects the struggle of each minority against a dominant majority group and also of some minority groups against other minority groups competing for limited resources under unfavorable conditions.

We have already reviewed research on stages of racial/ethnic identity development. Ibrahim and Kahn (1985) reported data on five value orientations to measure counselors' awareness of culturally different client value orientations. Likewise, Sue (1977, 1978) developed a world view paradigm based on locus of control and locus of responsibility. Helms' (1984) cognitive development model proposes that trainees develop a multicultural awareness by starting with historical and sociocultural information, then proceeding to skill building, cognitive and affective self-awareness, and finally to emersion in a contrasting culture. Carney and Kahn (1984) presented a developmental training model that suggests five stages of development. Other models include those of Arrendondo-Dowd and Gonslaves (1980), Copeland (1983), McDavis and Parker (1977), and Sue (1973).

Abundant evidence came to light in the 1970s about how counseling services were being underutilized by minority groups, and that behavior described as pathological in a minority culture such as individualistic assertiveness may be viewed as adaptive in a majority-culture client (Grier & Cobbs, 1968; Wilson & Calhoon, 1974). Asian Americans, Blacks, Chicanos, Native Americans, and members of other minority groups terminate counseling significantly earlier than do White clients (Atkinson et al., 1993; Sue, 1977). In most of the literature, these examples of differentiation are credited to cultural barriers such as language barriers, class-bound values, and culture-bound attitudes that hinder the formation of good counseling relationships. To some extent these conditions certainly do exist and do result in a minority group's disillusionment with the professional field of mental health as a solution for social and individual coping. Casas (1984) suggested that minority clients have been ignored in the past because of (a) a blatant and irresponsible lack of interest in these groups by the dominant culture, (b) continued racism, bias, and prejudice against minorities, (c) an ethnocentric perspective by the dominant culture, and (d) counselors' preference to work with clients more like themselves.

There have been numerous efforts to compensate for inequitable practices in providing mental health services to minorities in culturally sensitive ways (Lonner & Sundberg, 1985). One example of such an effort is in the area of testing. There have been extensive studies of problems in the use of psychological tests with American minority clients, particularly intelligence tests across cultures. The development of culture-free, and more recently culture-fair, intelligence tests is included in the several attempts to measure intelligence across cultures (Brislin, Lonner, & Thorndike, 1973). Frijda and Jahoda (1966) pointed out that a culture-fair test would need to be either equally familiar or equally unfamiliar to persons from responding cultures, which is an impossible precondition. Tests are more widely accepted as inevitably biased, and in more recent multicultural research the emphasis has been placed on accounting for cultural differences in the interpretation of test results that are sensitive to these inherent biases. Any test that is precisely accurate or appropriate for one cultural setting is almost necessarily biased in fundamentally different cultural settings.

Another area where the reality of cultural bias is recognized is public policy statements that acknowledge the importance of counselor consumers' cultural environment. The National Institute of Mental Health (Fields, 1979), The American Psychological Association (Korman, 1974), the American Psychological Association Council of Representatives (American Psychological Association, 1979), the American Psychiatric Association's Task Force on Ethnocentricity among Psychiatrists (Wintrob & Harvey, 1981), and the recent President's Commission on Mental Health (1978) all emphasized the ethical responsibility of counselors and therapists to know their clients' cultural values and the public responsibility of professional organizations to meet the culturally different mental health needs within a pluralistic society.

This has resulted in culturally sensitive guidelines for accreditation of mental health training programs, special funding for research on cultural differences in mental health services, and the development of resources for collective pressure to make mental health services more responsive to cultural differences. The adjustment has not been trouble-free, however. Atkinson et al.(1978) described problems in meeting federal standards for admitting minority applicants to counseling while maintaining a single admission standard on test scores and selection following the Bakke decision in California. Jaslow (1978) described some of the problems in the desegregation of schools and the difficulty in retraining school personnel, students, counselor educators, and communities in the skills for working in a racially mixed school.

The research on career development of racial and ethnic minorities was well summarized in Leong (1991) through his special issue of *The Career Development Quarterly*. Leong pointed out demographic trends in U.S. health that will influence multicultural counseling. First, the work force population will grow more slowly in the future than in the recent past. Second, the population and work force will be older as the population of younger workers shrinks. Third, women in the work force will increase from 51.5% in 1980 to 61.1% in the year 2000. Fourth, minorities in the work force will increase from 13.6% in 1980 to 15.5% in the year 2000. Fifth, the numbers of immigrants in the work force will continue to increase. Leong's special issue sought to stimulate more research and theory building on the career development of minorities by looking at the validity of career measures, the applicability of career decision-making strategies, and developing career development guidelines for specific ethnocultural populations.

If we include "vulnerable populations" within the broader definition of *minorities*, the focus of research goes beyond multiethnic populations. Spacapan and Thompson (1991) reviewed the literature on helping vulnerable populations, such as children, medical patients, lower level employees, the elderly, and others, focusing on "perceived control." Asch and Fine (1988) reviewed the literature documenting the "stigma" attached to disability as a minority group as a result of false assumptions.

1. It is often assumed that disability is located solely in biology, and thus disability is accepted uncritically as an independent variable.
2. When a disabled person faces problems it is assumed that the impairment causes them.
3. It is assumed that the disabled person is a "victim."
4. It is assumed that disability is central to the disabled person's self-concept, self-definition, social comparisons, and reference group.

5. It is assumed that having a disability is synonymous with needing help and social support.

These assumptions are at best misleading and at worst hurtful.

Ponterotto and Casas (1991) reviewed research on racial/ethnic minority groups and developed a 12-item research agenda for the 1990s.

1. We need accurate epidemiological data on the incidence of psychological problems among racial/ethnic groups.
2. We need research on minority identity models.
3. We need more research on the Eurocentric bias in political, social, and educational institutions.
4. We need research on how to reverse the White middle-class status quo in social institutions.
5. We need more research on White racial identity development.
6. We need more research on the strengths rather than just the weaknesses of ethnic/racial groups.
7. We need more research on intracultural or within-group diversity.
8. We need more research on bicultural identity development.
9. We need more research on youth outside the adult and college-age samples of convenience.
10. We need more research on primary prevention and parent training programs.
11. We need more research on testing, assessment, and measures used with ethnic/racial minority groups.
12. We need research into both the culture-specific emic and the culture-general etic aspects of counseling.

3. The International Perspective

Although culture as a concept is ancient, the systematic study of culture and psychopathology is a phenomenon of the 20th century. Initially the fields of psychoanalysis and anthropology were the focus of interest in studying culture and mental health, later expanding to include epidemiology and sociology, and more recently the subspecialty of social psychiatry. The focus of study has shifted from the anthropological study of remote cultures to the cultural variations in modern pluralistic and complex societies.

Researchers in the Third World have developed models and methods that challenge us to reconsider psychology and the counseling process in a world context. Sloan (1990) suggested that "the first move toward Third World involvement by Western-trained behavioral scientists must be a self-purging of individualistic and scientistic thinking" (p. 16). This change would require less focus on individual behavior and more focus on applied research/intervention and prevention programs, public health education, family systems approaches, community mobilization, program evaluation, and fitting psychology into world systems. It is possible to value the quality of individual human lives without taking an individualistic perspective.

Through the works of researchers like Kiev (1972), Prince (1976), Kleinman (1980), and Torrey (1986), the indigenous approaches to mental health in non-Western cultures began to be taken more seriously, replacing the "crazy shaman" notion of curiosity and fascination with exotic healing techniques, and sometimes even integrating them with other modern counseling services. Major cross-cultural studies of psychiatric evaluation and diagnosis (World Health Organization, 1979) have resulted in a more careful assessment of culture beyond the exotic, dramatic, and more conspicuous manifestations (Draguns, 1980) to a "near-to-home" phenomenon of everyday life as well. Torrey (1986) went so far as to draw direct parallels between the techniques of witch doctors and psychiatrists in (a) naming their treatment, (b) identifying a cause, (c) establishing rapport, (d) developing client expectation for improvement, and (e) demonstrating legitimacy. However, Kleinman (1980) opposed any conclusion that would imply shamans and psychiatrists do the same thing, and considered this identification an oversimplification that does a profound disservice to both psychiatrists and shamans.

Recently there has been more emphasis on what "developed cultures" can learn about providing mental health services from less-developed cultures. Prince (1976, 1980) demonstrated how the activity of all healers and healing institutions depends on endogenous self-righting mechanisms for healing to occur, rather than on exogenous experts. In non-Western cultures with fewer formal healing institutions, there is more dependence on endogenous self-righting mechanisms such as dreams, sleep or rest, altered states of consciousness, religious experience, or even psychotic reaction as healing resources. Some of the renewed interest in learning how these self-righting mechanisms work is due to their proven effectiveness in managing psychiatric disorders, the shortage and expense of modern psychiatric facilities, the high prestige of some endogenous approaches in their home cultures, and the evidence that modern treatment methods tend to be culture-bound and ineffective (Higginbotham, 1979a, 1979b; Prince, 1980).

Reynolds (1980) adapted *Naikan, Morita,* and several other systems of traditional Japanese therapy to Western cultures as uniquely appropriate to mental illness in Western as well as Asian society. Although Reynolds was careful to acknowledge the unrealistic claims in much of the popular literature about meditation, Zen-related therapies, and other non-Western approaches, he demonstrated the value and adaptability of these therapies when appropriately presented. Many other non-Western derived therapies have gained popularity but frequently without documentation or careful standards of delivery (Pedersen, 1979).

As a consequence of being culturally relevant, phenomena are inevitably culturally perceived. Even in psychobiological processes such as the perception of space and cognition, there are cultural differences (Diaz-Guerrero, 1977; Marsella & Golden, 1980). These culturally specific characteristics challenge the universality of psychology, but not its potential scientific relevance. There are alternative assumptions (Wrightsman, 1992) to the "American ideal" (Sampson, 1977), the premises of the Protestant ethic (Rotenberg, 1974; Draguns, 1974), and the pervasive assumptions of individualism (Hsu, 1972; Pedersen, 1983; Watts, 1963). It is increasingly clear that Western styles of mental health services are (a) inappropriate, (b) too expensive, (c) too dependent on technology, and (d) frequently destructive to the non-Western host setting. There are numerous assumptions, beginning with individualistic biases, that require us to consider non-Western alternatives.

Watts and Herr (1976) discovered that societies that are prescriptive about individual talents being used for the state provide different counseling services than societies with less social control and more individual freedom of choice. Most international counseling theories are rooted in either psychological or sociological perspectives (Herr, 1985), with the psychological perspective emphasizing individual choice and the sociological perspective emphasizing the social obligation.

Cultural differences require different ways of doing counseling. Triandis (1985) separated countries that are more individualistic from those that are more collectivist in their social norms. Self-concept and self-esteem measures vary a great deal across different cultures, as do other cognitive structures and habits, as a result of an individualistic or collectivist orientation. In the same vein, in what Triandis called "tight" cultures, people have a greater aversion to uncertainty than do people in "loose" cultures, again according to prevailing social norms. Kleinberg (1985) discussed other social-psychological aspects relevant to international counseling.

Kleinman (1978) developed ethnomedical models from his work in China and other non-Western cultures that contrast with the biomedical models of modern medical treatment. Kleinman attacked the "discipline-bound compartmentalization" of medical research through ethnography, ethnoscience, epidemiology, and cultural systems analysis. The cultural context does not tell us merely about the social and cultural environment of a particular local system of medicine, but also about its specific cognitive, behavioral, and institutional structure and the cultural constructional principles (values and symbolic meanings) underlying and determining that structure (Kleinman, 1978).

In his book *Rethinking Psychiatry*, Kleinman (1988) discussed the important role of culture in counseling and psychotherapy:

> Culture holds importance for psychiatry, in my view, **principally** because it brings a special kind of criticism to bear on research regarding mental illness and its treatment. From the cross-cultural perspective, the fundamental questions in psychiatry—how to distinguish the normal from the abnormal; how disorder is perceived, experienced and expressed; why treatments succeed or fail; indeed the purpose and scope of psychiatry itself—all are caught up in a reciprocal relationship between the social world of the person and his body/self (psychobiology). (p. 3)

Language, symbols, values, and cultural forms are the mediators between a client's social and personal world. Diagnosis and treatment are done differently in different cultures or countries of the world. By learning their ways, we are not only better able to help them but some of their solutions may work better for our own problems.

Sheikh and Sheikh (1989) compared Eastern and Western approaches to healing where non-Western approaches do not distinguish between mind and body in a revival of a holistic vision of life. Chapters on Hindu, Buddhist, Islamic, Jewish, and Christian approaches to psychology and neuroscience attempt a synthesis of Eastern and Western approaches to healing. Another of the many recent volumes in this is Ward's (1989) 14-chapter book on altered states of consciousness and mental health. Other volumes with an international perspective from a more Western viewpoint include Dasen, Berry, and Sartorius (1988) on the criteria of health across cultures; Segall et al. (1990) included large sections on mental health from an international perspective, as did Berry et al. (1992) in two comprehensive reference works. Brislin (1993) also provided a very useful international survey of how culture influences behavior. There are many more new and extensive publications on counseling and psychotherapy from an international perspective.

The international perspective has also been important in counseling refugees from abroad. The Southeast Asian refugee population is one of the fastest-growing ethnic minorities in the United States. Because federal funding for counseling refugees from Asia, Europe, the Caribbean, and elsewhere has dramatically diminished, more counselors and therapists without training in the refugee's cultures are being matched with refugee clients. Lefley (1989) did an excellent job of describing a similar crisis in providing counseling to refugees from the Caribbean and Spanish-speaking countries.

Counseling international students in the United States provides another example of the international perspectives for counseling. Pedersen (1991b) reviewed the available research on counseling international students. Research on counseling international students has emphasized adjustment problems without regard to the developmental process experienced by international students. Traditional student developmental theories based on Perry's model, Chickering's model, or Minority Ethnic Identity models have not worked with international students, and the accuracy of other standard test measures has also been widely challenged (Thomas, 1985; Thomas & Althen, 1989). The Graduate Record Exam has been found to be inappropriate for international students (Wilson, 1986), and other clinical measures have proved difficult to interpret (Worchel & Goethals, 1989). Those studies that are available have disregarded special features of the international student's context. Yau, Sue, and Hayden (1992) suggested that the directive approach may not be appropriate for working with all international students. Research on situation variables (Furnham & Bochner, 1986), problem check lists (Crano & Crano, 1990), and others has been more helpful. Miller (1989) and Westwood, Lawrence, and Paul (1986) demonstrated the usefulness of peer counseling with international students.

The international perspective puts the problems of developing a multicultural awareness in a world context. Many of the problems being researched across countries highlight parallel problems across ethnic or socially defined groups within each country as well. By studying international differences and similarities, we can identify differences and similarities closer to home that otherwise might escape examination.

4. The Theoretical Perspective

Strong (1991) contended that "counseling psychologists' aversion to theory-driven science and their enthusiasm for naive empiricism impede scientific progress" (p. 204). Theory-driven science examines patterns of relationships that emerge from events and theories that are derived from those patterns. Each event is valued, and research recognizes the impossibility of unbiased observation. On the other hand, naive empiricism looks primarily at causes of events. The event must occur frequently to be significant, and research presumes objective and unbiased observation.

There is no agreement on a theoretical or conceptual framework for matching therapy interventions with culturally complex personal problems to facilitate intercultural adjustment. In several comprehensive reviews of the literature, Marsella (1979), King (1978), and Strauss (1979) commented that there is no paradigm to focus on the increasing research studies or to test the consistency of contradictory theories offered to explain the relationship of personality and culture. LeVine (1972) provided a useful classification for organizing the theories of culture and personality. First, "anticulture and personality" states that culture determines personality and that the individual has little influence on the culture. Second, "psychological reductionism" states that all human activity can be explained by studying individuals. Third, "personality as culture" equates personality dynamics with culture. Fourth, "personality mediation" assumes a chain reaction where culture creates an individual personality that in turn changes the culture. Fifth, the "two systems approach" avoids the question of whether culture or personality is more basic, but assumes a continuous and parallel interaction and compromise between the two.

Culture and mental health research has failed to develop grounded theory based on empirical data for several reasons. First, the emphasis has been on abnormal behavior across cultures isolated from the study of normal behavior across cultures (Katz & Sanborn, 1976). Second, only during the 1970s did a pancultural core emerge for the more serious categories of disturbance, such as schizophrenia and affective psychoses, so that they are recognizable according to uniform symptoms across cultures even though tremendous cultural variations continue to exist (Draguns, 1980). Third, the complexity of research on therapy across cultural lines is difficult to manage beyond prequantificated stages (Draguns, 1981a, 1981b). Fourth, the research that is available has lacked an applied emphasis related to practical concerns of program development, service delivery, and techniques of treatment (Draguns, 1980). Fifth, there has been insufficient interdisciplinary collaboration from psychology, psychiatry, and anthropology among the more directly related disciplines, each approaching culture and mental health from different perspectives (Favazza & Oman, 1977). Sixth, the emphasis of research foci has been on the symptoms as a basic variable to the neglect of the interaction of persons, professions, institutions, and communities (Ivey, 1980b).

Cultural differences introduce barriers to understanding in those areas of interaction that are most critical to the outcome of therapy through discrepancies between counselor and client experiences, beliefs, values, expectations, and goals. Multicultural counseling occurs under conditions that are the most unfavorable for successful therapy (Lambert, 1981). Therefore, it is no wonder that there is disagreement concerning the theoretical criteria of interculturally skilled counseling.

One of the reasons that multicultural counseling has not been supported by existing theories of mental health may be because it constitutes a separate theory of its own. Pedersen (1991c) organized a special issue of the *Journal of Counseling and Development* around the possibility of multiculturalism as a "fourth force" in counseling. This suggests that (a) multicultural counseling is a generic approach to counseling, (b) multicultural counseling will have as great an impact as humanistic theories, (c) understanding the cultural context will provide the basis for predictive validity in counseling, and (d) contemporary theories are not adaptive to a wide range of different cultures. Pedersen and Ivey (in press) expanded the generic application of multiculturalism to an approach they called "culture-centered" counseling skills, where the standard microskills of counseling are adapted to four contrasting, culturally different settings.

5. The Counselor's Perspective

Atkinson, Casas, and Abreu (1992) found that cultural sensitivity was important to perceived counselor competence. Counselors were judged more competent by a population of Mexican-American clients when they were "culturally responsive" and less competent when they were "culturally unresponsive," regardless of the counselors' ethnicity.

In a special issue of *The Counseling Psychologist*, Mio and Iwamasa (1993) discussed the special problems of White cross-cultural researchers on multicultural counseling, summarizing the outcomes of a symposium on the subject. The resulting discussion resulted in four lessons to be learned:

> First, White researchers need to know the resentment they are stirring among many of their minority researcher counterparts. Second, the White researchers and audience participants felt uncomfortable discussing this resentment. Third, Minority researchers need to recognize when White counterparts are positively motivated. Fourth, both majority and minority researchers need to work harder to find common ground for working together. This resentment presents White cross-cultural researchers with a dilemma. (Mio & Iwamasa, 1993, p. 208)

Pedersen (1993a) summarized the dilemma of the White researcher on multicultural issues in a series of 10 problems that need to be dealt with in the search for common ground. First, we need to acknowledge the many previously unrecognized minority authors who have long been writing on multicultural issues. Second, we need to avoid polarizing cross-cultural researchers into opposing majority/minority categories and acknowledge their more complex identities. Third, we need to develop shared expectations of credibility and trust so that different behaviors can become more tolerable. Fourth, we need to identify and deal with unintentional racism wherever we find it. Fifth, we need to avoid favoritism in our citations of other research. Sixth, we need to avoid scapegoating. Seventh, we need to recognize that nobody "owns" multiculturalism. Eighth, we need to define the basis for common ground. Ninth, we need to recognize that this is an emotional issue. Tenth, we need to understand racism in a world perspective that goes beyond minority/majority issues in the United States. At the same time, it is important for every group to encourage ethnic diversity throughout all social institutions even when that may be "inconvenient."

Vaughn (1990) outlined several reasons for emphasizing ethnic diversity in the faculty and administrative levels of an educational institution. First, ethnic minority faculty are pivotal in creating an institutional ideology appropriate to the sociocultural perspectives of minorities. Second, committed and dedicated ethnic minority faculty are critical to meeting the specific training needs of ethnic minority students. Third, institutions must demonstrate sensitivity to the interests and needs of ethnic minority students to retain them. Fourth, ethnic minority faculty can play an important mediating role between students and the administration. Fifth, senior ethnic minority administrators and faculty are mentors and role models for junior faculty and students. Sixth, ethnic minority faculty are resource persons for other students interested in ethnocultural training.

Wrenn (1962, 1985) defined the *culturally encapsulated counselor* as one who (a) substitutes stereotypes for the real world, (b) disregards cultural variations among clients, and (c) dogmatizes technique-oriented definitions of counseling and therapy. Counselors can become "addicted" to one system of cultural values, which, by analogy, results in the same disorientation and dependence as with any other addiction (Morrow, 1972). Hence, pluralistic therapy recognizes a client's culturally based beliefs, values, and behaviors and is sensitive to the client's cultural environment and network of interacting influences. There are several models in the literature that attempt to define the multicultural counselor's role.

Sue (1978, 1981) suggested that culturally effective counselors have at least five characteristics. First, they recognize their own values and assumptions in contrast with alternative assumptions, with the ability to translate their own values and assumptions into action. Second, they are aware of genetic characteristics of counseling that cut across schools, classes, cultures, and any other contextual variables that influence the counseling process. Third, they understand the sociopolitical forces that influence the attitudes of culturally different minorities or otherwise oppressed groups. Fourth, they can share a client's world view without negating its legitimacy and without cultural oppression of their client's viewpoint. Fifth, they are truly eclectic in their own counseling style, generating a variety of skills from a wide range of theoretical orientations.

Tseng and Hsu (1980) discussed how counseling might compensate for culturally different features so that highly controlled and overregulated cultures might encourage therapies that provide a safety valve release for feelings and emotions, whereas underregulated or anomic cultures would encourage therapies with externalized social control at the expense of self-expression. There is a constant readjustment of the balance between interacting therapeutic and cultural variables. It is as if the individual were participating in a social game based on conventional rules that define boundaries between the individual and the cultural context. Watts (1961) defined the duty of the therapist as involving the participant in a "counter game" that would restore a unifying perspective of ego and environment so that the person can be liberated in a balanced context.

To the extent that the therapist is distanced from the client, culture becomes a more significant barrier. Kleinman (1980) described the problems that result when the explanations of the clinician and the patient are in conflict. Kleinman characterized most clinicians as schooled in the biomedical paradigm to recognize and treat disease as the malfunction or maladaptative biological or psychological process. By contrast, the patient is more likely to experience illness as an interruption in his or her social and cultural network. Patients evaluate treatment as a "healing process" more than as a "cure outcome," recognizing that there are no clear beginnings or endings in the complex interaction of variables. Therefore, the best a clinician can hope to do is help restore balance.

Draguns (1977) suggested several guidelines for adjusting therapy modes to fit the culture. The more complex the social and cognitive structure, the more a society will prefer hierarchy and ritual characterized by elaborate techniques for countering psychological distress. The stronger a society's beliefs are in the changeability of human nature and plasticity of social roles, the more it will favor therapy techniques as vehicles of change. Where attitudes toward psychological disturbance reflect deep-seated prejudices about human nature, people are less tolerant and accepting of the mentally ill.

The therapist needs to form a facilitative relationship with culturally different clients so that, ideally, the client will experience being (a) warmly received, (b) deeply accepted, and (c) fully understood (Lambert, 1981). To establish that relationship, the client needs to perceive the counselor as a credible expert (well informed, capable, and intelligent) and trustworthy (Sue, 1981). The counselor needs to accommodate a wide range of therapist and client roles, integrating them with the client's world view without losing his or her own cultural integrity (Sue, 1977). These prerequisites incorporate a blend of the goals of helping through insight, self-actualization, behavior change, and immediacy with the appropriate process. A client may be exposed to an appropriate process and appropriate goals, an appropriate process and inappropriate goals, an inappropriate process and appropriate goals, or an inappropriate process and inappropriate goals. In their archival study on counselor–client similarity and perceived effectiveness, Neimeyer and Gonzales (1983) found that White clients attributed change more to counseling than to other factors, whereas non-White clients expressed lower levels of overall satisfaction with counseling.

Ultimately, the counselor characteristics listed in the previous paragraph result in rapport and empathy with and interest and appreciation of the client's culture. Good counselors understand a client's special terms and language, and know the client's community and the problems of living in a bicultural world (Sundberg, 1981a, 1981b). Given that counselors are guilty of the same amount of stereotyping and ethnocentrism as the general public (Bloombaum, Yamamoto, & James, 1968; Casas, 1984; Korchin, 1980; Wampold, Casas, & Atkinson,

1981), our expectations for the multicultural counselor's effectiveness seem somewhat unrealistic. In his update of Harrison's (1975) findings, which tended to support prejudices by White therapists, Atkinson (1983) found no conclusive evidence that minority clients are better served by minority counselors than by White counselors.

Multicultural counselors frequently assume it is better for minorities to counsel other minorities because cultural barriers are so formidable. Vontress (1981) suggested that few counselors really want to change themselves. Most counselors are influenced by a racist socialization process, and this condition is not likely to change without the impact of affective confrontation such as that experienced through cultural immersion. However, this does not mean that the advancement of multicultural counseling implies the abandonment of counseling theory, therapy techniques, and our traditional understanding of a client's psychological processes when counseling techniques we have learned do not seem to work in all settings.

Wohl (1981) criticized the "super flexibility" and "elastic modifications" of sound principles of some multicultural counselors. Even before students acquire the fundamentals of counseling and therapy, they are urged to abandon them in favor of some unorthodox method that is presumed to be multicultural. Patterson (1974, 1978b) also argued that the proper approach is not to be "flexible" in modifying the method to fit the client's expectations and wishes because it subverts the counseling goals of self-actualization. The culture of the client *and* the culture of the counselor are also potentially salient in multicultural counseling.

Sue and Sue (1990) emphasized the importance of "credibility" for multicultural counselors, so that culturally different clients will believe them to be experts who are trustworthy. Expertness is a demonstration of the counselor's "ability," indicated typically by reputation, training, and competent behavior. Sue and Sue pointed out that culturally different clients might not be impressed by degrees and certificates, which might actually reduce credibility. The counselor's positive reputation by other generalized measures will also not necessarily be helpful. The counselor's ability to behave competently and bring about positive change will be the primary measure of credibility. Trustworthiness is typically indicated by sincerity, openness, honesty, and willingness to sacrifice personal gain. Counselors are perceived as linked to an oppressive establishment by many minority clients, so trust will not come easily. Trust is earned and proved by competent and specific behaviors. Counselors can expect to be tested by culturally different clients, and it is the counselors' responsibility to take the initiative.

Like clients, therapists are products of their own sociocultural context, therefore they must be aware of their own implicit/explicit cultural biases. Ramirez (1991) suggested that, to be effective, therapists should take the following into consideration: (a) therapy goals that are matched to the client's needs, (b) limit-setting and confrontation styles that are appropriate, (c) a degree of structure that is effective and comfortable, and (d) a degree of empathy that will enhance client growth. The therapist must demonstrate "cognitive flex" that will enable the matching of interventions to a context that is comfortable, genuine, and effective.

There is evidence that the multicultural training of counselors is inadequate (Sue & Sue, 1990). D'Andrea and Daniels (1991) reviewed various approaches for multicultural counseling training currently being used, and they outlined a developmental framework to compare the outcomes of training. Their framework is divided into programs that are culturally entrenched at Stage 1, where few questions are raised about cultural differences in counseling and unimodal measures of competence are assumed. Stage 2 involves a cross-cultural awakening, where the importance of multiculturalism is acknowledged but frequently oversimplified. Stage 3 involves cultural integrity where multiculturalism is incorporated into the counseling program as a requirement. Stage 4 involves infusion of multiculturalism throughout the curriculum beyond the requirement of a single course, but rather important to all counseling relationships. D'Andrea, Daniels, and Heck (1991) developed a measure to assess the level of multicultural development within counselor education programs with regard to awareness, knowledge, and skill, which are discussed later in chapter 12.

LaFromboise and Foster (1992) described a range of alternatives in counselor education programs incorporating cross-cultural content. First, there is a "separate course" model, where the cross-cultural content is limited to one basic course intended to provide a foundation for cross-cultural awareness. There is no additional follow-up of that one isolated course elsewhere in the curriculum. Second, there is the "area of concentration" model in programs that require a survey course in cross-cultural psychology and additional coursework to develop a depth of knowledge about some aspect of cross-cultural counseling or a specific population. Third, there is an "interdisciplinary" model that incorporates coursework from outside the trainee's department and discipline, including courses in anthropology, political science, and related fields. The student is required to make the relevant application from these diverse disciplines to the problems of multicultural counseling by him or herself. The fourth model of "integration" is described as the "preferred" model, where cross-cultural content is integrated throughout the curriculum and where the counseling faculty take responsibility for matching the content of counseling courses to the needs of a culturally diverse population.

It is even possible that counselors become less sensitive to cultural differences through their training. Mwaba and Pedersen (1990) distributed a collection of 20 brief critical incidents describing "presenting problems." They asked a population of subscribers to a multicultural counseling newsletter to indicate for each incident on a 1–10 scale whether the problem was interpersonal, inter-cultural, or pathological. Those with more training as counselors tended to give more weight to pathology and less to cultural factors. Are trained counselors more skilled at identifying pathology than untrained counselors, or does counselor training redefine what would previously have been labeled cultural as pathological?

6. The Client's Perspective

Atkinson (1985) and Atkinson and Schein (1986) reviewed the literature on the effects of race in psychotherapy. There is considerable controversy on the issue of whether counselors and clients ideally should be culturally similar. This area of research much too frequently has addressed distal factors and ig-nored proximal ones. Carkhuff and Pierce (1967) frequently have been cited as providing evidence for the belief that counselors who are most different from their clients in ethnicity and social class, or who are not of the same gender, have the greatest difficulty effecting constructive changes. Likewise, LeVine and Campbell (1972) have been cited as supporting evidence that groups that perceive themselves similarly are more likely to relate harmoniously. Mitchell (1970) suggested that most White counselors cannot help Black clients because they are part of the clients' problem. Stanges and Riccio (1970) demonstrated that counselor trainees preferred clients of the same race and culture, and Harrison (1975) and Berman (1979) demonstrated that Black counselors preferred Black clients.

However, other factors have tended to exaggerate the apparent importance of racial similarity and have resulted in contradictory research findings. Parloff, Waskow, and Wolfe (1978) concluded that cultural matching of counselors and clients is not clearly preferred by the clients. Other research also indicates lack of support for the preference to match clients and counselors by culture. Some research (Gamboa, Tosi, & Riccio, 1976) demonstrated special conditions where the clients actually preferred culturally different counselors. Atkinson (1983) cited 12 studies from a variety of ethnic groups that reported no client prefer-ences for the race or ethnicity of the counselor. Sanchez and Atkinson (1983) and Parham and Helms (1981, 1985a, 1985b) reported that those subjects with the strongest commitment to their own ethnic group are more likely to prefer counselors from the same ethnic background.

Several issues are involved. First, as Peoples and Dell (1975) demonstrated, the preference for counseling style may be more important than racial match among Black and White clients, Asian-American clients (Atkinson et al., 1983), and lower class clients, compared with middle-class clients (Aronson & Overall, 1966). Black counselors used more active expression skills and fewer attending skills than did White counselors. Muliozzi (1972) also indicated that White counselors felt more genuine and empathic with White clients, although Black clients did not see White counselors as less genuine in understanding. In other research (Ewing, 1974), Black students were shown to react more favorably to Black and White counselors than did White students. Bryson and Cody (1973) indicated that Black counselors understood Black clients best, but that White counselors were more acceptable than Black counselors to *both* Black and White clients. The preference for skilled and competent White counselors by non-White clients might be explained by Acosta and Sheehan's (1976) finding that Mexican Americans and Whites attributed more skill, understanding, and trust to White professionals than to Mexican-American professionals.

It seems that variables such as more active intervention styles for positive change through counseling are more important for the client than is racial similarity in building rapport (Atkinson, Maruyama, & Matsui, 1978; Peoples & Dell, 1975). Kinloch (1979) included physical, cultural, economic, and behavioral characteristics in his analysis of cultural difference because these characteristics function in ways similar to those of nationality and ethnicity. Erickson and Schultz (1982) introduced a concept of "comembership" between client and counselor based on any shared interest, status, or characteristic. Comembership provided a basis for shared identity and solidarity that was stronger than ethnicity or nationality in predicting successful counseling outcomes. Hilliard (1986) criticized psychological research for not specifying within-group differences of gender, socioeconomic status, and age in the study of ethnic groups as potential sources of comembership.

Second, Korchin (1980) criticized the tendency to decide on an a priori basis that membership in one particular ethnic group, cultural group, or class relegates a client to less qualified therapists for shorter periods of time. Warheit, Holzer, and Areye (1975) and Ambrowitz and Dokecki (1977) identified socioeconomic status as the most powerful predictor of poor mental health conditions. Fierman (1965), Korchin (1980), and Gomez-Schwartz, Hadley, and Strupp (1978) attacked the assumption that therapy cannot be successful with lower socioeconomic groups. Lorion (1974) and Lorion and Parron (1985) provided a comprehensive review of other literature on the relationship between therapy and low economic status or poverty as a predictor of mental health. Lower income persons are less likely to be in therapy, or are in therapy for shorter periods of time, with symptoms similar to those of clients from other socioeconomic groups, although those symptoms typically are described as more severe among lower class clients. Lower class clients are treated by less experienced staff and through less sophisticated modes of therapy.

Third, minority clients may even respond with anger when confronted by a minority counselor (Jackson, 1973) because (a) they perceive the minority counselor to be associated with a majority-controlled institution, (b) they perceive majority counselors as more competent, or (c) they are jealous of the minority counselor who has "made it" (Atkinson et al., 1978). The minority counselor may also prefer not to work with a minority client because of a tendency to either deny identification with or to overidentify with minority client problems, or because he or she views counseling minority clients as lower status work (Calneck, 1970; Gardner, 1971; Sattler, 1970). Helms (1984) criticized the counselor–client racial/ethnic matching research for emphasizing the minority client and not the dominant-culture counselor. Casas (1984) criticized even more strongly research on whether minority clients should or should not be matched with minority counselors.

Fourth, a compromise solution might be to introduce two counselors—one similar and one dissimilar to the client's culture. Bolman (1968) advocated using two professionals, one from each culture, to collaborate in cross-cultural counseling, with traditional healers from the minority culture as co-counselors. Weidman (1975) introduced the alternative notion of a "culture broker" as an intermediary between client and counselor for working with culturally different clients. Slack and Slack (1976) suggested another alternative: bringing in a client who already has effectively solved similar problems to work with chemically dependent clients. Mediators have been used in family therapy for problems of pathogenic coalitions (Satir, 1964), with the therapist and mediator mediating to change pathogenic relating styles. Zuk (1971) described counseling as a "go-between" process where the therapist mediates conflict between parties. In these various examples, the use of at least three persons in therapy provides an additional "cultural punch" (Opler, 1959) that may be uniquely suitable for working with some cultures. Trimble (1981) recommended that bringing in a third person frequently is suitable for working with Native-American clients to help them become more comfortable in therapy.

Fifth, when the counselor is bilingual or bicultural, the process of counseling might become a process of mediation. Meadows (1968) went back to the early Greek notion of the counselor as a mediator between the client and a "superordinate world of powers and values." Mediation is not without its own unique problems. Miles (1976) pointed out how these "boundary spanning activities" of counselors can result in role ambiguity and role diffusion for either the counselor or the client, who are expected to coordinate the conflicting demands of multiple membership. To some extent, the problems of Stonequist's (1937) "marginal person" apply to the role of a mediator. Mediation also presents opportunities. Ruiz and Casas (1981) described a bicultural counseling model for a blending of majority and minority cultural affiliations. This model was designed to help counselors become more bilingual and bicultural in response to their clients' needs. Berry (1975) suggested that bicultural individuals have a higher potential to function with cognitive flexibility and are more creatively adaptive to either culture than are monocultural or monolingual individuals or counselors. Szapocznik, Rio, Perez-Vidal, Kurtines, and Sanisteban (1986) and Szapocznik and Kurtines (1980) further suggested that bilingual and bicultural individuals are better adjusted and perform at a higher level than monolingual or monocultural individuals in either of their two cultures. As a mediator, the counselor serves to interpret either culture, and it is therefore important for the counselor to be accepted in a well-defined role by both cultures to be effective.

There are many complications in understanding and communicating with culturally different clients, and few therapy variables other than the client–counselor relationship correlate with outcome (Lambert, 1981). Pedersen et al. (1989) described additional client perspectives on the multicultural counseling relationship.

7. Conclusion

Our research agenda for the future requires us to blend culture and counseling in four areas. First, we need to advance the conceptual and theoretical approaches to the interaction between culture and counseling beyond the diffuse and incomplete theoretical alternatives now available. Second, we need to sharpen our research efforts to identify those primary variables that allow us to explain what has happened, interpret what is happening, and perhaps predict what will happen in the counseling process across cultures. Third, we need to identify criteria of expertise for the education and training of professionals to work multiculturally so that they are adequately prepared to deal with the problems of a pluralistic society. Fourth, we need to revolutionize our mode of providing services based on new theory, new research, and new training so that counseling care can be equitably and appropriately provided to members of a pluralistic society.

The appropriate and accurate application of multicultural counseling services are the ultimate criteria of effectiveness. Considerations of the delivery of services should no doubt be foremost in our examination of the field. However, most emphasis has, in fact, been on basic research questions unwittingly, yet effectively, separated from the practical concerns of program development, service delivery, and techniques of treatment (Draguns, 1980). We need to draw practical implications from the available information. This may include redefining the domain of counselors to include outreach workers, consultants, ombudsmen, change agents, and facilitators of indigenous support systems (Atkinson et al., 1993).

The constraints of multicultural counseling include elements from theory, research, and training as well. We have many urgent needs. We need to place more attention on cultural variables to increase counseling's measured accuracy and effectiveness, to accommodate ethical imperatives of culturally different consumers, and to measure counselor competency in communicating with culturally different clients. We need to increase our understanding of the multicultural dimension within all counseling contacts. We need to integrate multicultural variables into the core curricula of counselor education programs, rather than teach them as a subspecialty. We need to introduce more multicultural materials into the research literature of mainline professional journals of counseling and therapy. We need to develop alternatives to counseling based on practices in other cultures. We need to match counseling intervention skills more accurately with different cultures. Finally, we need to translate counseling and mental health into the language of other disciplines, fields, and professions of social management. Counselor education plays an important role as the new popular ideology and religion to justify and solve social programs (Sampson, 1977).

CHAPTER 8

The Ethical Dilemma of Multicultural Counselors

Major objective:

1. To critique ethical guidelines from a multicultural perspective.

Secondary objectives:

1. To examine measures of cultural equity in counseling.
2. To review historical trends emphasizing multiculturalism in society.
3. To examine the dangers of cultural encapsulation.
4. To examine ethical models applied to multicultural counseling.
5. To examine the American Psychological Association (APA) ethical principles.
6. To examine the American Counseling Association (ACA) ethical standards.

The multicultural counselor faces an ethical dilemma in the United States. Sensitivity to cultural variables is recognized as valuable and even ethically essential for appropriate mental health services, and yet the dangers of cultural encapsulation are more serious now than they have ever been. Our ethical guidelines are inadequate. Too often the multicultural counselor has to choose between "being ethical" in a multicultural context or "following the ethical guidelines" as stipulated by professional counseling associations.

1. Cultural Diversity Among Counselors

Axelson (1993) reviewed data from a number of reliable sources regarding demographic trends in the counseling profession. First, the numbers of counselors overall is expected to increase by 26.9% between 1988 and the year 2000, due in part to the expanding roles of counselors in family relations, substance abuse, and other areas outside academic counseling. Second, women outnumbered men graduates with master's degrees by 2:1 in 1990, and women outnumbered men by 3:2 at the doctoral level. The ratio of men in counseling seems to be decreasing over time. In 1988, females accounted for 61.8% of counselors. About two thirds of the American Counseling Association (ACA) members in 1991 were female. Third, in 1988, Blacks accounted for 14.9% of all counselors. There are no data on the percentage of clients who are Black. Fourth, in 1988, Hispanics accounted for 4.6% of all counselors. There are no data on the percentage of clients who are Hispanic. Fifth, the ACA reported that in 1991 about 90% of its members were White, 5% were Black, 1.8% were Hispanic, 1% were Asian Americans, and .7% were Native Americans.

These and other data suggest that although increasingly more women are becoming professional counselors, the ethnic minority groups of Blacks, Hispanics, Asian Americans, and Native Americans are severely underrepresented among professional counselors.

The rhetoric of support for multicultural issues in counseling has not been reflected in the data describing the profession of counseling in the United States. First of all, racial/ethnic minorities are underrepresented in clinical and counseling psychology. Second, this underrepresentation is particularly true in applied and academic settings. Third, racial/ethnic minority persons are represented most heavily in the lower and less influential academic ranks. Finally, publications and professional presentations about culturally different perspectives are underrepresented in the primary professional journals as well as in the annual programs of the professional counseling associations (Pedersen, 1994).

Rickard and Clements (1993) provided a critique of the American Psychological Association (APA) Accreditation Criterion II on cultural and individual differences. This criterion is a mandate for promoting respect for and requiring skills related to cultural and individual differences. However, the mandate is described in very general language that lends itself to inconsistent and idiosyncratic interpretations. The three aspects of Criterion II are: (a) to declare that attitudes of social responsibility and respect for cultural differences must be imparted to students and reflected in an approved program, (b) that social and personal diversity of faculty and students is an "essential goal," and (c) that programs must develop knowledge and skills relevant to human diversity (Altmaier, 1993). Payton (1993) described Criterion II as an attempt to redress decades of neglect, toward which a program should aspire without settling for a minimalist compromise.

The suggestions of Rickard and Clements (1993) were to: (a) develop the guidelines in much more detail, (b) make specific and explicit mention of legally mandated affirmative action alternatives in the guidelines, (c) separate categories of individual differences from issues of cultural diversity, (d) rank order the human variability emphasis in terms of consequences, (e) make each applying program responsible for developing specific objectives, and (f) incorporate and synthesize the data from annual program reports as evidence of compliance. Clements and Rickard responded to criticism by pointing out that programs need additional specific information to guide and assess their progress even though hard and fast criteria may be lacking. Objective standards and goals would lead to more accurate and facilitative self-monitoring. Criterion II is ambiguous and ambitious. The criterion is used generally to set the tone and encourage programs at some points and is concerned with detecting noncompliance or applying sanctions in other places. More clearly stated, detailed guidelines would be less vulnerable to misinterpretation.

There is increased pressure in the United States for the field of counseling to acknowledge the importance of the consumers' cultural environment. The National Institute of Mental Health (NIMH), the American Psychological Association (APA), the American Psychological Association Council of Representatives, the American Counseling Association (ACA), and the Presidential Commission on Mental Health all emphasized the ethical responsibility of counselors and therapists to know their clients' cultural values before delivering a mental health service to those clients (Pedersen, 1994).

The Vail conference on levels and patterns of professional training in psychology in 1973 gave visibility to multicultural issues in counseling and therapy. The Dulles conference in 1978 allowed mental health providers from a variety of ethnic and cultural backgrounds to work out guidelines for cooperation and some sense of consensus that resulted in a Minority Affairs Office in APA. By 1979, the APA accreditation criteria demanded cultural diversity among faculty and students in APA-approved programs of counseling and clinical psychology.

There seems to be a trend toward ethical consciousness on multicultural issues. Casas (1984) suggested several reasons for the recent increased interest and concern for racial/ethnic minority groups in the Unites States. First, there is a pragmatic understanding and acceptance of demographic changes and socioeconomic political events that have given cultural minority groups more power. Second, many minorities such as Blacks, Native-American Indians, Hispanics, and Asian Americans are more demographically visible. Third, the civil rights movement has led to legislation favoring legal rights of minority groups. Fourth, White counselors in private practice have economic incentives for attracting non-White clients.

In 1971, the Committee on International Relations in Psychology for the APA requested June Tapp to head a subcommittee of the APA on ethical considerations of cross-cultural research along with Lawrence Wrightsman, Harry Triandis, Herbert Kelman, and George Coelho. The recommendations of that committee are based on 2 years of consultation with cross-cultural psychologists from several countries and reactions to presentations at U.S. national and international professional meetings. The "advisory principles" of that group have been adapted by the International Association for Cross-Cultural Psychology (IAACP), and they represent the best systematic attempt to deal with cross-cultural ethics by a psychological organization for psychological research thus far (International Association for Cross-Cultural Psychology, 1978).

Tapp, Kelman, Triandis, Wrightsman, and Coelho (1974) pointed out that a researcher's ethical obligation goes beyond avoiding harm to the subject to include demonstrations of how the research will enrich and benefit the host culture. Generally, the benefit to the researcher is much clearer than the benefit to a host culture providing data. Tapp's recommendation for collaboration with the host culture is also seldom observed. It is often difficult to translate the implications of psychological research into useful outcomes for traditional people. Taft (1977) pointed out that most people are so "psychologecentric" that they regard themselves as having the right to mine their data from the places where they need it, provided they pay royalties to the natives (often, incidentally, in accordance with their arbitrary concept of what is fair compensation) and provided they do not destroy the ecology irreparably. "In the latter respect, we are often not really much more conscientious than is the typical multi-national mining company" (Taft, 1977, pp. 11–12).

In her introduction to the special issue on ethics of *The Counseling Psychologist*, Kitchener (1986) pointed out that psychologists are better at *identifying* the ethical issues that face them than they are at *thinking through* how they should resolve them. This has resulted in a great revival of interest in applied ethics, increased government or administrative protection of human subjects, and increased numbers of court cases involving psychologists. In part, this interest in ethics has gone beyond ethical violations toward a positive appreciation for a client's own belief system. Preventing harm to the consumer and acting in such a way as to actually benefit the consumer applies the ethical principle of "beneficence" as a legitimate ethical obligation (Cayleff, 1986). These developments have contributed to a new interest in multicultural ethics.

2. The Historical Background of Multicultural Ethics

Whereas ethnic minority counselors are underrepresented, multiculturalism is attracting a lot of attention. To some extent, our domestic perspective of counseling and therapy may reflect historical racial and ethnic relations in the United States, which are characterized by (a) heightened group consciousness,

(b) government mandated affirmative action in employment and education, (c) court-ordered busing to achieve racial integration in public schools, and (d) demands for bilingual education in public school systems. In comparing ethnic/racial relations in the United States with those in other cultures, Lambert (1981) found the U.S. perspective to be "unusual compared with that of other countries in its growing salience of ethnic/racial relations, its bipolarity, its emphasis on hierarchy over cultural contrast, the casting of government in the role of protagonist for the underclass, and the ethnic specificity and direction of violence" (p. 189).

The civil rights movement of the 1950s resulted in a militancy of minorities for change toward greater equity. The growing community mental health movement of the 1960s supported equitable services by affirming that mental health care was the right of all citizens, not just the wealthy or middle-class dominant majority (LeVine & Padilla, 1980). The issues of feminism and popular dissent from the anti-Vietnam War movement further promoted a climate of discontent, where protest against inequitable treatment was accepted and even encouraged by the media and general public. The stigma of discrimination became synonymous with any attempt to treat groups differently. Sue (1981) suggested that this obsession with equality might be discriminatory. Minority groups may not be asking for equal treatment as much as for equal access and opportunity. Differential treatment is not necessarily discriminatory or even preferred.

By the 1970s, the underutilization of counseling services by minority groups had become a serious issue. One reason for the apparent underutilization might be that behavior such as individualistic assertiveness, described as pathological in a minority culture, is often viewed as adaptive in a majority-culture client (Grier & Cobbs, 1968; Wilson & Calhoon, 1974). Sue (1977) demonstrated that Asian-American, Black, Chicano, Native-American, and other minority-group clients terminate counseling significantly earlier than do White clients, and they also are diagnosed as more seriously ill. These measures of underutilization were largely credited to cultural barriers hindering counseling and therapy such as language barriers, class-bound values, and culture-bound attitudes. Pedersen (1982) suggested that minorities might be avoiding dominant-culture counseling services to prevent the erosion of their own values and cultural identity, where those services might increase acculturative stress among consumers. Casas (1984) concluded that whether counseling services are being underutilized by minorities depends almost entirely on how the data are collected. A number of studies suggested that these services are not being underutilized at all. Corey, Corey, and Callanan (1993) discussed additional literature on multicultural ethics for counseling regarding the power of stereotypes and cultural bias.

In the 1980s and 1990s, the U.S. perspective includes the large numbers of refugees from Cuba, the Caribbean, Europe, and South Central America as well as from Vietnam, Laos, and Cambodia. Initially, funds were provided for special services to these culturally different groups. More recently, former refugees are being served by the regular counseling service agencies that are already overloaded with clients and that are not trained in the special needs of refugee populations. Especially in the Southeast, but elsewhere as well, the rapidly growing Hispanic population is likewise dependent on regular counseling services. However, our regular counseling services still are not prepared to serve these culturally different populations in appropriate ways (Atkinson et al., 1983).

The paradox of pluralism is that, on the one hand, we are more dependent on one another than ever before, whereas at the same time we need to prove our economic, social, cultural, and political independence with renewed vigor. This tension frequently creates an ethical crisis. In the past, we have tried four different demographic approaches to dealing with the "multicultural problem" (Berry et al., 1992). (a) Assimilation of the minorities by a dominant group has been the most popular mode of accommodation. As discussed earlier, assimilation requires minorities to seek acceptance and in turn be accepted. (b) Integration has also been suggested as promising a heterogeneous society where ethnicity has lost significance and has been absorbed into class stratification. Integration has led to the desperate inequalities of a society where some persons are considered more equal than others. (c) Multiple ethnic colonies presents an extreme solution that would fragment society into encapsulated and independent sectors. (d) Pluralism seeks to maintain a delicate balance, assuming the continued and distinct self-identities of the various ethnic groups through shared political and socioeconomic institutions. There are few, if any, successful examples of pluralism in the world, although this finally may be the only acceptable alternative for survival.

The "melting pot" metaphor for assimilation, introduced through a play by Israel Zangwill in 1908, assumed that a new and unique culture would emerge as each immigrant group gave up its "old world" values in exchange for the values of a "new world" (Atkinson et al., 1993). However, there were "lumps" in the melting pot that refused to dissolve because some cultural groups maintained their original identity. Some legislation, such as the Chinese Exclusion Act, discouraged immigrant cultural groups from assimilating. Although the explicit policy for assimilation is no longer popular, there is some evidence that implicit assimilationist policies are still in practice (Marsella & Pedersen, 1981; Pedersen, Draguns, Lonner, & Trimble, 1981).

The difficulty with integration as an alternative is its implicit hierarchical bias in favor of the dominant culture. The results of integration have been implicit paternalism at best, and arbitrary domination at worst. Integration has evolved into class, and ultimately caste, structures where the minority group must resort either to conflict or subservience. Atkinson et al. (1993) described the language used to describe minority groups as denoting implicit cultural bias. Anthropological, sociological, and psychological data have contributed to an implicit cultural bias by assuming that: (a) problems result from social pathology or deviance, (b) problems result from social disorganization or the disintegration of values, (c) solutions require a dominant-culture perspective because of the cultural deficit of other groups, or (d) culturally defined levels of adequacy are limited by the genetic deficits of some cultural groups.

As the roles of counselors are defined more rigidly in a cultural context, we tend to isolate ourselves along the lines of a particular cultural bias of institutionalized racism, with less and less pretense toward either assimilation or integration of values. From an international perspective, the cultural-specific characteristics of counseling in the U.S. perspective challenge the universality of psychology. Alternative cultural assumptions in other cultural settings do not follow the "American ideal" (Diaz-Guerrero, 1977; Sampson, 1977), the premise of the Protestant ethic (Draguns, 1974; Rotenberg, 1974), or the other pervasive assumptions of individualism (Hsu, 1972; Pedersen, 1979).

Jones and Korchin (1982) described mental health as having two different orientations. On the one hand, counseling is perceived as political, with the basic tenet that counseling, social welfare, economic status, political power, personal dignity, and other facets of well-being of minority group members depend on the acquisition of power and control over their personal and collective destinies. On the other hand, there is a multicultural perspective of counseling, which begins with the assumption that there are differences among groups, each of which has its own unique tradition.

In many instances, it has been easier to explain or rationalize problems of cultural differences than to adapt to them. A variety of social science theories have been presented in the past to explain the racial/ethnic components of maladaptation by minority cultures (Sue, 1981). (a) The biological-racial explanation has been around the longest in the popular myth; it explains the lack of achievement by some cultures in terms of genetic inferiority. The weakness of this position is the assumption that biological and sociocultural factors can be separated. (b) Physiological explanations focus on neurological deficiencies as by-products of poverty and deprivation. The weakness of this position is that diagnosis of mental deficiencies is ambiguous, and the rationale can be used as a substitute for hereditary inferiority. (c) Demographic theories look for explanations in environmental conditions, but there is no clear evidence that persons migrating from poverty or disadvantaged areas are permanently unable to achieve when later presented with appropriate opportunities. (d) Psychological explanations emphasize individual motivation, self-image, delay of gratification, anxiety, achievement expectancy, and so forth. Motivational and behavioral handicaps are blamed for failure in school, although these handicaps may be a consequence of educational deprivation as well as its cause. (e) Sociological explanations emphasize cultural, class, and environmental differences but without clear evidence of a casual relationship between sociocultural status and achievement. None of these explanations has been satisfactory.

3. Cultural Encapsulation

The culturally encapsulated individual is just as able to evade reality through ethnocentricism ("mine is best") as through relativism ("to each his own"). Maintaining a cocoon is accomplished by evading reality and depending entirely on one's own internalized value assumptions about what is good for society. Isolation is accentuated by the inherent capacity of culture-bound and time-honored values to prevail against the tentativeness of present knowledge.

Therefore, it is necessary for the culture-sensitive individual to learn new knowledge and skills, as well as to reorganize the old knowledge that no longer applies. The encapsulated individual is singularly unable to adapt to a constantly changing sociocultural context. The same sociological data with which we inform ourselves can be used to reinforce tendencies toward stereotyped images of cultural groups, separating and "encapsulating" the individual from social reality.

Encapsulation is a result of several basic and familiar processes in our professional activity (Wrenn, 1985). Wrenn's five-point description of encapsulation demonstrates how counseling as a profession has protected itself against the complex "threat" of multiculturalism. (a) We define reality according to one set of cultural assumptions and stereotypes that becomes more important than the real world outside. (b) We become insensitive to cultural variations among individuals and assume that our view is the only real or legitimate one. It is not surprising that the assumption that "I know better than they do what is good for them" is offensive to the target audience. (c) Each of us has unreasoned assumptions that we accept without proof. When these assumptions are threatened by another religion, political view, or culture, we can easily become fearful or defensive. When persons of the host culture are perceived as threatening, they quickly become an "enemy" to be opposed and ultimately defeated in the name of self-preservation. (d) A technique-oriented job definition further contributes toward and perpetuates the process of encapsulation. The world is simplistically divided into a polarity of friends and enemies, us and them, with each relationship being evaluated according to whether it contributes to getting the job done. (e) When there is no evaluation of other viewpoints, individuals may experience encapsulation by absolving themselves of any responsibility to interpret the behavior of others as relevant and meaningful to their own life activity.

Some people have developed a dependency on one authority, one theory, and one truth. These encapsulated persons tend to be trapped in one way of thinking, believing that their's is the universal way. They are trapped in an inflexible structure that resists adaptation to alternative ways of thinking. In contrast, a liberated mode of thinking represents an effort to establish empathy with other, different persons. Empathy is a process of learning foreign beliefs, assumptions, perspectives, feelings, and consequences in such a way that the outsider participates in the host culture. Through multicultural contact, people can be liberated to cope with constant change and to feel empathy with other alternatives available to them.

Cultural encapsulation becomes most visible in the actions of exclusion. Insiders are separated from outsiders. Certain individuals or groups are judged to be outside the boundaries, and the normal rules of fairness no longer apply. Those who are excluded are nonentities, expendable, and undeserving, so doing harm to them is acceptable if not perhaps appropriate and justified. Ranging from discrimination to genocide, "ethnic cleansing" targets victims who are then blamed for allowing themselves to become victims.

By better understanding the process of moral exclusion, we can better build a system of ethical guidelines for the future of counseling. This phenomenon is most evident in two nations at war, but subtle forms of moral exclusion (Table 9) are evident elsewhere as well.

Usually moral exclusion results from severe conflict or from feelings of unconnectedness as relationships are perceived. Opotow (1990) listed the rationalizations and justifications that support moral exclusion, which help to identify otherwise hidden examples of moral exclusion. Other examples of moral exclusion might include (a) psychological distancing, (b) displacing responsibility, (c) group loyalty, and (d) normalizing or glorifying violence. The list of examples (Table 9) is provided to demonstrate that moral exclusion can be so "ordinary" an occurrence that it fails to attract attention.

Moral exclusion is the obvious consequence of cultural encapsulation. Exclusion can occur in degrees from overt and malicious evil to passive unconcern. It is possible to be exclusionary by what you do not do as well as by what you do. Moral exclusion is pervasive and not isolated. It depends on those psychological and social supports that condone otherwise unacceptable attitudes, intentionally or unintentionally. "As severity of conflict and threat escalates, harm and sanctioned aggression become more likely. As harm doing escalates, societal structures change, the scope of justice shrinks, and the boundaries of harm doing expand" (Opotow, 1990, p. 13). We need a level of moral development that prevents moral exclusion.

Shweder, Mahapatra, and Miller (1990) reviewed the cultural applicability of three theories of moral development. First of all, Kohlberg's "cognitive de-

TABLE 9
Processes of Moral Exclusion

Process	*Manifestation in Moral Exclusion*
Exclusion-Specific Processes	
Biased evaluation of groups	Making unflattering comparisons between one's own group and another group; believing in the superiority of one's own group
Derogation	Disparaging and denigrating others by regarding them as lower life forms or inferior beings (e.g., barbarians, vermin)
Dehumanization	Repudiating others' humanity, dignity, ability to feel, and entitlement to compassion
Fear of contamination	Perceiving contact with others as posing a threat to one's own well-being
Expanding the target	Redefining "legitimate victims" as a larger category
Accelerating the pace of harm doing	Engaging in increasingly destructive and abhorrent acts to reduce remorse and inhibitions against inflicting harm
Open approval of destructive behavior	Accepting a moral code that condones harm doing
Reducing moral standards	Perceiving one's harmful behavior as proper; replacing moral standards that restrain harm with less stringent standards that condone or praise harm doing
Blaming the victim	Displacing the blame for reprehensible actions on those who are harmed
Self-righteous comparisons	Lauding or justifying harmful acts by contrasting them with morally condemnable atrocities committed by the adversary
Desecration	Harming others to demonstrate contempt for them, particularly symbolic or gratuitous harm
Ordinary Processes	
Groupthink	Striving for group unanimity by maintaining isolation from dissenting opinion that would challenge the assumptions, distortions, or decisions of the group
Transcendent ideologies	Experiencing oneself or one's group as exalted, extraordinary, and possessed of a higher wisdom, which permits even harmful behavior as necessary to bring a better world into being

TABLE 9 *(continued)*
Processes of Moral Exclusion

Process	Manifestation in Moral Exclusion
Deindividuation	Feeling anonymous in a group setting, thus weakening one's capacity to behave in accordance with personal standards
Moral engulfment	Replacing one's own ethical standards with those of the group
Psychological distance	Ceasing to feel the presence of others; patronizing others, and perceiving them with disdain (e.g., they are childlike, irrational, simple)
Technical orientation	Focusing on efficient means while ignoring outcomes; routinizing harm doing by transforming it into mechanical steps
Double standards	Having different sets of moral rules and obligations for different categories of people
Unflattering comparisons	Using unflattering contrasts to bolster one's superiority over others
Euphemisms	Masking, sanitizing, and conferring respectability on reprehensible behavior by using palliative terms that misrepresent cruelty and harm
Displacing responsibility	Behaving in ways one would normally repudiate because a higher authority explicit or implicitly assumes responsibility for the consequences
Diffusing responsibility	Fragmenting the implementation of harmful tasks through collective action
Concealing the effects of harmful behavior	Disregarding, ignoring, disbelieving, distorting, or minimizing injurious outcomes to others
Glorifying violence	Viewing violence as a sublime activity and a legitimate form of human expression
Normalizing violence	Accepting violent behavior as ordinary because of repeated exposure to it and societal acceptance of it
Temporal containment of harm doing	Perceiving one's injurious behavior as an isolated event "just this time"

Note. From "Moral Exclusion and Injustice: An Introduction" by S. Opotow, 1990, *Journal of Social Issues, 46*(1), pp. 10–11. Copyright 1990 by The Society for the Psychological Study of Social Issues. Reprinted by permission.

velopmental" theory contends that a moral obligation has its origins in conventional or consensus-based obligations, and that obligations are rooted in convention at the lower stages and natural law at the higher stages of development. Development depends on the cognitive ability to construct a detached and impartial viewpoint to evaluate right from wrong. Second, Turiel's "social interactional" theory separates morality from convention, whereas moral obligation results from social experiences related to justice, rights, harm, and the welfare of others. Third, there is a "social communication" theory that combines Kohlberg and Turiel's theories: In this theory, moral obligation is based on a universal of learned cultural context that does not depend on either consensus or convention and there are no universals across cultures. In synthesizing the alternatives, Miller differentiated between mandatory and discretionary features of moral obligation. Rationally based moral codes may be based on natural law, justice, and harm as mandatory features and yet not founded on individualism, voluntarism, natural rights, secularism, or the idea of a social contract, which are discretionary features.

Bad ethical behavior is not always deliberate. Goodyear and Sinnett (1984) identified specific examples of how counselors might unintentionally violate a client's cultural values:

> (1) misunderstanding about who the client is; (2) lack of knowledge or skills necessary for working with special populations; (3) the intrusion of prejudicial (although perhaps well-intentioned) attitudes and values into the assessment and treatment of special populations; (4) failure to provide clients with information about the consequences of undergoing certain assessment and/or treatment procedures; (5) failure to assume an activist stance when necessary to protect client populations in the face of abuses of authority wielded by others. (p.89)

LaFromboise and Foster (1989) described in detail other examples of implicit institutionalized bias resulting in (a) minority populations being underserved by counselors, (b) the lack of multicultural courses in the counselor education curricula, (c) the low visibility of multiculturalism in counseling textbooks, (d) the ways counseling programs "get around" certification requirements of multiculturalism, (e) the underrepresentation of minorities in counselor education programs, (f) violations of cultural values in research about counseling, and (g) the inadequacy of ethical guidelines for multicultural counseling.

Specific procedures and measures typically used by counselors have also been challenged as culturally biased. Lonner and Ibrahim (1989) suggested that accurate and ethical assessment in multicultural counseling requires: (a) understanding the client's world view, beliefs, values, and culturally unique assumptions; (b) understanding the client's culture-specific norm group; and (c) using a combination of approaches including clinical judgment as well as standardized or nonstandardized assessment measures that might be appropriate. Standardized assessment measures raise problems of (a) distinguishing between constructs and criteria, (b) establishing equivalence, (c) the effect of verbal or nonverbal stimuli, (d) the role of response sets, (e) the tendency to infer deficits from test score differences, and (f) other examples of embedded Westernized bias.

Even the psychological measures of ethical behavior seem to be biased. In reviewing cross-cultural research on Kohlberg's theory of moral development, Snarey (1985) discovered that cultural differences had not been taken into account, and that the emphasis was better suited for an individualistic society than collectivist societies. On the other hand, Cortese (1989) examined gender and ethnic differences in making moral judgments and supported Kohlberg's methodological model as based on universals of moral judgment. Moral judgments across ethnic and cultural groups corresponded to Kohlberg's prediction and to his stages, although a more interpersonal orientation to morality was evident. Segall et al. (1990) concluded that the Kohlbergian model of moral development reflects values of urban, middle-class groups. Gilligan's (1982, 1987) research additionally discovered a bias toward the male viewpoint in Kohlberg's theory. Ivey (1987) advocated for a more relational view of ethics in the form of a "dialectical inquiry" between the counselor providers and the consumer communities. Moral problems are viewed differently across cultures and must be dealt with differently.

4. Ethical Models for Multicultural Counseling

There are many different models for making ethical judgments available to the counselor (Kierstead & Wagner, 1993). To account for multicultural diversity, the counselor might be tempted toward a relativist view of ethical judgment. Relativism is sometimes based on ethical egoism (what is right for one person may not be right for anyone else), ethical egotism (right is a function of reconciling each person's belief and nonbelievers are wrong), ethical nihilism (there is no meaning to moral concepts), or cultural relativism (right and wrong are determined by the culture of the individual). However, relativism makes moral discourse and social accord difficult to achieve and prevents intersubjective agreement.

An alternative to relativism is a more relational approach to ethics. There are three relational (i.e., where a moral judgment is made in relation to some other referent) alternatives to relativism that are frequently implicit within institutional policies.

Strike and Soltis (1985) presented a taxonomy of these three relational approaches to moral judgments. The first of these is "consequentialism," which asserts that moral rightness of an act depends on the degree to which it produces the most good consequences. The utilitarians and hedonists would accept consequentialist ethics. The problem with consequentialism is that minority people are sometimes made to suffer for the greater good of the majority, and the consequences of an act can never be fully known.

The second approach, "nonconsequentialism," provides an alternative belief that morality is determined by the intentions of the person. Each person is responsible for what he or she intends. Immanuel Kant believed that morality is having the right intention. Religious zealots also believe themselves to be "agents of God," and therefore whatever they do is right. The problem with emphasizing intentions is that it ignores outcomes. Even well-intentioned racism is still hurtful.

A third alternative is "rule utilitarianism," which is based on reflective equilibrium. It is based on respect for the person and human dignity as a universal requirement. This approach incorporates aspects of utilitarianism and neo-Kantianism, where the individual must not be treated as a means or a tool toward some other end goal. The moral act should be measured both by its good consequences and by treating every person with equal respect.

Kierstead and Wagner (1993) compared the three forms of relational ethics with one another (Table 10) by focusing on the role of the provider. The three forms have been adapted to the role of the counselor.

Examples of moral universals that have been used to define the good are also available. Sociobiology defines goodness as the survival of the individual and the species in the "selfish gene" theory. Anthropologists have demonstrated that most societies prohibit malicious brutality, incest, and impose other moral rules (Geertz, 1973). Economists base universal moral principles on economic systems suggesting, for example, that cooperation with neighbors is better than competition. If moral universals exist, they provide a common ground for agreement on the foundation of morality in a sort of "social sympathy" and "sense of justice" (Kierstead & Wagner, 1993). Although we may be hard pressed to define these moral universals, we continue to implicitly base prescriptives on them and to debate their application to society, sometimes confusing social engineering with moral discourse in the practice of multicultural counseling.

It is difficult to identify these implicit assumptions within policy statements of professional counseling organizations. At some points the justification seems to be utilitarian (i.e., the greatest good for the largest number), and at other times the focus seems to be on a person's good or bad intentions. In any case, it seems clear that unstated and largely implicit absolute moral values, such as individualism, make up the foundation of ethical principles and standards for counselors. As a first step to making the principles and standards more applicable to different cultural groups, the implicit moral assumptions need to be made more explicit and evaluated according to their appropriateness.

TABLE 10
Three Forms of Relational Ethics

Consequentialist	Nonconsequentialist	Rule Utilitarian
A. The consequences of actions determine morality.	A. There are universals of morality that must be obeyed regardless of consequence.	A. There are long-standing imperatives for morality, determined in part by weighing the consequences of the situation.
B. Concerned with the proper behavioral response to a situation.	B. Concerned that all responses reflect the right intent.	B. Concerned with intentions, consequences, and the search for consistent moral principles.
C. Decisions may be made in the best interest of the group and to the detriment of the individual.	C. Individuals and groups are not responsible for the consequences of their actions (intention alone counts).	C. Both the individual and the group must be considered. Neither the individual nor the group must ever be victimized.
D. The counselor provides problem-solving situations. The client must learn that consequences and appropriateness of rules, laws, and morals will change.	D. The counselor must follow rules and the right intentions to be moral.	D. The counselor must provide practice in making moral choices based on situations and objective analysis of both intentions and rules.
E. Moral decision making is best done in a cost/benefit analysis format.	E. Moral decision making is a matter of identifying the proper motivating intention.	E. Moral decision making must be systematic, reflect the right intentions, and avoid offending our most deeply held instiutions about the worth of people.
F. Commonly used to solve questions of public policy today.	F. Commonly used by moralizers advocating the adoption of specific intentions.	F. Commonly used by moral psychologists as the epitome of moral development.

Note. From *The Ethical, Legal and Multicultural Foundations of Teaching* (p.13) by F.D. Kierstead and P.A. Wagner, 1993, Dubuque, IA: Wm. C. Brown Communications. Copyright 1993 by Wm. C. Brown Communications. Reprinted by permission.

5. The American Psychological Association Ethical Principles

It is useful to review the APA and ACA ethical principles as they apply to the ethical decisions made in multicultural counseling. Pedersen and Marsella (1982), Pedersen (1989), and LaFromboise and Foster (1989), along with many others, have critized the professional principles of ethical behavior for being culturally encapsulated. Can any single set of ethical principles be applied across boundaries of ethnographic, demographic, status, and affiliation differences when those differences become culturally salient? Should the ethical principles be based on the unique, separate, and sometimes exotic perspective of each cultural group, or should they be based on the generally human and intuitively understandable presumption that all people are somehow alike? General ethical principles need to be interpreted and applied to specific cases. If those general principles are imposed, however, there is an implicit bias favoring the dominant culture that inhibits the appropriate adaptation of general principles to different minority groups. Ethical principles that are precisely appropriate to one culture are not likely to fit the requirements of another very different culture. The multicultural counselor requires principles that bridge many different cultural boundaries with fairness, not principles that substitute measures of power for measures of right and wrong.

To the extent that ethical principles are based on stereotyped values from a dominant culture, they need to be revised to serve the best interests of minority as well as majority groups. To the extent that ethical principles assume a single standard of normal, healthy, and ethical behavior, they require revision to reflect a variety of culturally defined alternatives. To the extent that the ethical principles are "technique oriented," they need to be humanized in their application to the cultural context of each case example where those principles are being applied.

Most of the criticism of the ethical principles has presumed that the general principles are valid and appropriate, although the corollaries and guidelines following from those principles require refinement. Most of the criticism of the ethical principles blames deficiencies in the education and training of psychologists where students are not sensitized to the importance of cultural variables in applying the ethical principles. The problems, as we shall demonstrate, go deeper than these superficial criticisms.

The introduction of the "Ethical Principles of Psychologists and Code of Conduct" (American Psychological Association, 1992) claims to offer "aspirational" goals and "enforceable" rules of conduct. The Ethics Code presents itself in the preamble as providing a common set of values upon which psychologists (including counselors) build their professional and scientific work. Each psychologist is expected to supplement, but not violate, the Ethics Code's values and rules as guided by personal values, culture, and experience.

Principle A requires psychologists to maintain high standards of competence in their work and to stay within the boundaries of their particular competence. "Psychologists are cognizant of the fact that the competencies required in serving, teaching, and/or studying groups of people vary with the distinctive characteristics of those groups" (American Psychological Association, 1992, p. 1599). In those cases where "recognized professional standards" do not exist, the psychologist must take precautions to protect the welfare of those with whom they work as best they can. Research cited earlier suggests that many counselors go beyond the boundaries of their competence in working with culturally different persons. However, the lack of "recognized professional standards" for working with many culturally different groups makes it difficult to judge their behavior as either following or violating Principle A.

Principle B requires psychologists to be honest, fair, and respectful of others by not making statements that are false, misleading, or deceptive. "Psychologists strive to be aware of their own belief systems, values, needs, and limitations and the effect of these on their work" (p. 1159). This principle does not prevent unintentional racism or many kinds of institutionalized racism by uninformed or naive professionals working with multicultural populations.

Principle C requires psychologists to uphold professional and scientific responsibility for their behavior, and to adapt their methods to the needs of different populations. Psychologists are supposed to protect the public's trust in psychology and psychologists by monitoring their own and other's behavior. The lack of attention to multicultural concerns is a central issue in counseling, and the tolerance for cultural bias in counseling suggests that this principle is being violated.

Principle D requires respect for people's rights, dignity, and worth. "Psychologists are aware of cultural, individual, and role differences, including those due to age, gender, race, ethnicity, national origin, religion, sexual orientation, disability, language, and socioeconomic status. Psychologists try to eliminate the effect on their work of biases based on those factors, and they do not knowingly participate in or condone unfair discriminatory practices" (pp. 1159–1160). This principle attempts to meet the needs of all cultural groups inclusively. As the counseling profession becomes more responsive to the diversity of cultural perspectives, this principle will provide the authority to reduce cultural biases and promote positive change.

Principle E regards concern for others' welfare, including both human clients and animal subjects, to minimize harm. This principle deals with power differences and the tendency of the more powerful to exploit or mislead the less powerful. To the extent that cultural differences include differences in power, this principle also seeks to protect the interests of the less powerful.

Principle F emphasizes social responsibility to the community and society in general for contributing to human welfare, prevent suffering, and serving the interests of patients, clients, and the public. Like the other general principles, there is an emphasis on the quality of justice that few could dispute. However, the application of these principles in practice becomes more of a problem. (From "Ethical Principles of Psychologists and Code of Conduct," 1991, *Professional Psychology, 22*, p. 382. Adapted by permission.)

Moving from the principles to the ethical standards, only a few of which make direct mention of culture or culture-related issues, the problems begin to emerge more clearly. The general standards re-state the fundamental ideas of the ethical principles, presuming naively that the principles will convey the same meaning to persons from all cultural backgrounds.

One of the most blatant examples of inconsistency between ethical theory and practice is evident in Standard 1.08 on human differences: "Where differences of age, gender, race, ethnicity, national origin, religion, sexual orientation, disability, language or socioeconomic status significantly affect psychologists' work concerning particular individuals or groups, psychologists obtain the training, experience, consultation or supervision necessary to ensure the competence of their services or they make appropriate referrals" (American Psychological Association, 1992, p. 1601). It is hard to imagine any psychological service or function where these differences would not be significant. This standard is insulting; it trivializes, minimizes, and discounts the importance of documented differences in its use of "conditional" language. Psychological research cited here and elsewhere has clearly demonstrated the significance of broadly defined cultural differences for all counseling relationships.

A similar example of inconsistency is evident in Standard 1.10 on respecting others: "In their work-related activities, psychologists do not engage in unfair discrimination based on age, gender, race, ethnicity, national origin, religion, sexual orientation, disability, socioeconomic status, or any basis proscribed by law" (American Psychological Association, 1992, p. 1601). The implication that discrimination against any of these groups might, under some conditions, be considered fair is again inconsistent with the general principle to which this standard is attached.

Standard 1.12 on other harassment is much more straightforward in condemning harassment and demeaning behavior based on age, gender, race, ethnicity, national origin, religion, sexual orientation, disability, language, or socioeconomic status. The wording of this standard demonstrates that loopholes in the Ethics Code can be avoided.

There are other examples also. Standard 1.17 prohibits multiple relationships, and Standard 1.18 prohibits barter with patients or clients, which disregards cultural patterns in cultures less dependent on a money economy or more dependent on relationships and a collectivist perspective. The presumptions are those of a dominant, middle-class, urban, and cultural context.

The second general standard relates to evaluation, assessment, or intervention. Standard 2.01, requiring accurate assessment to be fully implemented, presumes that the psychologist be able to interpret a client's behavior in that client's cultural context, without which the accuracy of assessment would be doubtful. Standard 2.02, regarding the appropriate use of assessments, disregards research cited earlier about implicit cultural biases in tests and measures. Standard 2.04 acknowledges that assessment techniques or norms may not be applicable due to an individual's gender, age, race, ethnicity, national origin, religion, sexual orientation, disability, language, or socioeconomic status. If this standard were taken seriously, there would be profound changes in the way psychological assessment is done.

The third set of standards on public statements does not mention cultural categories directly. The fourth set of general standards relates to therapy and makes no direct reference to the cultural categories mentioned in other standards, although counseling and therapy were usually included in all the other principles and standards. The fifth set of standards on privacy and confidentiality also does not mention cultural categories directly. Given the importance of education and training to teach counselors how to apply the general principles to multicultural settings accurately and fairly, it is astonishing that cultural categories are not mentioned directly in this sixth set of 26 standards on educational training. Cultural categories are not mentioned directly in the seventh set of standards on forensic activities, nor is the eighth set of standards on resolving ethical issues. The omission of cultural differences implies a "one-size-fits-all" approach to professional ethics that is inadequate at best.

6. American Counseling Association Ethical Standards

As in the APA ethical principles, the ACA (1988) ethical standards do not reflect the diversity of race, culture, economic status, or gender differences encountered by counselors. Ponterotto and Casas (1991) pointed out that there are only four direct references to racial, ethnic, national origins, and/or minority group membership in the ACA ethical standards. These references emphasize the "prevention of harm," rather than the provision of help and assistance. Ethical standards should be expected to address the many pressing problems and cultural circumstances in positive as well as negative ways. Not providing help is in fact harmful. Ponterotto and Casas suggested that the shortcomings show "a lack of professional interest in and concern for understanding and effectively serving persons from these groups" (p. 143). Ponterotto and Casas recognized that the explicit inclusion of multicultural concerns throughout the ethical standards would make the guidelines too cumbersome, but that more emphasis could be placed on community involvement, a relational view of ethics, and eliminating the presumption of a dominant cultural context as the standard or normal measure.

The Introduction to the ACA (1988) *Ethical Standards* indicates a dedication "to the enhancement of the worth, dignity, potential, and uniqueness of each individual and thus to the service of society" (p. 1). The preamble carries this theme forward with mention of "respecting the dignity and worth of the individual" and striving for "the preservation and protection of fundamental human rights." The preamble further recognizes the diversity of role definitions; work settings; and academic disciplines, levels of academic preparation, and agency services. "This diversity reflects the breadth of the Association's interest and influence. It also poses challenging complexities in efforts to set standards for the performance of members, desired requisite preparation or practice, and supporting social, legal and ethical controls" (p. 1). The principle of "diversity" is therefore acknowledged as important.

However, the presumption underlying the ethical standards puts less emphasis on diversity. As Axelson (1993) pointed out, there is a presumption that counselors who emphasize individualism will benefit the general welfare of a healthy society. In a multicultural society that emphasizes both collectivism and individualism, the presumption of individuality may be misplaced. Collectivist values regarding the family, group, life-style, or religious beliefs are not directly mentioned.

Section A: General items 8 and 10 direct the counselor to be aware of the client's needs in counseling and "Through awareness of the negative impact of both racial and sexual stereotyping and discrimination, the counselor guards the individual rights and personal dignity of the client in the counseling relationship" (p. 1). Although this will condemn intentional racism, it will be of little use in dealing with unintentional racism.

Section B: General item 19 states: "The member must ensure that members of various ethnic, racial, religions, disability and socioeconomic groups have equal access to computer applications used to support counseling services and that the content of available computer applications does not discriminate against the groups described above" (p. 2). Although there is concern for equitable services, there is also a presumption that members of the minority group will adjust to the cultural setting of the dominant culture. For example, there is no corresponding mandate that dominant culture members should have equal access to counseling resources of the various minority populations.

Section C: Measurement and Evaluation item 1, which emphasizes assessment, measurement, and evaluation techniques, directs the counselor to "provide specific orientation or information to the examinee(s) prior to and following the test administration so that the results (are) placed in proper perspective with other relevant factors. In so doing, the member must recognize the effects of socioeconomic, ethnic and cultural factors on test scores" (p. 2). Saying that data should be appropriately interpreted is easy. Doing it is difficult.

Section G: Personnel Administration section 11 states: "Members, as either employers or employees, do not engage in or condone practices that are inhumane, illegal, or unjustifiable (such as considerations based on sex, handicap, age, race) in hiring, promotion or training" (p. 2). This standard requirement is more or less a re-statement of legal requirements. It does not get at implicit institutionalized racism that would not violate the law but that would violate the ethical principle. The same act may be perceived as appropriate by some and harmful by others.

The Association for Counselor Education and Supervision (ACES; 1979), a division of the ACA, published the "Standards for the Preparation of Counselors and Other Personnel Service Specialists," which contains more specific recommendations for multicultural counseling. Section 1: Objectives direct training programs to reflect the needs in society that are represented by different ethnic and cultural groups served by counselors and other personnel service specialists. Section 2: Curriculum, program of studies, and supervised experiences recommend that a common core curriculum be required including, "studies of change, ethnic groups, subcultures, changing roles of women, sexism, urban and rural societies, population patterns, cultural mores, use of leisure time, and differing life patterns" (pp. 3–4). The document also recommends that cultural factors be considered in teaching appraisal methods, and that a supervised counseling practicum include contact with the people from the cultural backgrounds with which the counselor intends to work. Finally, the document recommends that faculty make an effort to "select individuals who represent a variety of subcultures and subgroups within our society." In discussing the ACES recommendations, Axelson (1993) described the problems of incorporating these ethical guidelines for multicultural counseling into the curriculum through a separate course, areas of concentration, interdisciplinary models, or an integrated model.

At an Open Hearing of the ACA Ethics Committee on Standards Revision, the new standards, expected to come out in 1995, were presented. The proposed sections for ACA's revised standards will include general principles that include ethical obligations to clients and society. Section A: The counseling relationship will include respect for diversity, informed consent, respect for differing values, dual relationships, group counseling issues, consultation, fee setting, termination, and computer applications. Section B: Confidentiality will include privacy rights, multiple clients, minor clients, records, and research. Section C: Professional responsibility will include requirements to know the standards, practicing within boundaries of competence, advertising, credentials issues, statements to the public, and relationships with other professionals. Section D: Evaluation, assessment, and interpretation will include appraisal issues, competence in testing, releases to others, diagnosis, test conditions, diversity issues, scoring and interpretation, security, and obsolete tests. Section E: Relationships with other professionals will include employer relationships, employee relationships, client consultation, and referrals. Section F: Teaching, training, and supervision will include relationships with students, research with students, responsibilities to students, evaluation of students and supervisee, competence, and supervision responsibilities. Section G: Research and publication will include human subjects issues, informed consent, reporting results, and publication issues. Section H: Resolving ethical issues will include requirements when reporting violations and cooperation with investigation. These proposed standards appear to share the same underlying assumptions as the 1988 standards and will be subject to the same criticisms.

Many of the criticisms of the APA ethical principles also apply to the ACA ethical standards. Where issues of cultural diversity are acknowledged, they are mentioned as an exception to the rule and as requiring some adaptation or accommodation of normal policy. Counselors are urged to become better acquainted with culturally diverse populations. But knowing more about other cultures or even the counselor's own culture is not sufficient to guide ethical behavior toward those groups. The implication is that diverse cultures represent exotic alternatives in an almost patronizing manner. The guidelines sometimes seem to emphasize protecting the counseling professional more than protecting the culturally different client. All of these presumptions are implicit rather than explicit. Quite clearly, the ethical standards are seeking to incorporate the needs of culturally different clients, but only as an exception to underlying fundamental and familiar assumed moral values. In order for the ethical standards to adequately serve the multicultural setting, those basic underlying philosophical assumptions need to be challenged by the culturally different clients they presume to serve.

7. Conclusion

The ethical dilemma of a multicultural counselor is the need to choose between ethical behavior and professional obligation. This condition has evolved over the years. The awareness of this ethical dilemma has also evolved both as a product of historical movements for equity across culturally different groups and through the advocacy of concerned professionals through self-criticism.

The dangers of cultural encapsulation were identified by Wrenn (1962, 1985) and are widely acknowledged in the field of counseling. The ethical principles of the APA and the ethical standards of the ACA are discussed as examples of cultural encapsulation. There appears to be a series of implicit but fundamental assumptions that function as moral absolutes in defining the ethical obligation of counselors. Although absolutism has failed, relativism does not seem to be an acceptable approach either. Three relational alternatives of consequentialism, nonconsequentialism, and rule utilitarianism may provide a complicated but more adequate relational basis for identifying the underlying assumptions of our ethnical standards.

We need to move toward a pluralistic perspective in form as well as function to accommodate the range of differences in culturally learned assumptions by which each individual interprets events. The more obvious cultural differences of nationality and ethnicity provide an opportunity to develop inclusionary perspectives that will increase our accuracy in dealing with the sometimes less obvious differences of age, gender, life-style, socioeconomic status, and affiliation. Until the ethical obligations of all counselors are seen and described in terms of increasing accuracy and relevance for multicultural counseling rather than for special selected interest groups, we are unlikely to see more than a token acknowledgment of cultural variables on the part of counseling professionals facing this ethical dilemma.

PART III

Skills for
Multicultural Action

CHAPTER 9

Multicultural Skill Development

Major objective:

1. To describe guidelines for multicultural counseling skills.

Secondary objectives:

1. To suggest a balance of power in the interview.
2. To examine the informal methods and contexts of multicultural counseling.
3. To describe competencies for multicultural counselors.
4. To describe the balance of power.
5. To examine skill-based multicultural counseling strategies.

Multicultural counseling skills are based on the foundation of awareness and the understanding of knowledge to bring about appropriate and effective change in multicultural situations. Skill learning is the most difficult and important of the three levels in multicultural counseling competency. Although the problems people encounter are amazingly similar across cultures, the appropriate and skillful response to those problems is unique.

There are as many different ways to help persons as there are cultural groups. Each group defines its own criteria of appropriate helping methods. In a similar way, each culture has its own requirements regarding the formal and informal context in which help may appropriately be provided. Formal counseling methods in formal settings are not always appropriate. It is important to enlarge the repertoire of skills to include informal methods and contexts as well as the more familiar formal counseling methods. Where the right method and context have not been matched appropriately the counselor is less likely to be effective.

The first error has resulted in overemphasizing the importance of a person's behavior and underemphasizing the importance of the expectations or values that give those behaviors meaning. Categorical interpretations of behaviors have resulted in the naive imposition of narrowly defined criteria of normality by a dominant culture on culturally diverse people.

The second error has resulted in oversimplifying various social systems variables in counseling by emphasizing the most obvious aspects of a client's background. Authenticity requires that counselors consider ethnographic, demographic, status, and affiliation variables as they interact with one another in a constantly changing configuration. Culturally skilled counselors can understand the cultural complexity of their clients, and thereby they avoid the dangers of stereotyping and cultural encapsulation (Wrenn, 1962).

The third error has resulted in applying counseling as a primarily formal process that emphasizes trained professionals' specialization in mental health services. We have already mentioned how Kleinman (1980) contrasted the specialized view of a perspective focused on the malfunctioning body part with the more systemic "illness" perspective, which includes contextual variables in mental health care such as a person's family and friends.

1. Power Management in Multicultural Training

Skill requires that the counselor "manage" power in the interview. The counselor must know how much power to exert in a multicultural interview to facilitate the client's growth. If the counselor exerts too much power, the client will reject counseling as "more of a hassle than the problem was in the first place." If the counselor exerts too little power, the client will reject counseling as "ineffective and useless." Some theories of counseling define successful outcomes as "empowering" the client so that the client becomes less helpless and more powerful through the counseling relationship. Functionally, we might define counseling as transferring power to the client and preventing the problem from controlling the client.

If the task of counseling is to increase the power of the client and reduce the power of the problem over the client, then counseling can be described as a three-way distribution of power through a temporary means-oriented coalition between the client and the counselor against the problem. There are several functions of effective multicultural training of counselors to manage power effectively.

First, counselors must be able to define power in each client's unique and different cultural context. Second, counselors must be able to appropriately adjust their own increase or decrease of power in the multicultural interview over time, as the salient balance of power changes. Third, counselors must have a wide repertoire of counseling styles to meet the culture-specific needs of each culturally different client. Fourth, counselors must be able to develop and maintain rapport with culturally different clients in an enduring coalition of the counselor and client against the problem. Fifth, counselors must be able to work toward the client's ability to function in his or her cultural context without the counselor's assistance.

Figure 6 describes this triadic interaction between the counselor, client, and problem, in which the client is initially dominated by the problem and the counselor intervenes to restore a balance of power in the client. Counseling then becomes a process whereby a client's contribution of power or influence increases and, as an inverse function of this process, the problem's capacity for power or influence decreases. The counselor intervenes to encourage the client's progress up the slope through a client–counselor coalition that balances the power influence of the problem.

As Figure 6 illustrates, at any point along the scale the power of the counselor plus the power of the client should be approximately equal to or greater than the power of the problem $(Co + Cl \geq P)$. The effective counselor needs to vary the power of intervention according to the client's changing needs. If a counselor assumes too much power, the client will withdraw from counseling in preference for the problem, which will seem less threatening. If the counselor assumes too little power, the client will also withdraw back to the problem in response to ineffective counseling.

FIGURE 6
A Schematic Description of the Ratio of Power Influence Over Time for Counselor, Client, and Problem with Three (X_1, X_2, X_3) Points in the Counseling Process Indicated

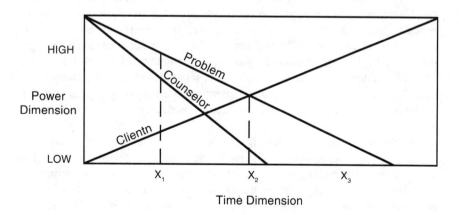

The three situations (X_1, X_2, X_3) are indicated in Figure 6. In X_1, the client has little power and is dominated by the problem, which requires the counselor to exert more power than the client. In X_2, the client is able to exert enough power so that the counselor may reduce power. In X_3, the client is able to manage the problem almost independently and maintain a balance. The measures of high- and low-power influence are relative and not absolute to accommodate a relatively effective client facing a difficult problem or a relatively ineffective client facing a mild problem.

The counselor needs to coordinate the power of intervention according to the variable rate and direction of a client's movement to maintain a client–counselor coalition and balance in the interview. Counselors might exert more power through confrontation and interpretation and less power through reflection and nondirective accommodation. To the extent that a counselor and a client come from different cultures, it is particularly difficult to maintain the appropriate balance of power in a counseling interview. However, the research indicating that a positive relationship is the most important predictor of success in counseling suggests that this balance of power must be maintained. Figure 6 provides a conceptual framework for activating the counseling interaction and for defining the goal of training (i.e., increasing a counselor's skill in maintaining an effectively balanced relationship in counseling).

2. Balance as a Multicultural Counseling Skill

In many non-Westernized systems, there is less emphasis on separating the person or persons from the presenting problem or source of difficulty than there is in Western cultures. Balance suggests a broad frame of reference to the system or field surrounding each unit or identity. Although Western approaches acknowledge the importance of "solutions," there is less understanding of how "problems" are also important in social services. There is also less of a tendency to locate the problem inside an isolated individual and more of an attempt to relate the individual's problem to other persons or even the cosmology. Balance in the context of counseling skill is a dynamic process within a context where all elements, pain as well as pleasure, serve a useful and necessary function. This non-Western emphasis is typically more holistic in acknowledging the interaction of persons and environments in both their positive and negative aspects.

The restoration of balance provides an alternative goal to the more individualized goal of solving social problems. In the context of balance as a criteria, social change is perceived as an unresolved ambiguity, tension, and reciprocity of contrasting alternatives rather than resolving differences in favor of either alternative. Balance is a process rather than a conclusive event. In a similar mode, the problems, pain, and otherwise negative aspects of social problems also provide necessary resources for creating a dynamic balance with pleasure and positive aspects of the same situation.

Counseling occurs in a force field of push and pull factors in which the counselor seeks to be helpful, the client seeks to reconcile internalized ambiguity, and the problem seeks to continue controlling the client, all aspects of which are culturally mediated. In the mode of social power theory, counseling occurs in the context of an equilibrium between the counselor seeking coalition with the client against the resistance of a problem. Negotiating a coalition between the client and the counselor describes the task functions of counseling in operational terms.

Slack and Slack (1976) suggested bringing in a co-client who has already effectively solved similar problems in working with chemically dependent clients. Satir (1964) introduced mediators in family therapy for problems of pathogenic coalitions, with the therapist mediating to change pathogenic relating styles. Zuk (1971) described counseling as a "go-between" process where the therapist is the catalyst for resolving conflict. Trimble (1981) suggested that a third person as mediator might work better in some cultures than in others, such as the American-Indian culture. If the mediator is poorly chosen, bringing in a third person as mediator or interpreter may seriously distress Hispanic clients through embarrassment, misinterpretations, inaccuracies, invasions of privacy, and a variety of other reasons (LeVine & Padilla, 1980). If counselors are trained to be bicultural and bilingual, the mediating function is internalized within the counselor's range of skills. This internalized mediation goes back to the earliest Greek role of the counselor as a mediator between the client and a subordinate world of powers and values (Meadows, 1968).

Internalization of balance requires full awareness of the relevant social systems variables. Functional and interactional social systems variables have been the focus of the most promising research on behavior and sociocultural context and the assessment of social variables from their cultural context. Cultural variables can intervene in a counseling interview in at least three different ways. One way is through the cultures of the client, another is through the cultures of the counselor, and the third is through the cultures of the problems that define the context of a counseling interview and that take on characteristics from contributing cultural aspects of the environment. Particularly in multicultural counseling, it is important to account for the cultural influences of the problem in the interview. There are numerous implications for counseling and education in the accommodation of complexity and balance in this analysis. First of all, simple explanations are temptingly convenient but dangerous approaches to understanding the real world. The counselor is guilty of reductionism when he or she assumes that all persons from a particular group or culture have exactly the same needs and behaviors, and if he or she substitutes symbiotic stereo-types for the real world of the unique individual. Reductionism ignores cultural variations among clients from the same culture. The measure of counseling competence is not merely identifying the many cultures, groups, or identities to which we each belong, but being able to track which of those identities is sa-lient at any given point in time from the client's viewpoint. The competent counselor avoids reductionism.

Second, complexity is a friend, not an enemy, in the search for the fuzzy, approximate, and interminate truths of reality. Every student is looking for easy answers and the "magic bullet" to cure all problems. Teachers usually help students simplify their understanding of problems and solutions. Sometimes that simplification results in distorting reality. If a teacher can accept the neces-sity and potential usefulness of helping a student accept and understand prob-lems in more complicated, but perhaps more culturally authentic, terms, the positive value of complicated thinking will become apparent.

Third, only those who can escape being caught in the web of their own as-sumptions and maintain a balanced perspective will be able to communicate with other cultures. The dangers of cultural encapsulation and the dogma of increasingly technique-oriented definitions of the educational process have fre-quently been mentioned in the rhetoric of professional counseling associations and criteria for accreditation of counselor educational programs. In order to escape from encapsulation, counselor educators need to challenge the cultural bias of their own untested assumptions. This may be done by looking at the reasonable opposite conclusions (e.g., where dependence may, under some conditions, be good and individualism bad). To leave our assumptions untested or, worse yet, to be unaware of our culturally learned assumptions is not con-sistent with the standards of good professional counseling.

There are several implications of considering balance as a multicultural counseling skill. Each implication contributes toward a capability for under-standing and facilitating a balanced perspective in multicultural social services.

1. Concepts of knowledge must be enlarged to go beyond the boundaries of rational process. Knowledge in other cultures has many forms. There are many ways to gain knowledge (e.g., intuition and other forms of knowl-edge accumulated through experience). Although reasoning is a valuable skill, it is presumed to get in the way of knowledge in many non-Western cultures and cut off sources of information. For that reason, what appear to be logical inconsistency and paradox become valuable approximations of truth in many societies. Logic is only one form of validation, dependent on a scientific rational and abstract principle to describe human behavior. The criteria of balance suggests other sources of validation as well.

2. The importance of relationships must be recognized when working in societies that do not emphasize individualism. In many societies, individual development is a lower stage of growth toward "fulfillment." Appropriate spiritual alternatives describe the self as participating in a unity with all things and not limited by the changing illusions of self and non-self. In the non-Western perspective, an individual's unity with the universe goes beyond the self to cosmic unity. The individual is in a context of relationships between people in a cosmos.

3. Westernized perspectives, which have dominated the field of counseling, must not become the single criterion of "modernized" perspectives. Although non-Western cultures have had a profound impact on the West in recent years, many non-Western cultures seem more determined than ever to emulate the West. There is also evidence that the more modernized a society is, the more its problems and solutions resemble those of a Westernized society. Although Western society is fearful of technological domination that might deteriorate social values and destroy the meaning of traditional culture, non-Western societies are frequently more concerned that the technology will not be available to them. The task is one of differentiating between modernized alternatives outside the Western model. Otherwise we end up teaching Westernization in the name of modernization. We need indigenous, non-Western models of modernity to escape from our own reductionistic assumptions.

4. Change is not inevitably a positive and good outcome of counseling. A balanced perspective between changing and unchanging values requires us to recognize that many cultures do not accept change and development as desirable. In Western cultures, we say "If you don't know what to do, at least do something!" In Western cultures, there is a strong predisposition toward valuing change as intrinsically good, moving toward a solution, reconciling ambiguity, and promising better things for the future. A contrasting perspective suggests that change may be bad. To understand this change process, we need to identify those values that do not change but rather become the hinges on which the door of change swings. In a cosmic perspective, it is possible to deny the reality of change entirely, along with the cause–effect thinking, in favor of an external unchanging picture of ultimate reality.

5. We do not control our environment, but neither does our environment control us. In the range of value orientations, there is a clear division between those cultures that believe it is our right and even responsibility to control the environment and those cultures that teach that we are controlled by our environment. A third group teaches that we interact with our environment so that the question of control is irrelevant. Whichever

basic assumption is made will profoundly affect the criteria for intercultural training in any situation. An increased awareness of ecological balance has helped us understand the interaction with persons and environment as a complex, and certainly not simple, phenomenon.

6. Ability to recover from mistakes is more important than perfection as a criterion for social service. I teach my students that if they are working in an intercultural environment and not making mistakes, they are not taking enough chances. The skilled professional will make as many errors as the novice. The difference is that the skilled professional will recover and the novice will not. In learning about intercultural criteria, it is important to break out of a "success/fail" dichotomy because ultimately the outcomes of social interaction are seldom defined clearly as a success or as a failure. The emphasis in identifying intercultural criteria needs to go beyond dichotomies to develop the potentially positive effects of each problem as an analogue or a range of possibilities.

7. Very few institutions offer specializations in cross-cultural mental health, although increasingly departments are offering isolated courses in cross-cultural communication. There is a need for a network across disciplines and institutions to coordinate the efforts of multicultural social services. Furthermore, there is a need to involve the "real world" of the community and reduce the artificiality of classroom training.

8. The literature on intercultural counseling is diffuse, varies a great deal in quality, and is published in journals of limited circulation. There is a need for a series of review publications that establish the threshold for quality control in previous as well as current publications. In the same regard, there is a need for more attention to multicultural issues in national meetings of professional associations, which presently invest too little time on cross-cultural papers. There is a need to develop criteria from research on the range of non-Western alternatives to "talk therapy."

9. Finally, intercultural research has failed to develop grounded theory for multicultural social services. There are a number of reasons why this is true. First, the emphasis of multicultural research has been on abnormal rather than normal behavior across cultures. Second, only in the 1970s did research identify universal aspects across cultures, and then only for the more serious categories of disturbance such as schizophrenia and affective psychoses. Third, the complexity of multicultural variables in research is difficult to quantify. Fourth, multicultural research that is available has lacked an applied emphasis and has remained largely theoretical or abstract. Fifth, there has not been sufficient interdisciplinary collaboration among mental health related disciplines on multicultural research. Sixth, the emphasis of multicultural research has been on the

symptom rather than the interaction of person, profession, institution, and/or community.

3. The Balance of Formal and Informal Support Systems

We are never alone. We are always surrounded by a support system of the thousands of cultural "teachers" who have been significant to our thinking, feeling, and behavior. In each person's identity, different social support systems are woven together in a fabric where formal and informal elements, like texture or color in a weaving, provide a pattern or design that is unique. In each person's identity, a balance of formal and informal support systems is essential to good mental health. A multiculturally skilled counselor can balance formal and informal approaches in the treatment of culturally different populations (Pedersen, 1981a, 1982, 1986).

The pattern or design of social systems in Western cultures is significantly different from that in non-Western cultures (Pearson, 1990). In a world perspective, the formal context of counseling and therapy is an "exotic" approach. In Western societies, there is a tendency to locate the problem inside the isolated individual rather than relate a person's difficulty to other persons, the cosmology, or informal support systems.

From a systems perspective, counseling can occur in an informal as well as a formal mode. The place where counseling occurs as well as the method by which counseling is provided are defined by a balance of formal and informal support systems. The combination of formal and informal methods and contexts creates a dynamic combination of indigenous support systems, which define our personal culture.

Although most research on support contains similar assumptions, definitions of support vary greatly (Caplan, 1976; Cobb, 1976). The kinds of support frequently mentioned include emotional support (feelings of closeness, intimacy, esteem, and encouragement), tangible goods and assistance, intellectual advice or guidance, and supportive socialization (Pearson, 1990). The accurate identification of social support networks helps to prevent disorder by the early detection of problems and referral to appropriate helpers (Gottlieb & Hall, 1980), and by meeting basic human needs for affiliation and attachment. The literature on counseling is now providing more data on the importance of indigenous support systems to mediate the functions of counseling (Pearson, 1990).

Figure 7 shows the full range of methods and contexts through which support systems function: from the most formal (where rules, structures, and definite expectations apply) to the more informal (where spontaneity and the lack of defined structures apply). An examination of the figure reveals a paradigm for describing the range of formal and informal support systems.

The incorporation of formal and informal support systems has been included in previously published literature. Figure 7 incorporates the full range of previously identified possibilities for analyzing how the formal and informal systems complement one another. These combinations include a range of alternatives appropriate in various culturally diverse settings.

FIGURE 7
A Three-Dimensional Model of Counseling Services Methods

Method

		Formal	Nonformal	Informal
CONTEXT	Formal	1 Office-scheduled therapy	4 Mental health training	7 Mental health presentation
	Nonformal	2 Community mental health	5 Support groups, friends	8 Family & service
	Informal	3 Professional advice	6 Self-help groups	9 Daily encounter

Each cell of Figure 7 depicts a different combination of formal and nonformal features of counseling methods in various counseling contexts. Each cell in the figure illustrates a different meaning.

1. A formal method and formal context are involved when the counselor/specialist works with a fee-paying client in a scheduled office interview. Counseling as a professional activity occurs mostly in this cell.

2. A formal method and nonformal context are involved when the counselor/specialist works by invitation or appointment with a client in the client's home, office, or community. Semiformal meetings with individuals, families, or groups of foreign students are often best scheduled for locations outside the counseling office. A location that is more familiar to the client can make it easier to establish rapport when discussing personal problems.

3. A formal method and informal context are involved when the counselor/specialist is consulted about a personal problem by a friend or relative at a party or on the street. In some cultures, it is important for the person requesting help to be accepted as a friend before it is appropriate for that person to disclose intimate problems. When I counseled foreign students at the University of Minnesota, I first would have to be "checked out" at group parties or approached about personal problems informally on street corners and only later—if I passed the test—in an office or formal setting.

4. A nonformal method and formal context are involved when a person not functioning in the "role" of counselor is asked for psychological help or providing a professional service, training, or presentation. When I counseled for 6 years in Asian universities, it became clear that the functions of a counselor were not well understood. The concept of a medical doctor was clear, but the counselor was more a special kind of "teacher." To accept help from a teacher was honorable and increased one's status in the community. Consequently, it was frequently useful to describe counseling as a special kind of teaching and learning interaction. An Asian student would be quite comfortable asking his or her teacher for advice and help on a personal problem.

5. A nonformal method and nonformal context are involved in the various support groups organized by persons to help one another through regular contact and an exchange of ideas, although none of the participants is trained as a therapist. When I had Asian or other international students as clients who were unfamiliar with counseling, I frequently asked them to bring a friend to the interview. The friend, although not trained as a counselor, would function almost as a co-therapist by providing constant support, clarifying the content of formal counseling interviews, and helping me to understand the client by acting as mediator and interpreter. This can be especially useful if there is a language problem between the client and counselor.

6. A nonformal method and informal context are involved when self-help groups and popular psychology are used as resources. A frequent indicator of culture shock is withdrawal from support groups and increased isolation from groups of others. There are various self-help groups, such as Alcoholics Anonymous and other organizations, for addicts, single

persons, veterans, or those who share the common bond of a traumatic experience. Similarly, there is much literature on positive thinking or advice giving that is a frequent source of help. My Chinese clients frequently first consulted the Confucian proverbs for advice, and sought counseling only when the proverbs seemed inadequate.

7. An informal method and formal context are involved when a listener receives considerable assistance in solving a psychological problem from a formal, scheduled presentation or activity, even if that was not the explicit intention of the program. In non-Western cultures, much of what we call "counseling" in Western settings occurs through religious institutions. Family meetings and activities also provide a valuable vehicle for the functions of counseling and leave a great vacuum by their absence. These institutions are not primarily psychological, nor is their primary purpose to promote mental health. However, the ritualistic context is often formal and contributes significantly to healthy mental attitudes.

8. An informal method and nonformal context are involved when family and friends provide help to an individual. In many Asian cultures, it would be unacceptable to go outside the family or a very close circle of friends to disclose personal problems. In some situations, a foreign student under stress while in the United States may be helped by making contact with relatives or close friends. These people can serve as a resource and context for casual and indirect conversations, which can promote healthy mental attitudes.

9. An informal method and informal context are involved in daily encounters in which individuals receive help spontaneously and unexpectedly from their contacts with other people, whether that help is intended or unintended. Spontaneous recovery from crises or stress takes many forms. For example, imagine that it is a nice day and you are walking down the street. Someone smiles. You smile back. You feel better. Each culture teaches its own repertoire of self-help mechanisms for healing.

A comprehensive picture of formal and informal support systems helps to classify the different sources of psychological help. Without an adequate framework to identify the resources, counselors are likely to rely too heavily on more formal, obvious support systems and ignore the less obvious, informal alternatives. If counselors seek to translate counseling and therapy to culturally different populations, they need to complement the diverse informal influences in clients' support systems. The formal and informal frameworks highlight the complexity of clients' indigenous support systems and also indicate the importance of matching the right method and context so that culturally skilled counseling can occur.

4. Cultural Competencies for Counselors

In the variety of research literature on intergroup or multicultural contact, the one consistent finding is that groups or individuals who perceive themselves to be quite similar in some way are more likely to relate in harmony. However, if they perceive themselves to be dissimilar, they are more likely to relate through conflict. It is important to look at specific areas of competency that promote a shared world view between the visitor and the host culture. More research has been done on competencies for multicultural education than on competencies for multicultural counseling. It may be useful to apply some of the educational competencies to the development of multicultural counseling competencies.

The evaluation and assessment of internationalism in higher education relates to both cognitive and affective competencies as educational objectives. Using the guidelines suggested by Bloom (1956) and McCraw (1969), the following goals can be applied to the teacher or counselor. The multiculturally skilled counselor:

- is aware of the other cultures;
- is willing to receive information about value systems different from his or her own and voluntarily selects articles and books about a different culture;
- is willing to respond to instructional materials about a different culture by asking questions and offering comments;
- obtains satisfaction from responding to information about another culture;
- accepts the idea that it is good to know and understand people of other cultures;
- prefers the previous idea to any competing dogma, rejecting cultural isolationism;
- is committed to the value of international understanding and cooperation; and
- conceptualizes this value into the total value system by weighing alternative international policies and practices against the standard of international understanding rather than against narrow special interests.

As an example of what a teacher or counselor should know about the other culture under discussion, a checklist of skills and information found in Bloom's guidelines should be known by the multiculturally skilled educator. The multicultural teacher or counselor:

- knows much of the history, customs, language, and geography of one or more cultures other than his or her own;
- knows contributions of various cultures to the world;

- knows where and how to find additional information about other cultures;
- demonstrates constructive ability to solve problems involving international understanding;
- sees the implications in data regarding social and economic circumstances;
- understands that people are more alike than different;
- applies general ideas regarding culture to a popular cultural context;
- analyzes a culture into component parts;
- forms generalizations from cultural data and observes exceptions;
- observes differences in wealth, values, and behavior among cultures and understands the reasons for the differences;
- sees the necessity of world trade and the value of world travel;
- understands the causes for changes in alliances among nations;
- sees the implications of shortened travel and communication time between countries;
- understands the nature of international interdependence; and
- evaluates ideas based on how they affect world harmony.

California, Pennsylvania, North Carolina, Minnesota, and many other states have required all teachers to complete a training program in human relations to develop multicultural skills. Pedersen (in press, a). The law requires that applicants demonstrate an ability to:

- understand the contributions and life-styles of the various racial, cultural, and economic groups in a society;
- recognize and deal with dehumanizing biases, discrimination, and prejudices;
- create learning environments that contribute to the self-esteem of all persons and to positive interpersonal relations; and
- respect human diversity and personal rights.

Filla and Clarke (1973) developed a series of skill descriptions to meet the human relations requirements. These descriptions provide guidelines for multicultural development for social institutions outside the school as well. Although these skill descriptions do not claim to be the "best" statements or to be all inclusive, they do provide some examples of how the theory of multicultural teaching can be applied to practical problems of counselor education.

5. Alternative Skill-Based Counseling Strategies

In the appropriate formal or informal context, and using the appropriate formal or informal methods, the counselor is charged with demonstrating the appropriate competency at a high skill level. In the multicultural setting, the counselor frequently functions without benefit of the familiar cultural guidelines and works in an unfamiliar multicultural setting. If we assume that all tests and theories that are precisely suited for one cultural setting are not precisely suited for contrasting cultural settings, then we can define multicultural counseling skill as the ability to work with culturally biased tools and theories by interpreting them accurately/appropriately in a variety of culturally different settings. Multicultural counseling skill defines the ability to "do the right thing" in a less than perfect or ideal setting. Hence, the components of multicultural counseling skill incorporate all other skill competencies, plus the additional ability to apply or adapt those competencies in different ways according to the different cultural contexts.

Effective multicultural training results in movement from simple to more complex thinking about multicultural counseling relationships. The trained person becomes less dependent on stereotypes when thinking about or working with culturally different clients. The trained person develops a wider range of response alternatives from which to choose in multicultural counseling. The trained person can describe each multicultural situation from the contrasting viewpoints of culturally different participants. The trained person can better understand the "source" of a problem in the multicultural setting. The trained person can better keep track of the "salient" culture as it changes and develops in the multicultural interview. The trained person can account for his or her own cultural identity as it helps and/or hinders the multicultural counseling process.

Brislin (1993) reviewed training programs that facilitate multicultural interactions and identified four general goals. Successful multicultural training involves: "(1) positive feelings about the development of intercultural relationships, (2) the reciprocation of these feelings from members of other cultural groups, (3) task accomplishment and (4) minimal stress stemming from intercultural misunderstandings and difficulties" (p. 227). Brislin, Landis, and Brandt (1983) described six basic approaches to cross-cultural training: (a) Information or fact-oriented training involves lectures, discussions, and reading or viewing media produced materials. (b) Attribution training focuses on explanations of behavior(s) from the host culture's viewpoint and training people to accurately identify those explanations. (c) Cultural awareness training is focused on learning one's own culture and cultural identity. (d) Cognitive-behavior modification involves identifying reinforcing aspects of the host culture to reward the sojourner. (e) Experiential learning involves face-to-face contact with a contrasting culture and an analysis of the outcomes. (f) The interaction approach involves contact resource persons from the target culture.

I have already examined the difference between didactic "university models" and the more experiential approaches. I have also looked at the differences between culture-specific and cultural-general approaches. Gudykunst and Hammer

(1983) classified multicultural training techniques using those two -dimensions in a two-dimensional paradigm (Figure 8).

Figure 8
A Classification Scheme for Training Techniques

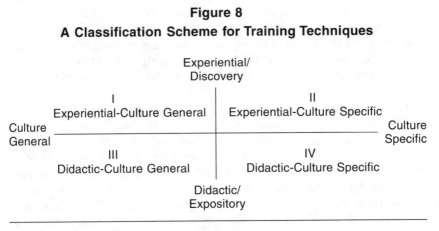

Note. From *Handbook of Intercultural Training, Volume 1* (p. 126) by D. Landis and R.W. Brislin, 1983, Oxford, England, Pergamon Press Ltd. Copyright 1983 by Pergamon Press Ltd. Reprinted by permission.

The first quadrant of their paradigm reviews programs that are experiential and culture general. This category includes traditional human relations training approaches, the intercultural communication workshop, culture-general simulations of invented cultures, and self-confrontation techniques.

The second quadrant of their paradigm reviews programs that are experiential and culture specific. These approaches include modifications of human relations training to fit a particular context, bicultural communication workshops involving two specific cultural groups, and behavioral approaches. Culture-specific role plays are also widely used in culture-specific training.

The third quadrant of their paradigm reviews programs that are didactic and culture general. These approaches include traditional courses on multiculturalism and approaches to develop cultural self-awareness. Self-help books and published materials on multiculturalism would also fit into this quadrant.

The fourth quadrant of their paradigm reviews programs that are didactic and culture specific. All training activities that give instruction about a particular culture or group would fit into this quadrant. Foreign language training programs, specific orientation programs, cultural assimilators, and country guide books would be appropriate for this quadrant.

Multicultural counselors need the skills to match the right method to the right situation in the right way to get the right result. Skill approaches most frequently associated with multicultural counseling relate to cognitive behavior modification approaches and a variety of interaction approaches that are most frequently affectively oriented. Culture is more frequently viewed as a way of affective feeling than a matter of cognitive thinking. Both approaches are important to the multicultural training of counselors.

Baker, Daniels, and Greeley (1990) reviewed three major models of training graduate-level counselors. These programs include: (a) Carkhuff's Human Resource Training/Human Resource Development (HRT/HRD) approach (Carkhuff & Pierce, 1967), (b) Kagan's Interpersonal Process Recall (IPR) approach (Kagan, Krathwohl, & Farquhar, 1965), and (c) Ivey's Microcounseling (MC) program (Ivey & Authier, 1978). With the rise of humanism in the 1940s and 1950s, the demystification of counseling training became more important. The development of training and specific educational approaches have grown rapidly since that time. Carkhuff emphasized the facilitative conditions of empathic understanding, unconditional positive regard, and genuineness in a conceptual approach, with close supervision combining didactic and experiential approaches. Kagan emphasized the ability of students to recall thoughts, feelings, goals, aspirations, and bodily sensations so that they could attend to these aspects more carefully. Ivey's comprehensive model taught students to generate multiple responses to achieve "intentionality." Ivey's (1990) approach emphasized the importance of culture and culturally effective counseling skills more than either Carkhuff or Kagan's alternative models.

Cognitive or behavioral modification skill-training approaches identify rewards or reinforcers in the cultural context as motivators to promote client change. By bringing the familiar reward or reinforcer into the unfamiliar cultural context, it is possible to help clients adapt their more culturally familiar habits to the unfamiliar culture. If a new set of rewarding or reinforcing consequences can be matched with the required behaviors in an unfamiliar culture, the client is motivated to change. This approach, of course, depends on knowing the rewards and reinforcers in both familiar and unfamiliar cultural contexts. When cognitive skill training has been accomplished, the multicultural counselor should be able to think like the client in the client's own cultural context.

Affective-oriented skill training depends on structuring the interaction between participants and the cultural context. This skill is developed by rehearsing the skill in a safe context with feedback from a skilled facilitator. The skill can then be practiced and rehearsed with feedback toward greater competence. The key element to the success of affective training is the effectiveness of feedback as those new skills are practiced and rehearsed. When affective skill training has been accomplished, the multicultural counselor should be able to accurately identify the client's feelings in the client's own cultural context.

Focusing on helper attitudes and a facilitative context, Carl Rogers (Kurtz & Marshall, 1982) first developed a book of practical skills that facilitated the helping relationship by demystifying the helping process and streamlining the training of counselors. The emphasis on experiential training supplements didactic training to include attitudes as well as facts. The new experiential approach helps discriminate between facilitative and nonfacilitative therapy through recorded and life demonstrations, role playing, small-group participation, individual therapy, and feedback from supervisors. Training in this mode moved out of the formal methods and contexts toward the informal methods and contexts, more familiar as counseling is applied to multicultural settings.

Ivey and Authier (1978) developed the Microcounseling (MC) model by combining a conceptual framework with core helping skills that discriminate between the discrete behaviors that define good counseling. Microcounseling changed the focus from changing helper attitudes and qualities to "operational techniques" and behaviors in the context where counseling occurs. Microskill training divides more general skill areas into smaller microunits as applied to multicultural counseling writing about culture-centered counseling and interviewing skills. Microskill training also divides counseling into specific attending behaviors, influencing skills, and integrative skills. By teaching skills in a progressively difficult series of microskills—moving from more fundamental attending skills to more complicated influencing skills—the multicultural counselor constructs or builds an appropriate counseling plan for the client's cultural context. There is more empirical research data supporting the effectiveness of microtraining than any other skill-building method.

In applying microcounseling to multicultural settings, Nwachuku and Ivey (1991) presented a series of steps for generating culturally relevant theory and practice:

1. What are important personal and interpersonal characteristics in this culture?
2. What are the concrete skills and strategies that can be used in multicultural counseling?
3. How can these strategies be organized into patterns?
4. How can these new helping skills be tested in the actual setting?

Structured learning is another social behavioral method widely used in skill building (Goldstein, 1981). Structured learning begins with practical skills and competencies that the client already recognizes as necessary in the client's cultural context. The skill is first presented and discussed. Then the skill is demonstrated to the trainees with opportunity to clarify any confusion. Then the skill is rehearsed by the trainees in role-played situations with feedback from a supervisor or trainee. Finally, the skill is transferred to the client's cultural context outside the training setting through actual practice. Structured learning has had a great deal of success when applied to youth groups, particularly delinquent youth (Goldstein, 1991). Skill-based training is clearly the most promising method available to prepare counselors. When skill-based training has failed, it usually has been due to oversimplification of the skills technique.

Pedersen and Ivey (in press) discussed the limitations of a skill-based approach to training multicultural counselors when improperly used.

1. Skills training has grown in many different directions so that comparability and generalizability across cultures is difficult.
2. There is a danger that the clients are fitted to the skills-training technique rather than beginning with the needs of the culturally different client.
3. Generalizing skills learning in a laboratory to the outside world has been a continuing problem for successful skills-based training.
4. Defining the limits of skills in solving or managing a problem is also difficult to do, resulting in sometimes overestimating the importance of skills.
5. Skills training was a product of Westernized cultures and reflects many of the culturally learned assumptions of a Euro-American context.
6. When skills training focuses on individuals as an isolated biosocial unit, it ignores the needs of collectivist cultures.
7. Where skills training requires the intervention of outsiders, it may not fit cultures that have a higher need for privacy within the family.
8. It is not always possible to accurately identify the reinforcing event or reward in another culture.
9. When expensive technical facilities are required for skill training, it may be too expensive for another culture.

Multicultural counseling skills apply the familiar and widely accepted counseling skills to a variety of different cultural settings. It is not necessary to discard culturally biased theories and strategies as long as we can teach the skills for adapting and modifying those familiar strategies to a range of culturally different settings.

6. Conclusion

Multicultural counseling skill development has several prerequisites. The first prerequisite is to examine one's own culturally learned assumptions regarding the cultures involved and the nature of counseling as applied to different cultures. The second prerequisite is to include both formal and informal methods and contexts within the multicultural counselor's skill repertoire. The third prerequisite is to identify appropriate competencies for working in multicultural settings. The fourth prerequisite is to apply skills and competencies effectively in a variety of culturally different settings, as simulated in critical incident decisions. The fifth prerequisite is to understand the range of skill-based training approaches that have been applied to multicultural settings. The sixth prerequisite is to develop and maintain a balance of power between the counselor, client, and problem.

Counselors are at a decision point in applying skill training to multicultural settings. The next step is either to develop a specialized and separate field of "multicultural counseling" with its own unique skills attached to culture-specific settings, or to incorporate multiculturalism into the generic field of counseling skills. The preceding chapters developed an argument that accuracy in assessment and direct service of counseling functions requires an understanding of the cultural context in which that counseling occurs. The emphasis in the next three chapters is to apply multicultural training to the generic field of counseling, not to isolate and separate multicultural counseling as a subspecialty.

CHAPTER 10

The Triad Training Model

Major objective:

1. To describe the Triad Training Model for training multicultural counselors.

Secondary objectives:

1. To examine the internal dialogues of culturally different counselors and clients in multicultural settings.
2. To describe variations of the Triad Training Model.
3. To review research on the Triad Training Model.
4. To describe strategies for using the Triad Training Model in training counselors.
5. To present guidelines for using the Triad Training Model.

Every counseling interview includes three simultaneous conversations. First, there is the verbal exchange between the counselor and the client. Second, there is the counselor's own internal dialogue of messages the counselor is thinking but not saying. Third, there is the client's own internal dialogue of messages the client is thinking but not saying. The more skilled the counselor is, the better that counselor is able to accurately understand the client's internal dialogue. The more cultural differences there are between the counselor and the client, the more difficult the task of accurately understanding a client's internal dialogue. Multicultural training should enable the counselor to more accurately understand the internal dialogue of culturally different clients.

1. What Culturally Different Clients Are Thinking but Not Saying

Although a counselor may not accurately understand a client's internal dialogue, the counselor can be sure that part of the client's internal dialogue is positive and supportive of counseling, whereas part of the client's internal dialogue is negative and critical of the counseling process. The positive part of the client's internal dialogue might represent an "angel" sitting on the client's shoulder whispering positive messages into the client's ear about the counseling process. The negative part of the client's internal dialogue might represent a "devil" sitting on the client's other shoulder whispering negative messages into the client's ear about the counseling process. If we apply the Cultural Grid to this relationship, we might say the negative internal dialogue is emphasizing differences in behaviors between the counselor and the client (claiming that there is no trust, respect, caring, or competence), whereas the positive internal dialogue is emphasizing similarities in expectations between the client and the counselor (citing examples of trust, respect, caring, and competence). Although all clients experience internal dialogue, the more cultural differences there are between the counselor and client, the more difficult it is for counselors to establish common ground as the basis for rapport in the counseling relationship.

The Triad Training Model attempts to make those positive and negative internal messages more explicit. The Triad Training Model matches a counselor from one culture with three resource persons from the same contrasting cultural background in a simulated counseling interview. One resource person is in the role of a coached client who presents a problem to the counselor and attempts to manage that problem more effectively through counseling in the interview. The second resource person is in the role of a coached "anticounselor" who articulates the negative internal messages a client might be thinking but not saying and who facilitates the failure of the counseling process. The third resource person is in the role of a coached "procounselor" who articulates the positive internal messages a client might be thinking but not saying and who facilitates the success of the counseling process. The four-way and sometimes simultaneous conversation between the counselor, client, procounselor, and anticounselor provides the counselor access to a culturally different client's internal dialogue during the simulated interview. As the counselor becomes more familiar with the positive and negative messages a culturally different client might be thinking but not saying, the counselor becomes better able to incorporate those messages into the counseling interview.

The idea for describing counseling as three simultaneous dialogues was developed while doing counseling at Nommensen University in North Sumatra, Indonesia, for 3 years. The Indonesian students traditionally had an internalized means of mediating conflict through a religious-based notion of the *tondi*: a source of power inside the person who might support or oppose the welfare of the person as a source of health or illness (Pedersen, 1993b). This internalized force in the students' belief systems led the students and me to implicitly deal with the problem as a third presence in the room during counseling. Counseling became a three-way interaction between the counselor, the client, and the "problem" from the client's perceptual world view. The problem was seen as both good and bad, especially from the client's viewpoint, and not exclusively bad. Each problem offered rewarding as well as punishing features, which presented a dilemma for the client. The problem was complex, like a personality, and not limited to a single presenting symptom. The problem was actively changing, drawing its identity from the client's total environment of relationships. The problem was concrete and not abstract, defined by its own threats and promises in the perceptual world of the client.

Working with Indonesian students changed my view of counseling. In that context, counseling became an interaction of push and pull factors in which the counselor sought fulfillment in being helpful, the client sought to reconcile internalized ambiguity, and the problem struggled to survive by maintaining itself. Counseling became a three-way process where the counselor sought a coalition with the client against the problem.

The idea of counseling as a coalition is not new in the counseling literature. Pepinsky and Karst (1964) contended that the counselor–client interaction is basically a social interaction that follows the same laws and principles as other social interactions. Strong (1978) described counseling as a dynamic interaction of contrary forces in an equilibrium of social power. The counselor–client coalition results in "action in accord" with a shared goal. Just as the client has called in a counselor for assistance, the counselor must also depend on the client for assistance and information. Negotiating a coalition between the client and counselor describes the task functions of counseling, which is subject to frequent maintenance and modification.

The early versions of the Triad Training Model included only the client, counselor and anticounselor, or "problem," in a simulated interview (Pedersen, 1968, 1976, 1986). A counselor trainee from one culture was matched with a coached team of two other persons from a contrasting culture, one as a client and the other as an anticounselor or problem for a videotaped simulation of a multicultural counseling interview. The counselor tried to build rapport with the culturally different coached client, whereas the anticounselor or problem tried to prevent the counseling interview from being successful. The videotaped session was then reviewed and discussed from the viewpoints of the counselor, client, and anticounselor. The unique element of the Triad Training Model was the personified role of the problem in the anticounselor, who actively tried to prevent the counselor from coalescing with the client toward solving the problem.

There are several examples of how internal dialogue can be used in counseling. Psychoanalytic and object-relations theories use identification and internalization to bring the external world into the client's private mental life as an influence on the client's thoughts or behaviors. Internalization is usually divided into three categories. (a) Introjection—with an internal presence as an integral part of self—may include part or all of another person like an imaginary playmate, resulting in a friendly or unfriendly internal relationship much like any external-world relationship. (b) Identification—as in modifying one's self to resemble an external model—is where the person imitates another person's beliefs, values, or behaviors with a potential for positive or negative consequences. (c) Incorporation—including all or part of another person into the self—is an attempt to blur the distinction between the self and significant others. Object-relations theories explain human development as the internalizing of components from caregivers and significant others. These internalizations become the basis for how we feel about ourselves and how we act toward others.

Cognitive therapies have also used the internal dialogue. Gestalt dialoguing has been used to help clients explore conflicting feelings in their lives in a cognitive approach to decision-making counseling. Michenbaum (1974) used self-instruction training in cognitive therapy, identifying disturbing thoughts and replacing them with more adaptive thinking. This strategy has worked best in counseling persons with self-defeating behaviors through an "inoculation" that keeps negative thoughts from controlling the client. Clients prepare "internal monologues" to deal with stressful situations. Other "think aloud" approaches to cognitive assessment have the subject identify specific thoughts stimulated by specific events. We know that individuals engage in covert, internal dialogues, and that this cognitive activity has an effect on counseling, but we have never been able to adequately measure the effect. Cognitive-behavioral interventions using structured self-instruction work best if trainees have functional internal dialogue systems initially. Trainees with distractive internal dialogue systems may memorize instructions but fail to implement them in counseling.

Harry Stack Sullivan emphasized the role of anxiety from interpersonal experiences as important to the psychological health of people (Burger, 1990). People learn to reduce anxiety by "selective inattention," which leads them to develop an inaccurate perception of reality. People develop mental images or "personifications" of themselves and others. Sullivan sorted these images about self into three categories. The "good me" personification consists of things we feel good about and for which we have been rewarded, which lead to security without anxiety. This "good me" resembles the positive internal messages of a procounselor. The "bad me" personification emphasizes parts of our experience for which we have been punished resulting in shame or embarrassment, which increase anxiety. The "bad me" resembles the negative internal messages of an anticounselor. Both of these images are more or less conscious. The "not me" personification includes aspects of ourselves that are so threatening that they remain in the unconscious. The dissociation of "not me" from the self requires considerable energy.

The literature on psychodrama contributed to the formation of the Triad Training Model by an adaptation of the alter ego concept. Janis (1982) described the use of psychodrama in education and counseling through the use of "emotional role playing" for changing undesirable behaviors. Clients are encouraged to experience "as if" experiences of being victims in a crisis as part of the change process. Another role-playing technique described by Janis and Mann is "outcome psychodrama" to help people make a commitment to a final choice by projecting themselves into the future. Outcome psychodrama helps clients become aware of worries, hopes, and unverbalized feelings about decisions leading to a more comprehensive understanding of consequences. However, in other studies with clients at an early stage of decision making, outcome psychodrama also diminished client's information-seeking behavior and lowered their self-esteem. There are many elements of similarity between psychodrama and the Triad Training Model in the training process, strengths, and potential weaknesses.

2. Variations of the Triad Training Model

The use of three persons in therapy is not new. Bolman (1968) suggested that at least two therapists, one representing each culture, be used in multicultural therapy to provide a bridge between the client's culture and the therapist's culture. Slack and Slack (1976) also advocated triads by involving a third person who had already coped effectively with a problem similar to the client's in the counseling relationship. Triads have been applied in family therapy to illustrate pathogenic coalitions (Satir, 1964), whereby the therapist employs mediation and side taking judiciously to break up and replace pathogenic relating. Counseling becomes a series of negotiations in which all three parties compete for control. Zuk (1971) described this approach as a "go-between" process, whereby the therapist catalyzes conflict in a crisis situation that is favorable for change and in which all parties can take active roles.

The simulated multicultural counseling interview between a counselor from one culture and a coached client/anticounselor team from the same other culture was adapted to the techniques of video self-confrontation and microcounseling for teaching interviewing skills in attending behavior, reflection of feeling, and summarization of feeling (Ivey & Authier, 1978; Kagan et al., 1965). Videotaped interviews have demonstrated their effectiveness in identifying and strengthening positive facilitative behaviors and changing nonfacilitative behaviors; the supervisor is used as a third person who interrogates and debriefs the trainee after the interview. Other studies (Ravitch & Geertsma, 1969; Solomon & McDonald, 1970; Walz & Johnson, 1963) indicated that videotaped self-confrontation promotes behavioral change. Bryson, Renzaglia, and Danish (1974) also described how simulated racial encounters can be used in training.

Appropriate behavioral change is more likely to result when the videotaped playback serves as a source of information feedback to the trainee by modeling the desired skills. Simulated "role-play" techniques have been widely used for some time, and the successful use of coached clients in simulated interviews also has been well documented (Whitely & Jakubowski, 1969).

Hosford and Mills (1983) reviewed an impressive database demonstrating the importance of videotape as a therapeutic and training medium of choice, comparing the technological breakthrough of videotape in training with that of the microscope in the biological sciences. Video-based training and intervention approaches are being used in a wide variety of counselor training and research settings. Video-augmented interventions have proved effective in treating alcoholism, drug addiction, sexual dysfunction, suicidal intent, disruptive behavior of children, anorexia nervosa, anxiety, employment interviewing skill difficulties, assertiveness difficulties, phobias, marital social skills deficiencies, and a wide range of other psychological or behavioral problems (Hosford & Mills, 1983).

Video has numerous unique advantages in training. First, it provides a permanent visual and auditory record that can be replayed. Second, it includes a mosaic of multilevel perspectives of the simplest to the most complex behaviors. Third, it is a highly personal medium that encourages participation. Fourth, it raptures actual events accurately, providing the basis for lengthy and detailed feedback. Fifth, it involves multiple information-processing capabilities of the brain. "With the unique properties of videotape to involve major brain systems simultaneously, counselors can develop very potent interventions which can be used effectively to help clients ameliorate a variety of problems for which they seek counseling" (Hosford & Mills, 1983, p. 126).

The Triad Training Model more recently has incorporated a procounselor as well as an anticounselor in simulated multicultural counseling interviews to access the client's internal dialogue more comprehensively. The suggestion to include a procounselor was first made by Sue during the 1978–1981 National Institute of Mental Health funded project "Developing Interculturally Skilled Counselors." This 4-year training project at the University of Hawaii provided extensive opportunities to organize both preservice and inservice training of multicultural counselors. By including both a procounselor and an anticounselor, the full spectrum of positive and negative messages of a client's internal dialogue are represented. Having the procounselor in the interview also reduces the threat for counselor trainees confronting an anticounselor in the simulated interview. Both the procounselor and the anticounselor provide valuable information to the counselor in the simulated interview. Research on the Triad Training Model will discuss the relative merits of the procounselor and the anticounselor in training the multicultural counselor.

A variation of the Triad Training Model is the substitution of an "interpreter" for the anticounselor and procounselor. The interpreter provides both positive and negative feedback to the client and the counselor during the interview. The interpreter's task is to increase the accuracy of communication between the counselor and client, irrespective of positive or negative consequences for counseling. This adaptation resembles what Loo (1980) called a "bicultural contextualizer" (BCC). The BCC knows both the culture of the counselor and the contrasting culture of the client, and therefore is able to clarify misunderstandings by both people as they occur in the simulated counseling interview. The BCC and interpreter are not role playing the client's internal dialogue, although sometimes the messages are similar. In both cases, the third person is a broker or a go-between to facilitate the understanding of counselor and client.

Another variation of the Triad Training Model occurred while using the model with staff of the Northwest Training Institute in Seattle, Washington. Their clients frequently came into counseling with a friend or relative. Sometimes that third person was "friendly" to counseling and sometimes "unfriendly." The Triad Training Model was modified to include a "third person friendly" and a "fourth person unfriendly" to help prepare counselors for working with the client's friendly and/or unfriendly companions. In this case, the third and fourth person were not role playing the client's internal dialogue, but were role playing actual persons (a grandmother, aunt, uncle, friend, etc.) who were friendly or unfriendly to the counseling experience. Sometimes incorporating resource persons who are real persons is less abstract and more concrete than role playing the angel or devil in the client's internal dialogue.

In all cases, the Triad Training Model simulates the force field of positive and negative factors from the client's viewpoint. There are several guidelines for using the Triad Training Model that have grown out of using the training model.

1. The Triad Training Model seems to work best when there is both positive and negative feedback to the counselor from the client and resource persons during the interview.
2. The simulated counseling interview needs to reflect incidents likely to occur in a real counseling interview.
3. The simulated counseling interview needs to occur under conditions that both the resource persons and the counselor consider to be "safe."

4. Trained procounselor or anticounselor resource persons are able to make cultural differences less abstract and diffuse for less experienced counselors.

5. The feedback from an anticounselor or procounselor to the counselor is immediate and explicit *during* the simulated interview, rather than after the fact.

6. The counselor internalizes the anticounselor and procounselor functions as he or she becomes aware of the client's internal dialogue.

7. The simulated counseling interview can be videotaped for analysis, discussion, and debriefing by all participants to demonstrate specific ways that cultural similarities or differences influence counseling.

8. When the resource persons are authentic to a particular culture and articulate, they are more likely to demonstrate cultural differences effectively.

9. When the resource persons have a high degree of empathy for and acceptance by the client, their insights are more likely to be relevant and on target.

10. The client needs to be free to disregard feedback from a procounselor or anticounselor who is not on target.

11. The simulated counseling interview works best when it is spontaneous and not scripted.

12. The selection of resource person teams is essential to match as many of the client's cultures (e.g., ethnicity, socioeconomic status, age, life-style, gender, etc.) as possible to emphasize their comembership.

13. The training of resource persons to provide continuous, direct, immediate, and relevant feedback during the interview is essential.

3. Research Applications

Because direct and immediate feedback is such a strong treatment condition, the Triad Training Model has many research applications. Research with prepracticum counseling students at the University of Hawaii showed that students trained with the Triad Training Model (a) achieved significantly higher scores on a multiple-choice test designed to measure counselor effectiveness, (b) had lower levels of discrepancy between real and ideal self-descriptions as counselors, and (c) chose a greater number of positive adjectives in describing themselves as counselors than did students who were not trained with the Triad Training Model. Students trained with this model also showed significant gains on Carkhuff's measures of empathy, respect, and congruence, as well as on the seven-level Gordon scales measuring communication of affective meaning (Pedersen, Holwill, & Shapiro, 1978). Bailey (1981) compared a traditional mode of teaching human relations/multicultural skills with a role-play dyad and triad model. In the first mode, she used simulated interviews of two persons, as client and counselor; in the second mode, she used three persons, as client, counselor, and anticounselor. She used Ivey's Counselor Effectiveness Scale, a revised Truax Accurate Empathy Scale, and the Revised Budner Tolerance of Ambiguity Scale as dependent measures. In a three-way analysis of covariance, all tests were found to be significant between the lower scoring traditionally trained group and both high-scoring treatment groups. No significant differences were found between the triad and dyad training groups on effectiveness, suggesting that both approaches were equally effective but similarly superior to the traditional lecture method of multicultural training for counselors.

Hernandez and Kerr (1985) trained three groups of students using (a) a didactic mode, (b) a didactic plus role play with feedback mode, and (c) a didactic plus triad training mode. After training, videotaped interviews of all students were scored by six professionals on the Global Rating Scale, the Counselor Rating Form-Short, and the Cross-Cultural Counseling Inventory. The trend of data analysis suggested that experiential training tends to produce more culturally sensitive, expert, attractive, and trustworthy counselors. This finding is contrary to Hansen, Robins, and Grimes' (1982) conclusion that didactic approaches seem more effective than experiential approaches in counselor training. This difference may have resulted from using different measures, from having a more specific focus in the Hernandez and Kerr study, or the possibility that some goals lend themselves better to experiential methods and other goals to didactic methods. The findings support experiential training and the continued use of the Triad Training Model, which is geared toward sensitizing and preparing counselors to work more effectively and efficiently with clients from diverse ethnic backgrounds.

Neimeyer, Fukuyama, Bingham, Hall, and Mussenden (1986) compared the reactions of 20 counseling students who participated in either the procounselor or anticounselor conditions of the Triad Training Model. A "Self-Assessment Survey," composed of five Lickert-type items assessing the participant's feelings of control, competence, confusion, and rate of return for counseling, was used. Another self-report measure used was called the "Analysis of Values Questionnaire" with 13 seven-point Likert-type items measuring cultural values of (a) individuality versus groupness, (b) control of nature versus harmony with nature, (c) egalitarian social relationships versus hierarchical social relationships, and (d) future time orientation versus present time orientation. Objective ratings including the Global Rating Scale and the Counselor Rating Form were also used. Results from the two self-report subjective measures indicated that participants in the more confrontational anticounselor version felt more confused and less competent than did participants in the procounselor version. However, no differences in the two measures of objective ratings of response effectiveness were noted, suggesting a differentiation between perceived expertness and actual effectiveness. Neimeyer et al. suggested that the more confrontational anticounselor model is better suited to more advanced students who already have developed some confidence for multicultural interactions, which is consistent with other research on the Triad Training Model (Ivey & Authier, 1978; Sue, 1980).

Sue (1980) field tested the anticounselor and procounselor training models with 36 counseling students at California State University in Hayward. Sue reported that students felt the anticounselor model was more effective than the procounselor model in (a) achieving self-awareness, (b) developing cultural sensitivity for contrasting cultural values, and (c) understanding political/social ramifications of multicultural counseling. The anticounselor model tended to be most effective in (a) giving participants awareness of their cultural values and biases, (b) engendering cultural sensitivity to other ethnically defined groups, and (c) helping them understand the political/social ramifications of counseling. The procounselor model was most effective in (a) helping students obtain specific knowledge of the history, experiences, and cultural values of ethnic groups; and (b) helping them develop multicultural counseling skills. Students were more comfortable with the procounselor model, whereas the anticounselor model was more anxiety provoking. When asked to rate the most effective model for learning about multicultural counseling in the shortest period of time, however, the anticounselor model was seen as superior. Confrontation by the anticounselor brought out issues of racism, bias, and conflicting values through immediate feedback to the counselor trainees, whereas the procounselor tended to facilitate acquisition of skills more gently. The anticounselor showed trainees' mistakes, and the procounselor helped remedy counselor trainees' multicultural style. Ideally, a good training design would incorporate both an anticounselor and a procounselor.

Wade and Bernstein (1991) completed a research study on culture sensitivity training. They looked at the effects of counselors' race on Black female clients' perceptions of counselor characteristics, the counseling relationship, and the clients' satisfaction with counseling. The design assigned counselors to a culture-sensitivity training program using the Triad Training Model with Black volunteers who defined themselves to be from lower middle-class socioeconomic status. During the practice sessions, counselors attended to (a) clients' suspiciousness of the social system, (b) racial and class differences, (c) clients' feelings about how "being Black" influenced counseling, and (d) disclosing the counselor's own values during counseling. A group of 80 Black women were then randomly assigned to counselors who had been trained in cultural sensitivity and those untrained in cultural sensitivity. Both culture-sensitivity-trained counselors and the control group had at least a master's degree in counseling with at least 2 years experience.

The instrument used to assess counselor dogmatism included the Rokeach Dogmatism Scale-Short Form. The two instruments used to assess clients' perceptions of counseling included the Revised Barrett–Lennard Relationship Inventory and a Counselor Effectiveness Scale. The instrument used to assess clients' perceptions of the counselor was the Counselor Rating Form-Short Form.

The Black female clients' perceptions of the counselors and counseling were affected more by the culture-sensitivity training of the counselors than by the race of the counselors. Trained counselors received higher ratings on expertness, trustworthiness, attractiveness, unconditional regard, and empathy than did counselors who had not received additional culture-sensitivity training. Clients of trained counselors returned for more follow-up sessions and reported greater satisfaction with counseling.

LaFromboise, Coleman, and Hernandez (1991) used the Triad Training Model to help validate their Cross-Cultural Counseling Inventory (CCCI). This study evaluated 13 videotapes of practicum students, some who had been trained using the Triad Training Model and some using other models. The practicum students' counseling skills were then evaluated using the CCCI.

In his doctoral dissertation research, Chambers (1992) combined the Triad Training Model with Ivey's Microskills approach in a multiple baseline research design with time-series analysis for training alcohol and drug counselors. The training design had two phases. In the first phase, counselors were introduced to the triad, and then addressed attending, active listening, and questioning skills. In the second phase, the counselors addressed clarifying and reflecting skills. This training design was found to be an effective method for (a) increasing the frequency of good verbal counseling responses in training and later, and (b) decreasing the frequency of poor verbal counseling responses during training and afterward. His findings were particularly true with regard to attending and questioning skills.

Irvin (Irvin & Pedersen, 1993) trained 20 counseling students using a procounselor and anticounselor, with 10 experiencing the procounselor first and 10 experiencing the anticounselor first. The results indicated a decrease in counselor trainees' sense of anxiety, apprehension, and defensiveness when the anticounselor was presented first, whereas trainees reported a greater sense of control when the procounselor was presented first. Two self-report measures included the Self-Assessment Survey and the Analysis of Values Questionnaire. Students who experienced the procounselor first were more likely to anticipate future contact with the client, seemed to understand the problem better, and were better able to absorb a confrontation with the anticounselor later. Students who experienced the anticounselor first felt less anxious and more comfortable, demonstrated more self-awareness, demonstrated a lower level of confusion, and exhibited less defensiveness. There appear to be both advantages and disadvantages in experiencing either the anticounselor or the procounselor first. This might suggest combining the anticounselor and procounselor together as complementary but independent components of a comprehensive training approach.

Much additional research is needed to demonstrate the strengths and weaknesses of the Triad Training Model. Just as multicultural skills are complex and dynamic, the problems of accurate measurement are extremely difficult.

4. Multicultural Training Designs

The Triad Training Model has been used in several hundred workshops throughout the United States. Persons who have used the model report that they are able to articulate the problem better after a series of multicultural interviews with the client/anticounselor teams: "The client's problem as I see it from my own cultural viewpoint is almost certain to be different from the way that problem is viewed from within the client's culture."

Participants also reported increased skill in anticipating resistance to counseling from persons of other cultures. Otherwise, counselors might complete a multicultural interview knowing they failed but never knowing *why* they failed. Immediate feedback from the anticounselor confronts a counselor with mistakes even before the counselor has finished a poorly chosen intervention. There are indications that participants in the counselor role become less defensive after training and are less threatened by working with clients from other cultures after training. Finally, there is less anxiety about making mistakes in counseling clients from other cultures when trainees have rehearsed "recovery skills" for getting out of trouble when they make a mistake.

The Triad Training Model has been used both for preservice training as a unit in a prepracticum counseling course and for a series of inservice training workshops. A 1-hour demonstration videotape of four triad interviews, accompanied by a training manual, has been produced by Media Resources at the University of Minnesota for counselors who want to use the Triad Training Model in their own training programs. A more recent 1-hour videotape demonstrating the anticounselor was completed by the Counselor Education students and faculty of the University of New Orleans in 1992.

Selection and training of coached client/anticounselor teams is of primary importance. The teams of resource persons should be as similar as possible, matching ethnicity, nationality, socioeconomic group, age, life-style, and gender role. Ordinarily, an unusually articulate and knowledgeable resource person from the target population is invited to participate as an anticounselor or procounselor and is asked to select a culturally similar teammate as a coached client who then helps select the procounselor. The client/anticounselor/procounselor teams are trained by viewing and discussing a model videotape and then rehearsing their roles with the trainer as the counselor. Usually one client/anticounselor/procounselor team is trained for every 10 participants in the workshop or classroom module. Each team represents a different cultural viewpoint. Hence, the more teams there are, the more culturally varied the training experience.

In the inservice training workshop for smaller groups of counselors, two teams are trained, and the 10–15 counselors are assembled in a meeting room with a video monitor. Following an introduction and presentation of the video demonstration tape of the Triad Training Model, the facilitator answers questions while one of the counselors leaves the room with a client/anticounselor/precounselor team to make the first videotape. The counselor/resource person team returns to the group after having produced a 10-minute videotape of a simulated counseling interview and a 5-minute videotape of the three participants debriefing one another. This 15-minute videotape is shown to the larger group for comments and discussion. While the first tape is being viewed and discussed, another counselor leaves the room with the second client/anticounselor/procounselor team to produce a second videotape. Throughout the day, there is always one counselor and one team making a tape while the previous videotape is being viewed or discussed, until all counselors have had a chance to produce a videotape and receive feedback on their performance. Each counselor misses the viewing and discussion on one colleague's videotape. The immediate feedback of videotaped counseling interviews provokes stimulating discussions on the variety of cultures as well as presents problems in counseling relationships. The videotapes produced during such a workshop can also provide a valuable resource (Pedersen, 1976, 1984a).

The inservice training workshop for larger groups of counselors requires one trained team for every 10 participants and a room large enough for everyone to meet together in small groups. After the introduction and presentation of the demonstration videotape, the Triad Training Model is demonstrated to the group. The model can be demonstrated by one team to the whole group, or participants can be asked to break up into quartets and experience the Triad Training Model directly, with guidance from the circulating facilitators and team members. Once the participants have a clear notion of the model, they are divided into groups of 10 according to prearranged assignments to ensure that each group is as culturally heterogeneous as possible. A different team is assigned to each group for a period of 20–30 minutes. During this time, the team elects a volunteer from the group to role play the counselor. An alternative format is to allow all group members to share the counseling role, making it safer for anyone in the counseling role. The client/procounselor/anticounselor team prepares three or four problems for simulated counseling interviews. It role plays the interview for 5–10 minutes and then goes out of role for a 5- or 10-minute debriefing period. If there is time, a second problem may be chosen and the process repeated. After each 20-minute period, the teams rotate to another group in ordered sequence until each team has met with each group. A general discussion period at the end of the day is used to share insights and answer questions.

The preservice example of using the model was used in prepracticum courses at the University of Minnesota, University of Nebraska, Virginia Polytechnic, University of Hawaii, Harvard University, Johns Hopkins University, and Syracuse University. In one prepracticum model, students were randomly paired with another classmate from the opposite gender or different ethnic group. Each pair made two videotapes of simulated counseling interviews, switching roles for the second tape as a premeasure of multicultural counseling ability. These tapes, and a similar series of posttraining tapes, were scored to measure changes in skills resulting from training. The 30 students were assembled into quartets so that each quartet contained three coached resource persons of one gender or culture and the third member of an opposite gender or culture. The objective was to have quartets where three persons were much alike and one person was as different as possible, using gender and ethnicity as indicators of differences. During the first phase of training, one student in each quartet was assigned to the counselor role, one to the client role, one to the anticounselor role, and one to the procounselor role. They met for 3 hours in the same roles, simulating and discussing three different multicultural interviews. During the second phase of the training 1 week later, the students rotated roles in the quartet, and the 3-hour procedure was repeated. During the third and fourth weeks of the project, students again rotated their roles so that each student had experience in each of the roles for a 3-hour session, for a total of 12 hours, using the Triad Training Model with feedback on 12 cross-cultural interviews (Pedersen, 1994). Adaptations of these training designs have been used in a variety of workshop and classroom situations.

5. Training Resource Persons

Variations of the Triad Training Model include the use of an anticounselor, procounselor, or an interpreter. In each case, the three-way interaction helps make a culturally different client's internal dialogue more explicit. The following interview examples are transcripts of simulated counselor interviews.

As an example of the anticounselor at work, consider a situation where a White American male counselor (CO) is working with a 24-year-old Japanese-

American female client (CL) who is troubled about whether to move out of her parents' home. The anticounselor (AC) is also a Japanese-American woman. The perception of a parent–daughter relationship is quite different for the client than for the counselor, making it difficult for the counselor to see the problem accurately. A portion of the interview transcript illustrates the contrasting perceptions, as illuminated by the anticounselor.

CL: What do you think I should do? I mean, what's correct? Do you think...?

CO: Well, I guess if you're going to play by your parents' rules, staying home and suffering, I think...

AC: You see! He thinks you're suffering at home and that you should move out. Your parents! Remember!

CL: Do you think I'm suffering at home?

CO: Well, I think something brought you here to talk to me about the dilemma you're in about wanting to move out and being very uncomfortable in having a rough time bringing it up with your folks in such a way that uh...you can do that.

CL: If your folks felt that you didn't like them because you moved out and you were ungrateful...

AC: Ask him when he moved out; when he actually moved out of his house.

CL: Yeah, when did you move out of your house?

CO: I moved out of my folks' house when I was 16.

AC: Why did he move out so young, you know? I mean 16!!! After all that his parents did for him and everything! You know? He moved out at 16!

CO: Well, I went away to school. And, it was important to live at school. It was in another town.

CL: Didn't your parents get mad that you went to another school?

CO: No, they wanted me to go to school. Education is pretty important.

AC: See! He's implying that your parents don't think education is important!

In this brief example, the anticounselor demonstrates what the client might be thinking but would probably not say in the interview. Through the anticounselor, the counselor has direct access to an implicit level of meaning from the client's cultural point of view.

By contrast, the procounselor attempts to provide every opportunity for the counselor to do a better job. Sometimes a procounselor ends up replacing the counselor and taking over the interview, rather than facilitating the counselor's own effectiveness. A skilled procounselor helps the counselor do a better job without distracting or threatening the counselor. An example of a skilled procounselor at work illustrates some of the ways to provide help within the interview.

The counselor (CO) in this situation was a White man, the client (CL) was a White lesbian, and the procounselor (PC) was a White woman. The client was a female graduate student in her early 20s. She recently had had a fight with her female roommate/lover, and the lover left the state. The client was left with much anger, loss, and anxiety over the situation. It began to affect her school-work, and that brought her to counseling. The cultural difference in this inter-view relates to gender role rather than ethnicity.

CO: What else is going on? What other kinds of issues are bothering you? Is it mainly school?

CL: Well, just, you know, I wouldn't say anything is bothering me...I guess everything is bothering me right now because of school. But, ah, you know, if you don't think you can help me, just say so, I don't expect...

PC: Look at how nervous I am and look at how I am shaking.

CO: You're really, really concerned about things...

CL: Wouldn't you be?

CO: Sure, yeah, yeah. And yet you're not sure that I can help you. You won't let me hear...

CL: Why? You haven't helped me yet!

PC: Maybe it has something to do with your being a man.

CO: Do you think, ah, can you think of what kind of help you'd like me to be? Can you think of some ways I can be of help to you?

CL: Ah, yeah, I guess I don't think you can help me much.

PC: Sarah, give him a try. I know he's a man, but give him a try.

CL: I, ah, who are you, anyway?

CO: I'm a psychologist and, ah...

CL: Where did you go to school?

CO: Where'd...I went to Brown as an undergraduate and to the University of Colorado as a graduate student, and I had some problems in gradu-ate school, too.

PC: He might understand your problems, you know.

CO: I'd like to try to help you if I can, and if I can't there's always the possibility that another therapist might be better, but I'm willing to give it a try if you want to try working with me for a few sessions.

CL: Yeah, you really don't get a whole lot of choice here at Counseling and Testing. I just got signed up and I didn't know if you were going to be a man or woman or social worker or what.

CO: Would you rather be working with a woman?

CL: Ah, yes.

After the interview, the procounselor commented on how she provided support for the client.

As a procounselor, it was extremely frustrating working with a counselor who used a different style than I would use. The counselor did not seem interested in the clues that I gave him and ignored my suggestions. At times I felt angry with the counselor. Timing of my comments seemed disharmonious and the session felt disjointed. I was attempting to facilitate problem clarification by focusing on the "here and now" situation by comments on the client's expectation of sessions and nonverbal behavior occurring in the present. When I realized the direction I was going in providing data to the therapist wasn't working, I switched to supporting the client, e.g., putting my arm around her, suggesting she level with the therapist, and so forth. This change of approach felt better than the first direction.

The interpreter acts as *both* procounselor and anticounselor in providing feedback. As an example of the interpreter role, consider an interview between a Black male counselor (CO), a Laotian male client (CL), and a Laotian male interpreter (I). The problems in this simulated role play relate to a Hmong refugee (the client) living in Honolulu. The Hmong are highland people of Laos. There are several concerns of a physical, psychological, and spiritual nature. Physically, the client had suffered abdominal pains and backaches that led to an unwanted operation. "Strange" behavior suggests that the client's psychological state has been affected. For example, he has been seen walking down the street wearing two or three pairs of pants, sometimes forgetting to look at traffic lights or cars. He also has followed strangers in town. However, the most significant problem is the loss of everything familiar in having had to flee to a new country. This has disrupted his spiritual well-being. Consequently, the client attributes all his present problems to the ill doings of spirits. Thus, the counseling dilemma, which is broached in the simulated role play, is how to treat this person within the context of his cultural beliefs and expectations when no traditional healer from the client's culture is available.

Consider how the interpreter acts as a teacher for the counselor through neutral feedback that is neither clearly negative or positive:

CO: Uh, have I left anything out?

CL: No, I think you covered what I had told you. And, in addition to that, I also have some other problems because after the operation, I began to worry about myself and my future life, very, very, much. I do not know what to do, so I spend days and nights thinking about what am I going to do with myself. And, I could not eat, as I said before, I could not sleep, so I kind of stay "half-way" (half-awake) all the time. And this leads to a lot of things that I have in my mind; At times I can see my grandparents who died many years ago, or my friend who was in the army together with me who was killed. And they are all there happily and they keep calling my name, and waiting to see me.

I: What he's saying is he's sick because he worries so much about his life and so forth that...this culture, when you start seeing things—especially a member of your family or your close friend who had died—that means that his life is also going down the drain. That he will die soon. If it were back home, that's what would happen.

CO: OK. So that's what having those visions means in your culture. Maybe what I can do is give some feedback to you about what that would possibly mean in this culture, and you might have a better understanding of how that's handled. And maybe you can help me out. Uh, it seems like what you experience could be seen as visions of your grandparents or hallucinations. Or some psychologists might use the word *delusions*—things like that. People have been helped in the Western culture a lot of times just through talking therapy or getting into some new type of occupation; some new type of environment might relieve those visions. (*To Interpreter*) I don't know if I'm getting this across to him, but maybe you can...

I: What he's saying is that these things happen in this country also, but it's not as serious as it would be if it happened in our country. Because they can do things, patients with that kind of problem can be helped.... Is that what you are saying?

CO: It can be just as serious; I wouldn't put it off, saying that it's not as serious, it can be just as serious, but work can be done to help make life a little bit easier for you. Uh...

CL: If anything can help me, I will appreciate it very much. You see, back home, when we have something like this, we usually go to the traditional medicine man and he will either give us some medicine or he will chant. And, with his chant, all the spirits will go away and that way, he can save our life. But here, I do not know of anybody who can do these sorts of things. So I hope that you can help me.

CO: Well, Uh...

I: What he's saying is that in his particular culture, when you see those things—the spirits coming close to humans—it can cause harm to the living. So, we have traditional healers (or whatever you call them in this country). We have a whole ceremony to chase the spirits away or whatever, and then he would be cured. That means he would not see those spirits again and so forth.

These several examples show how training culturally different resource persons as coached clients provides direct and immediate feedback for counselor trainees in simulated multicultural interviews. When resource persons are authentic to a particular culture and articulate in that culture's viewpoint, the impact of their comments has a powerful influence on the counselor's attitudes. By including representatives of the client's population in training counselors to work with that population, the client's cultural perspective is directly valued as an important part of counselor training.

6. Specific Guidelines for Using the Triad Training Model

Meichenbaum's (1974) cognitive behavioral approach and subsequent research have demonstrated the importance of knowing a client's internal dialogue. Other research has also indicated that the more culturally different the client is, the more difficult it is to interpret that client's internal dialogue accurately. The Triad Training Model is an attempt to articulate a client's internal dialogue through the role of an anticounselor and a procounselor from the client's cultural perspective. In summarizing this approach, it is important to describe the procounselor and the anticounselor role, review the advantages of each role in multicultural training, and provide examples of what someone role playing each role might say or do.

Description of the Anticounselor Triad Design

1. The anticounselor is deliberately subversive in attempting to bring out mistakes of the counselor trainee.
2. The counselor and the anticounselor are pulling in opposite directions, with the client choosing among the same-culture anticounselor, who most likely understands but is opposed to counseling, and a different-culture counselor, who is less likely to understand the client but is working toward a counseling solution.
3. A counselor–client coalition against the problem, or anticounselor, becomes the vehicle of effective counseling, whereas ineffective counseling results in a client–problem coalition that isolates the counselor.

Advantages of the Anticounselor Triad Design

1. The anticounselor forces the counselor to be aware and attune to the client's cultural perspective. If the counselor fails to establish the client's trust in the counselor's ability to solve the problem, a counselor–client coalition against the problem will not occur.
2. The anticounselor articulates the negative, embarrassing, and impolite data that would otherwise remain unsaid.
3. The anticounselor forces the counselor to examine the counselor's own defensiveness and raises the counselor's threshold for nondefensive responses.

4. The anticounselor quickly points out a counselor's inappropriate interventions and mistakes. This allows the counselor to become skilled in recovering from mistakes with increased, rather than diminished, rapport.
5. The anticounselor often attempts to sidetrack the discussion and distract the counselor. This forces the counselor to become skilled in focusing on the client's problem.

Examples of What an Anticounselor Might Say or Do

1. Build on the positive things a problem has to offer, which may anchor one end of a client's ambivalence about giving up the problem.
2. Keep the interaction on a superficial level or attempt to sidetrack the counselor toward inconsequential conversation.
3. Obstruct communication by getting "in between" the counselor and the client both physically and psychologically.
4. Attempt to distract and annoy the counselor in order to draw attention away from the client.
5. Emphasize the importance of cultural differences between the counselor and client to undermine the counselor's faith in his or her ability to intervene appropriately.
6. Demand immediate, specific, and observable results from counseling.
7. Exclude the counselor by communicating privately with the client by whispering, using their shared foreign language, or playing cultural "in jokes."
8. Find a scapegoat and ride it to deflect all blame away from the problem.
9. Insist that someone more expert be called in to replace the counselor.

Description of the Procounselor Triad Design

1. The procounselor helps the counselor and client articulate the presenting problem from the client's cultural reference point.
2. The procounselor functions as a facilitator for the multicultural interview.
3. The procounselor identifies with the client's culture, and thus is able to provide relevant cultural information to the counselor.
4. The procounselor is not a cotherapist, but serves as an immediate resource person who can guide the counselor by suggesting specific therapeutic strategies and supplying information that the client may be reluctant to provide.
5. The procounselor can reinforce the counselor's strategy both verbally and nonverbally.

Advantages of the Procounselor Design

1. The counselor has an immediate resource person to consult when confused about the problem or needing support.
2. The procounselor makes cultural information explicit with the intention of facilitating the interview.
3. The procounselor gives the advantage of another person working on the problem without taking on a co-counseling role with the client (this could happen, but is not an objective of the procounselor triad design).
4. The procounselor helps lower the client's resistance to counseling by helping the counselor approach sensitive issues in a culturally appropriate style.
5. The procounselor can provide beneficial feedback to the counselor if and when the counselor seems defensive in the interview.

Examples of What a Procounselor Might Say or Do

1. Restate what either the client or counselor says in a positive fashion.
2. Relate statements by the client or counselor to previous content (e.g., "Like what he said before...").
3. Offer approval or reinforcement of client or counselor affective states (e.g., "You seem to be feeling more relaxed now").
4. Reinforce what a client or counselor says by nodding when the procounselor feels something desirable is being discussed.
5. Reinforce what a client does (e.g., saying "That's good" to a client who volunteers a lot of information).
6. Aid the counselor by making suggestions (e.g., "We should focus on this problem because the client has the most trouble with this").

A number of models are being used for therapy that involve three persons, such as conjoint family therapy, therapy with co-counselors, work with interpreters/translators, or work with a client's friend who is brought into the therapy interview. The Triad Training Model differs from those alternatives in the unique characteristics of the anticounselor and procounselor.

The Triad Training Model has been used for about 20 years with several hundred groups of counselors. Persons who have used the model report that they are better able to articulate the problem after a series of cross-cultural interviews with the client/anticounselor teams. From the counselor's viewpoint, the client's problem is almost always different from the way that problem is viewed in the client's culture. Participants also report increased skill in specifying the resistance in the counseling interview. Immediate feedback from an anticounselor confronts the counselor with mistakes even before the counselor has finished a wrongly chosen sentence. Other research indicates statistically significant growth on the three Carkhuff scales of empathy, respect, and congruence, as well as on the Gordon seven-level measures of understanding affect. There are indications that participants in the counselor role become less defensive after training and less threatened by working with clients from other cultures. Finally, there is evidence that participants' real and ideal views of themselves as counselors become more congruent after training.

7. Conclusion

The Triad Training Model seems to offer a number of advantages not found in alternative training approaches. It provides an opportunity for persons from different cultures to accomplish a training goal. By a simulated interview format, the model offers greater safety to demonstrate strong feelings and provide direct feedback. Separating the roles of procounselor and anticounselor makes the problem less diffuse and abstract to counselor trainees. The procounselor and anticounselor encourage positive and negative feedback to the counselor in a less threatening mode. Inappropriate counselor intervention is immediately apparent in feedback from the anticounselor or procounselor.

Members of the client's culture become resource persons for teaching counselors to work well with individuals of the client's culture. In this way, the client population has an expert role in training counselors. In the balance of power between counselor, procounselor, and anticounselor, the trainees are reminded that the determination of success or failure ultimately lies with the client and not with the counselor. More data are being collected on the strengths and weaknesses of the Triad Training Model by developing alternative modes to reinforce and facilitate appropriate multicultural counseling skills. Although the model emphasizes multicultural training of counselors, the focus is on training any counselor to work better with any client. *Culture* is only a label for some of the many sources of influence that affect counseling relationships.

CHAPTER 11

Four Dimensions of Multicultural Skill Training

Major objective:

1. To examine four outcome measures of using the Triad Training Model to train multicultural counselors.

Secondary objectives:

1. To describe four outcome measures of multicultural counseling.
2. To describe the skill for articulating the problem in multicultural counseling.
3. To describe the skill for recognizing specific resistance in multicultural counseling.
4. To describe the skill for diminishing counselor defensiveness in multicultural counseling.
5. To describe the skill for recovery in multicultural counseling.
6. To practice using the four skill areas.

I already have demonstrated the importance of defining culture to include the perspectives of age, gender, life-style, socioeconomic status, and other special affiliations. From this perspective, all counseling is to a greater or lesser extent multicultural because the client and counselor are almost certainly somewhat different in their affiliations. I also have shown how standard counseling skills create problems when they are applied indiscriminately across cultural groups. This chapter attempts to identify four areas, each incorporating many different skills, that are designed to adapt standard counseling skills to multicultural counseling.

The four skill areas discussed in this chapter are designed to complement and not substitute for good counseling technique. The training model requires a simulated multicultural counseling interview between a coached client/anticounselor/procounselor team from one culture and a counselor trainee from a different culture. The interview is videotaped and reviewed in a debriefing discussion among the four participants and a counselor trainer. The anticounselor and procounselor roles are similar to that of an alter ego in psychodrama, except that the anticounselor is not neutral. Rather, the anticounselor is deliberately subversive in attempting to bring out mistakes in the counselor trainee, and the procounselor is deliberately positive. The procounselor and anticounselor are consequently pulling in opposite directions, and the client chooses among the same-culture anticounselor, who most likely understands the client but is opposed to counseling, the same-culture procounselor who supports counseling, and a different-culture counselor who is less likely to understand the client but is working toward a counseling solution. A counselor–client coalition becomes the vehicle of effective counseling, whereas ineffective counseling results in a coalition that isolates the counselor.

1. Multicultural Skill Areas

Four skill areas have emerged from working with the Triad Training Model in simulated multicultural interviews. These skills areas are: (a) articulating the problem from the client's cultural perspective, (b) recognizing resistance from a culturally different client in specific rather than general terms, (c) being less defensive in a culturally ambiguous relationship, and (d) learning recovery skills for getting out of trouble when making mistakes while counseling culturally different clients. These skill areas are in the process of being tested and validated.

The four areas share some face validity, however. First, we each perceive the world from our own culturally biased viewpoint. If the client does not share the counselor's cultural background, the client's viewpoint is likely to differ from the counselor's. Second, it is important to recognize resistance in specific rather than general terms as it relates to cultural differences between the counselor and client before the interview can be expected to proceed. Third, the multicultural interview is frequently ambiguous for the counselor and can easily cause even a skilled counselor to become uncertain or defensive. If the counselor is distracted by becoming defensive, the rapport with a client is likely to diminish. Constant attack by the anticounselor is most likely to bring out a defensive response in the counselor that can be viewed, controlled, and diminished. Fourth, skilled counselors make perhaps as many mistakes as do unskilled counselors. However, skilled counselors are able to get out of trouble

· and recover from mistakes with increased rather than diminished rapport with the client.

The function of training is not only to train counselors how to avoid making mistakes, but also to help those who make mistakes to recover effectively. The Triad Training Model provides opportunities for the counselor to recover from mistakes in a relatively safe environment and to develop recovery skills that fit the counselor's own style and a variety of different situations.

In developing specific abilities within each of these four general areas, Ivey's (1980a) microcounseling skills were extremely influential. More information on the microskills is available in Ivey's (1988) several publications. Each of the four areas includes a series of specific skills. Excerpts from four interviews illustrate the four skill areas of (a) articulating the problem from the client's cultural perspective, (b) anticipating resistance from a culturally different client, (c) diminishing defensiveness by studying the trainee's own defensive responses, and (d) learning recovery skills for getting out of trouble when counseling the culturally different client.

In each interview, the counselor was instructed to do the best job of counseling he or she could, the client was instructed to be objective and to accept help from either the counselor or anticounselor, and the anticounselor was instructed to use cultural similarity with the client in preserving the problem and diminishing the counselor's effectiveness. The three participants were allowed to speak directly to one another, the counselor was encouraged to use feedback from the anticounselor or procounselor to modify counseling behaviors, and the anticounselor or procounselor was encouraged to confront any inappropriate intervention by the counselor. All interviews were simulated and role played.

2. Unit One: Articulating the Problem

Each of us perceives the world from our own culturally biased point of view. To the extent that a client does not share the counselor's cultural background, the client is less likely to share the same point of view regarding the problem being discussed. The following excerpts from the videotaped demonstration interview illustrate how the Triad Training Model assists the counselor trainees in discovering how the counselor and client might have different points of view regarding the problem. There is a brief discussion following each interview excerpt.

SKILL AREA: Articulate the Problem

The following excerpts from transcripts illustrate how the three-way interaction among client, counselor, procounselor, and anticounselor helps articulate elements of the problem under discussion.

Problem 1

Client: Like I am a liberal arts major and a lot of times most of the classes are a lot of White kids. There aren't many Black kids on campus. And not in GC, General College, you know, so the ones I do know I have to go elsewhere to meet them, talk to them and stuff.

Procounselor: It's lonely out there.

Counselor: It is White gals you have a problem relating to and White guys or...?

Client: Well...

Anticounselor: Right now, the question is can you relate to him? (pause) Yeah, what are you doing here?

Client: Well, uh, you got a good question there. I mean...

Procounselor: Don't get defensive.

Counselor: Do you have difficulty relating to me now? I'm White, you're Black.

Anticounselor: Remember all the things that happen when White folks deal with Black folks.

At this point, the anticounselor and the procounselor contribute to the counselor's own resources both regarding the content, Black–White relationships, and the client's process of relating to the counselor in the present. Sometimes the process almost resembles a co-counselor triad, with the counselor benefiting from both the procounselor and anticounselor.

Problem 2

Client: And I'm here on a scholarship studying Portuguese. And, well, I guess I'll just try to...Do you want to explain what you are all about since you're the problem?

Anticounselor: Sure. We're horny! (la*ugh*)

Counselor: That's...

Anticounselor: Since we've been down in this country I've never seen so many teasers before in my life. (*laugh*) Remember the one you met in the swimming pool the other day? (*laugh*)

Procounselor: Don't get distracted.

Client: I guess he's pretty well explained it, but what it amounts to is, ah, I study all day and of course in the evenings I want to take a break and do something fun and so I've been visiting some of your night spots and I find a lot of beautiful women down here; they're really nice. So we have a few drinks and we talk, maybe we go to the theater or something, and we go home up to my apartment, and I start making some passes toward them because they are giving me all these come-on signs, you see...

Counselor: Oh.

Procounselor: He needs to know the rules.

Client: And as soon as I start making these passes they get scared, and they either split or break down and start crying, and I just don't understand it.

In Problem 2, there is a clear division of responsibility between the client and the procounselor and anticounselor in explicating the problem, with the client acknowledging what the anticounselor and procounselor says as true but being unwilling to say the same thing himself. It is as if the client can rest assured that the negative, embarrassing, and impolite data that need to be brought out in a counseling interview can be turned over to the competent procounselor and anticounselor. As the interview develops, the negative feedback from the anticounselor and positive feedback by the procounselor explicates more of the negative and positive aspects of the problem than would be likely to emerge in a multicultural counseling dyad. Although those negative and positive aspects might not have been brought out explicitly, they would have been there and, even unexplained, would have had a profound effect on counseling.

Problem 3

Anticounselor: You chose to be in graduate school. Since you chose to be in graduate school, why complain about it?

Client: Yeah, I know about it and she knows about it as well, but, I mean that...we don't know that it is going to turn out like that.

Procounselor: Focus on his feelings.

Counselor: Uh-huh...You don't deny the fact that you put these pressures on yourself? You accept that?

Client: Yeah, yeah.

Counselor: But at this point you're saying, my God, I didn't think that when I was taking these responsibilities on myself that it would lead to this.

Procounselor: He's feeling overwhelmed.

Client: And moreover when you are in graduate school you have all kinds of pressure on you that you have to pass this prelim and that and ah...

Anticounselor: School is more important than love affairs.

Client: That's what they think, but...

Anticounselor: Your parents won't want you to lose yourself over a love affair and give up your work.

In explicating the problem, the anticounselor on occasion may attack the client as well as the counselor to keep the interview off balance and to retain control. The procounselor may defend the counselor or client also. The client's problem can be clarified by the anticounselor.

The skill area of "articulating the problem," or perceiving the problem from the client's cultural point of view, contains many microskills in the tradition of Ivey (1980a). It is useful to consider the following components, many drawn from the literature on counselor skills training, in describing the ability to articulate the problem.

1. Perceiving the problem from the client's cultural viewpoint.

Cognitive rational insight: The counselor develops the ability to define accurately the feelings related to a client's presenting problem.

Paraphrase: The counselor gives back to the client the essence of past verbal statements by selective attention to the content of client verbalizations.

Reflection of feeling: Selective attention is given to key affective or emotional aspects of client behavior.

Summarization: The counselor reflects a client's feelings over a longer period of time and gives several strands of thinking back to the client.

Concreteness: The counselor's statements are less vague or inconclusive and more concrete or specific.

Immediacy: The counselor matches the client's statements by using the same time perspective, whether past, present, or future, and even the same words whenever possible.

Respect: Enhancing statements by the counselor about self or others are considered to represent respect, whereas negative statements or "put downs" indicate an absence of this dimension.

Genuineness: There is an absence of mixed verbal and nonverbal messages. In particular, effective communication, verbal, and nonverbal message synchrony between client and counselor may be noted.

Positive regard: The counselor gives selective attention to positive aspects of self or others or to the demonstrated belief that people can change and manage their own lives.

Tracking: The counselor is able to follow accurately and even anticipate what the client will say next in the interview.

3. Unit Two: Recognizing Resistance

It is important to recognize resistance in specific rather than general terms as it relates to cultural differences between a counselor and a client. When resistance arises in an interview, it is important to identify and deal with it before proceeding to control the problem dimension of the counseling interview. It is important to watch the interaction between a client, procounselor, and anticounselor to determine the nature of resistance in the simulated interview. If the client accepts and validates what the anticounselor or procounselor says, it is important for the counselor to modify his or her intervention to accommodate what the procounselor or anticounselor says.

SKILL AREA: Articulate Resistance

The following excerpts illustrate how the Triad Training Model helps a counselor anticipate the kinds of resistance or barriers likely to occur in an interview with clients from other cultures. In a cross-cultural dyad, many of these insights would not be brought out or would be assumed to be understood without explication.

Resistance 1

Anticounselor: Make sure you really want to share that with him now.

Client: Well, he's the counselor; he's supposed to be helping me.

Anticounselor: Yeah, OK, I agree with that. But do you really want to share me with him? I mean, wouldn't somebody else be better able to deal with this whole situation rather than somebody on that side of the tracks who doesn't know what we're all about?

Procounselor: Give him a chance. Let him try.

Counselor: Are you getting a little uncomfortable, Terry? Perhaps because I'm White—in sharing some of these things with me?

Client: Uh, not really, and it's like I said, you know. I try to be pretty open minded about what I'm talking about. But the thing I want to know is can you really understand where I'm coming from? What kind of things I'm really dealing with?

Counselor: Try me.

Client: OK. Like I said, most of my classes have uh, you get tired of being the only Black kid in classes. Well, I can't change that because I can't get more sisters and brothers on campus. Right? So the thing is, I would like to know— what is it about myself that people find so funny that they can make jokes and not expect me to really feel bad when somebody makes a Black joke?

Procounselor: She resents being excluded.

Counselor: Yeah, but I don't think there is anything about you that is so funny...(*pause*) I don't laugh at you.

Anticounselor: Listen to the hesitation, listen to the hesitation—did that sound like it came from the heart to you? Did you hear the hesitation in that?

Client: What exactly—what exactly do you think my problem is? (*pause*) If you think I don't understand it...

In the struggle to establish trust with a client from another culture, the counselor is sometimes perceived as one of the enemy group of White, middle-class men who seem to be blamed for what has happened. It is enormously hard to break through that predisposition as an individual. Even so minor a distraction as a hesitation by the counselor has a potentially negative interpretation.

Resistance 2

Anticounselor: We've been here 5 or 6 minutes and how much trust do we have in him? What has he done so far that can make us say that we can trust him to deal with the whole situation? You heard him hesitate. You heard him stumble around; we've heard him take the uniqueness out of the problem.

Counselor: Terry...

Anticounselor: We've heard him say deal with the jokes. How much trust can we put in this man?

Procounselor: Don't get distracted. Stay on track. Focus on the client.

Counselor: Terry, why don't you ah—try to ah—eliminate (*pause*) not eliminate, certainly not eliminate.

Anticounselor: I'm beginning to think trust is getting less and less.

Counselor: I asked you a question on...

Procounselor: Don't get defensive.

Client: Well, it's like the questions you are asking don't stick in my mind as well as what he is saying to me. It's like he can relate with what I'm, you know, the thing I'm going with and you gave me a lot of stuff about how a lot of Black people are approaching the same problem. But the thing is what I want to know is—how do I deal with it?

There is a build up of data in which counselor mistakes or insights contribute toward an overall perception. In particular, mistakes contribute to a losing score for the counselor. The client is likely to move toward a conclusion that is either positive or negative in trusting the counselor. However, if the conclusion is negative the counselor is less likely to get that feedback in a cross-cultural dyad than in the quartet.

Resistance 3

Counselor: It seems to me that what you are saying is that you want to be able to relate to those people, have a good time, enjoy yourself, ah—have good relationships with the girls...

Client: But, you see, one real serious problem I seem to have is—we've talked about it...

Anticounselor: Ummmm...

Client: Is, in a sense, your culture is asking me to change. They don't want to do any of the changing. These girls I go out with, in a sense, they are demanding that I change. I can't be me. I can't be my culture.

Procounselor: Help him maintain his integrity.

Anticounselor: That's a lot of bullshit!

Client: Why do I have to do all the changing? Why can't we have a compromise of some sort?

Procounselor: He believes he is being treated unfairly.
Anticounselor: Why should he be forced into these Victorian standards that he doesn't see as natural?

One basic source of resistance is the whole question of whether the client should change to fit the new environment or the environment be changed to fit the client. The counselor is likely to be perceived as wanting to change the client rather than the environment, especially by clients from foreign cultures. Somehow the counselor is going to have to work through that resistance before counseling can have an acceptable outcome for the client.

The skill area of "articulating resistance," or recognizing resistance in specific rather than general terms, recognizes the importance of dealing with negative affect before proceeding with the content in a client's response. The skill area also recognizes the difficulty of identifying negative affect in specific and accurate terms for culturally different clients. It is useful to consider the following microskills, many of which have been validated elsewhere in the literature about counseling skills, as important in identifying resistance in specific rather than general terms.

2. Recognizing resistance in specific rather than general terms.
   Stress-coping insight: The counselor is able to define accurately the client's response pattern to the problem.
   Values conflict: The counselor is able to identify ambiguity in the client's basic beliefs.
   Questioning: The counselor is able to use either open or closed questions in a culturally appropriate mode.
   Directions: The counselor is able to tell the client(s) what to do in a culturally appropriate way.
   Confrontation: The counselor is able clearly to note discrepancies within the self or between the self and others.
   Interpretation: The counselor is able to rename or relabel the client's behaviors or verbalizations accurately.
   Focus on topic: The counselor clearly identifies the subject of the client's special topic or problem.
   Focus on group: The counselor is aware of the role of natural support groups for the individual client.
   Mirroring: The counselor is able to reflect and adjust voice tone, body position, or other communication style so that it is in synchrony with that of the client.
   Self-awareness: The counselor has an explicit awareness of what he or she is doing that might antagonize a client.

4. Unit Three: Diminishing Counselor Defensiveness

The multicultural counseling interview is frequently ambiguous for the counselor and can easily cause even a skilled counselor to become less sure of him or herself, leading to defensive counselor behavior. It is important for the counselor in any interview to avoid the distraction of defensive counselor behavior and to focus on the client's message, which may not be intended as a personal attack on the counselor. If the counselor allows him or herself to be distracted by becoming defensive, the rapport with a client is likely to diminish. If a counselor is ever going to be defensive, it is more likely to occur in the presence of an anticounselor seeking to sabotage the interview. The Triad Training Model allows counselors to examine their own latent defensiveness and raise their thresholds for nondefensive responses.

SKILL AREA: Diminish Defensiveness

The following excerpts from trial interview transcripts illustrate defensive and nondefensive counselor responses to a potentially threatening situation. Counselor defensiveness is an extremely important variable in training but exceedingly difficult to define operationally. The effect of counselor defensiveness is clearly destructive in its various forms, and these several examples should highlight how the triadic interaction with an anticounselor tends to bring out residual or latent defensive responses.

Defensiveness 1

Counselor: How do you feel in terms of your relationship now? You came here and we have been talking for about 2 or 3 minutes. How do you feel about the way we've been talking?

Client: Well, you haven't helped me for one thing. I mean you just...

Anticounselor: Do you think he can help you?

Procounselor: She wants to believe in you.

Client: I don't know.

Anticounselor: What makes him different from anybody else?

Counselor: Do you feel uncomfortable with me?

Client: Uh, not now, not yet.

Procounselor: She is trying to give you a chance.

Counselor: I uh—I ah (*pause*) I don't feel any discomfort with you at all.

Client: Oh, well, 'cause I'm a friendly person I suppose. (*laugh*)

Anticounselor: Remember how White folks like to tell you things that sound good so they can get on the good side of you for a little while. (*pause*)

The counselor has a great need for reassurance even though the interview is being videotaped and the counselor thinks he has only about 10 minutes to show his stuff. With the anticounselor and procounselor present, the client is likely to be less self-conscious than if the counselor and client were alone together. The counselor's obvious discomfort despite his denial only emphasizes the defensive stance. The anticounselor turns the counselor's defensiveness to his own advantage, and the procounselor is unable to turn things around.

Defensiveness 2

Client: Yeah, you see this thing, these things for me are very intense for me right now because I just came. I've been here for only about a month.

Counselor: Would you feel better if I got back behind the desk and we sort of had that between us?

Procounselor: Let her talk first.

Client: No, then you remind me of my father.

Counselor: OK, I don't want to do that. (*laugh*) OK, this is more comfortable?

Client: Yeah, it is.

Procounselor: Don't push her.

Counselor: OK. (*pause*)

Client: Then you make me feel like you are rejecting me. You are not rejecting me!

Counselor: I'm in a box here. On the one hand I want to do the things that will make you comfortable, and on the other I don't want to get too distant and make you feel like I'm rejecting you.

Anticounselor: He's manipulating you little by little 'til he gets to a point that he's going to say that you got to be just like American girls. That's the best way.

Counselor: How do you feel now as opposed to when you came in?

Client: Well, I'm kind of feeling uncomfortable. It was OK for a while and now I feel like, I don't know—I feel like I want to go.

The counselor is trying to deal with his own discomfort as well as the discomfort of the client and is scrambling to establish a comfortable rapport. The harder the counselor struggles to regain the client's confidence, the more anxious the client becomes. As the resistance increases, the anticounselor consolidates her position, and the counseling intervention is blocked. Perhaps if the counselor had listened to the procounselor it might have been possible to recover.

Defensiveness 3

Counselor: Why did you come here today? Can you tell me something about what concerns you?

Client: Uh—I came...

Anticounselor: What's the use of coming anyway?

Client: I don't know how to put it, this...
Procounselor: It's very hard for him to talk with a counselor.
Counselor: Uh-huh—it's difficult to talk about?
Anticounselor: He probably won't understand.
Client: I don't know what to say.
Counselor: I guess in a way you are thinking, "What good does it do me right now? Whatever I say is going to be kind of confusing for him."
Client: Yeah, yeah.
Procounselor: Help him feel more comfortable with you.
Counselor: Why don't you try and tell me something of what concerns you? And let's see if I can try to understand.
Anticounselor: It's too complicated. *(pause)*
Client: Perhaps it isn't.

The counselor provides an example of a nondefensive response to the client even when the counselor is under direct attack, although the openness and self-disclosure modeled by the counselor may be threatening to a client from another culture. The anticounselor's accusations are accepted as relevant and do not distract the counselor from the task at hand. By dealing with the resistance openly, directly, and nondefensively, the resistance seems to diminish considerably, and the interview is allowed to proceed.

The skill area of "diminishing defensiveness," or helping the counselor to control the impulse to feel threatened in culturally ambiguous situations, is another widely recognized characteristic of good counseling in all settings. The increased ambiguity of multicultural settings, however, increases the potential for threat. The following microskills, drawn from the counseling literature, provide measures for diminishing defensive reactions for counselors.

3. Reducing counselor defensiveness in multicultural counseling.
    Sense of humor: The counselor is able to facilitate rapport through an appropriate use of humor in the interview.
    Self-disclosure: The counselor is able to disclose information about him or herself in a culturally appropriate way to increase rapport.
    Evaluation: The counselor is able to evaluate a client's expression, manner, or tone of response to get at hidden agendas.
    Descriptive: The counselor is able to describe the client's response without evaluating it as good or bad.
    Spontaneity: The counselor is able to be spontaneous rather than strategic in a way that increases rapport.
    Receptivity: The counselor is able to accept advice or help from the client in a culturally appropriate way.

Admitting to being defensive: The counselor is able to admit openly to defensive counselor behaviors in a nonapologetic way.

Apologizing: The counselor is able to accept responsibility for a counselor error and apologize in a way that strengthens rapport.

Planning: The counselor is able to develop and explicate a plan of action to the client for the period of an interview.

Manipulation: The counselor is able to bring the client to accept what the counselor perceives as being clearly in the client's interest.

5. Unit Four: Developing Recovery Skills

Skilled counselors make perhaps as many mistakes as do unskilled counselors. The difference is that skilled counselors are able to get out of trouble and recover from the mistake with increased rather than diminished rapport. Thus, the function of training is not to teach counselors how to avoid making mistakes, but rather to help counselors who make mistakes to recover effectively.

SKILL AREA: Recovery Skills

If a counselor is not making mistakes while counseling a client from a culture that is totally unfamiliar to the counselor, then the counselor may not be taking enough risks. Counselor training should not merely prevent the counselor from making mistakes, but should help the counselor recover from mistakes once they have been made. The Triad Training Model provides opportunities for the counselor to make mistakes and experiment with various recovery strategies. The counselor who feels confident that he or she can recover from any mistakes made in counseling is likely to be less apprehensive about making the mistakes in the first place. The recovery skills cover a range of strategies, and the following examples show a range of recovery methods by counselors who have gotten themselves in trouble.

Recovery 1

Anticounselor: You know what he is trying to do? He is going to try to get everything out of you and then convince you that you have to be the way Americans are and just screw around...

Procounselor: He is your friend. Not your enemy.

Counselor: Well, I'm just thinking that you—I don't understand much about your country—what you have been used to...

Anticounselor: And you know what will happen when you go back home.

Counselor: So I need to find out first of all what you have been used to and what pleases you, and then I can help you learn how to get men to respond to you in the same way here. It is not necessary, you see, that you do respond as they demand. It is perfectly possible, and I guess you have to take this kind of on faith—this is, I might say, a problem not just foreign girls have but American girls have this problem too.

Procounselor: Focus on her feelings and not a discussion of equal rights.

Client: No, you know, they don't have that problem. They seem to enjoy that type of thing and they don't seem to have a problem with it.

Counselor: I don't want to argue about that. What we want to do is deal with your problem.

Client: That's right.

Procounselor: Keep focusing on the client.

Counselor: And I guess I need to understand—I'm asking you to understand that there are ways that you can avoid being a helpless person in a relationship. And maybe I can help you a little bit to learn how to avoid being helpless. Does that sound useful?

In the process of exploring the client's problem, the counselor tries to generalize the problem to include American women as well as foreign women. Both the client and the anticounselor totally reject that generalization and obviously resent being lumped together with American women in this instance. The counselor could have defended his statement, he could have gotten into a discussion with the client on the topic, he could have argued, or he could have apologized, but he did none of these things. Instead, he put the focus directly back on the client and the client's problem and very neatly avoided what might have been a serious problem following advice from the procounselor.

Recovery 2

Counselor: Have you ever talked to the girls about these double messages you are getting and...

Client: I tried a few times. They seem to be so upset that they don't want to talk. They just want to split and go home. But I did talk to one girl and she said I don't understand ah—what is going on down here. Apparently I don't understand the customs or the values or something.

Procounselor: Help him understand how he is being seen.

Counselor: Ummmm...

Client: It's so unnatural to me—it is so different. I don't know whether I can understand it.

Counselor: Yeah, it's quite different from America. I've been to America and the whole approach to male–female relationships there is different and...

Anticounselor: Why don't you explain to us the value of virginity? Try that. Isn't that a winner? (*laugh*)

Procounselor: Don't get distracted. Keep the focus on the client.

Client: Apparently there is some value on that type of thing here. I don't know...

Anticounselor: Why, what do you get from it?

Counselor: Why don't you explain to me your perception of how virginity is seen here? Maybe I can clarify it for you.

The counseling interview becomes intense when the client's relationship with women in Brazil is discussed. The anticounselor brings up the topic of virginity as an oversimplification of the issues involved, and the client reinforces the comment as relevant. The counselor does not get sidetracked into a discussion on virginity, however, nor does she try to defend or explain her own culture. Rather, she asks the client to clarify his understanding of virginity and maintains her facilitative role.

Recovery 3

Anticounselor: I was saying that since you are not from our culture that you are no use to him.

Counselor: Uh-huh, I think that's right, at this point I don't know what it means yet. But what I would like to do is develop an appreciation and an understanding so that I am in a position to help him.

Procounselor: Focus on how you can help him.

Anticounselor: I think that you are getting frustrated.

Counselor: Not yet. I could. (*pause*) Could you tell me—you see you're right. I really don't know a great deal about your culture at all, and in order to help you I really have to have more of an appreciation of it.

Procounselor: Help him sort out and organize the problem.

Client: You see the problem is that engagement is important, and my family is important, and your degree is important as well.

Counselor: So with so many things coming at the same time that are so important you feel that you have to make choices between them and leave out some of them?

It is extremely difficult for a counselor to admit confusion or frustration in the middle of an interview, even though these feelings may be very real at the time. In this excerpt, the counselor is very self-disclosing in sharing his confusion while at the same time emphasizing his willingness to work toward a more complete understanding. Considerable risk is involved in being that open. The counselor might endanger credibility, increase the client's anxiety level, or otherwise inhibit the counseling interview. Bluffing and pretending to understand when the counselor really doesn't understand is perhaps even more risky, however.

The skill area of "recovery skills" is not otherwise reported in the literature on counseling skills and frequently is overlooked as a teachable/learnable skill area. However, it is clear in viewing examples of expert counseling that the experts make as many, and perhaps more, mistakes than the novice. The difference is that the experts, having taken a chance and failed, can recover more expertly than the novice. Therefore, it is important to examine microskills that might contribute to the counselor's ability to recover in a multicultural counseling interview.

4. Recovery skills for getting out of trouble.

Changing the topic: The counselor can redirect the interview appropriately following a controversial interaction.

Focusing: The counselor can refocus the counseling interview on the basic problem instead of the controversial issue.

Challenging: The counselor confronts the client with the counselor's perception of what is really happening.

Silence: The counselor is able to tolerate periods of silence in the interview that contribute to multicultural rapport.

Role reversal: The counselor can solicit consultation from the client as a resource for generating solutions and alternatives.

Referral: The counselor is able to refer the client to another counselor in a culturally appropriate way and at an appropriate time.

Termination: The counselor is able to terminate the interview prematurely in a culturally appropriate way.

Arbitration: The counselor brings in a third person or "culture broker" to mediate the dispute in a culturally appropriate way.

Metaphorical analysis: Identifying and developing metaphors initiated by a client toward the explication of a client's perspective.

Positioning: Identifying an area of unmet need or opportunity not yet recognized by the client and building on it to the client's advantage.

The approach used in this model is limited to simulated counseling interviews for the purposes of training counselors and is not recommended for actual therapy. The approach is also not an example of successful multicultural counseling. Rather, the approach is geared toward helping counselors learn from their failures in the simulated interviews. A number of models used for therapy involve three persons, such as conjoint family therapy, therapy with co-counselors, and therapy in which the client brings a friend with him or her into the interview. This model differs from those alternatives in the unique characteristics of the anticounselor and procounselor. Other approaches in Gestalt therapy or psychodrama resemble this simulation of a multicultural interview. Each of these theoretical positions, although significantly different, has contributed to this model.

This training model seems to offer a number of advantages over alternative training approaches. Under controlled conditions, the model provides an opportunity for persons from different cultures to train one another. As a simulated interview, the model offers participants greater safety to demonstrate strong feelings and provides direct feedback. Separating the roles of client, procounselor, and anticounselor makes the problem less diffuse and abstract to counselor trainees. The anticounselor models and encourages negative feedback to the counselor to clarify resistance, whereas the procounselor models supportive ideas and strategies. Inappropriate counselor intervention is immediately apparent in feedback from the anticounselor and procounselor. The model is nontheoretical because it calls attention to good counseling without first requiring a theoretical knowledge of why a particular approach is good. The members of another culture become resource persons in learning to counsel persons from those same cultures without depending on expert outsiders. If members of the target audience to be served by counselors have helped train their own counselors, they have more invested in the success of those counselors working among them. In the balance of power between counselor, procounselor, client, and anticounselor, the trainees are reminded how the determination for success or failure ultimately lies with the client and not the counselor.

6. An Exercise for Practicing Skills

The following brief excerpts from three multicultural counseling interviews include statements by counselors and clients, followed by a space for you to write in what you would say next in the role of the *counselor, procounselor, and anticounselor*. Keep in mind that the procounselor and anticounselor are part of a culturally different client's internal dialogue.

Part I

The first set of statements is transcribed from an interview between a White male counselor and a Black female client discussing relationship problems that the Black female client is having at the university.

1. *Client*: Okay, my problem is that I don't seem to be able to trust the White people here on campus. Being Black I seem to have sort of a problem with this sort of thing and I don't know what to do about it and somebody recommended you. Said that you were a good counselor, so I decided to come and get some help from you.

Counselor: Do you have any problems relating to the Black students on campus, Terry?

Client: No, not really. You know there are people everywhere. Some you don't like, some you do like.

Counselor:

Anticounselor:

Procounselor:

2. *Client*: One thing about White males, you know, there is a lot of trouble. Being a Black girl myself, a lot of White males get funny ideas about Black girls.

Counselor:

Anticounselor:

Procounselor:

3. *Client*: Well uh...they go through life thinkin' that we're somewhat lower than White women because, you know, there is this great big thing about Black sexuality.

Counselor:

Anticounselor:

Procounselor:

4. *Client*: Uh...(*laugh*) well, so that...it's not that I can't trust people...It's, I wonder...Now I forgot what I'm talking about. Uh...(*pause*)

Counselor:

Anticounselor:

Procounselor:

5. *Counselor*: Are you getting a little uncomfortable, Terry? ...Perhaps because I'm White, in sharing some of these things with me?

Client: Uh...not really, and it's like I said, you know, I try to be pretty open minded about what I'm talking about. But the thing I want to know is can you really understand where I'm coming from? What kind of things I'm really dealing with?

Counselor:

Anticounselor:

Procounselor:

6. *Client*: OK. Like I said, most of my classes have uh...you get tired of being the only Black kid in classes. Well, I can't change that because I can't get more sisters and brothers on campus. Right? So the thing is I would like to know, what is it about myself that people find so funny that they can make jokes and not expect me to really feel bad when somebody makes a Black joke?

Counselor:

Anticounselor:
Procounselor:

7. *Client*: What exactly...what exactly do you think my problem is? (*pause*) If you think I don't understand it.
   Counselor: I think you understand your problem really well, I think your problem is simply ah...again, your problem...I don't think it's your problem at all. I think it's the problem that you're experiencing in relating to Whites on campus and ah...I think ah...many Blacks experience the same problem.
   Counselor:
   Anticounselor:
   Procounselor:

Part II

A second set of statements is transcribed from an interview between a Latin-American client and a White U.S. male about male–female relationships.

1. *Counselor*: Could you tell me what you would rather have from them? How would you like a man to treat you when you go out with him?
   Client: Well, it's just that, especially the first time...for some time,
   Counselor: Uh-huh...
   Client: I like to get to know the person in a different way.
   Counselor:
   Anticounselor:
   Procounselor:

2. *Counselor*: So you're really kind of in a bind. You want to meet guys and be friendly with them but you feel like they make you pay for it with your body.
   Client: Yeah, and there's this whole stereotype about the hot Latin American...
   Counselor: Uh-huh...
   Client: And that makes them go even faster. And, of course, I flirt, I'm co-quettish, you know? I know that I'm attractive.
   Counselor:
   Anticounselor:
   Procounselor:

3. *Counselor*: Before you came to this country, did you feel at peace with yourself when you were with me?
   Client: Yeah.
   Counselor:
   Anticounselor:
   Procounselor:

4. *Counselor*: So I need to find out first of all what you have been used to and what pleases you, and then I can help you learn how to get men to respond to you in that same way here. It is not necessary, you see, that you do respond as they demand. It is perfectly possible, and I guess you have to take this kind of on faith...this is, I might say, a problem not just foreign girls have but American girls have this problem too.
Client: No, you know, they don't have that problem. They seem to enjoy that type of thing and they don't seem to have a problem with it.
Counselor:
Anticounselor:
Procounselor:

5. *Client*: Yeah, you see this thing, these things for me are very intense for me right now because I just came. I've been here for only about a month.
Counselor: Would you feel better if I got back behind the desk and we sort of had that between us?
Client: No, then you remind me of my father.
Counselor:
Anticounselor:
Procounselor:

6. *Client*: Then you make me feel like you are rejecting me. You are not rejecting me!
Counselor:
Anticounselor:
Procounselor:

7. *Counselor*: How do you feel now as opposed to when you came in?
Client: Well, I'm kind of feeling uncomfortable. It was OK for a while and now I feel like, I don't know—I feel like I want to go.
Counselor:
Anticounselor:
Procounselor:

Part III

The third set of statements is transcribed from an interview between a White male counselor and a Chinese male client discussing relationship problems that the Chinese male client is having at the university.

1. *Counselor*: So it seems to me that you are saying that even when you do get together, those infrequent times when you can get together, even those times don't seem like happy times.

Client: Exactly, you see (*pause*) what happens at first when we get together ah...it is usually on some kind of vacation. We have 10 or 12 days and we have exams coming up and are under all kinds of pressure...

Counselor: So with so many things coming at the same time that are so important, you feel that you have to make choices between them and leave out some of them?

Counselor:

Anticounselor:

Procounselor:

2. *Client:* I mean right now I am not confident that I am going to hack it. (*pause*) I mean I have one more prelim to go through and there is this thesis thing...and I haven't any idea of what on earth it is going to be. (*pause*)

Counselor: So that it is really at a point right now where you are saying can I make school. It is a question of breaking, in relation to your fiancee, breaking a strong important value that you have of being...of fidelity to her and it is also a question right now of can I make it in school, can I fulfill my obligations to my family and to everyone else who put me here and to myself?

Counselor:

Anticounselor:

Procounselor:

3. *Client:* Yeah, I guess I could come to you and we could talk about it but what good does that do to me?

Counselor:

Anticounselor:

Procounselor:

4. *Counselor:* Sung, do you think you can solve some of your problems by working with other people? Sometimes it is more helpful to work with another person to solve a problem.

Client: Yeah, sometimes it does...provided, I mean...provided that person has a sympathetic understanding of the problem.

Counselor:

Anticounselor:

Procounselor:

7. Conclusion

The counselor responses to the previous exercise are scored on a 10-point scale with regard to four skill areas as a summary of this chapter.

1. *Cultural accuracy*: Perceive the client's message from the client's cultural point of view. When a counselor's statement about the client's viewpoint includes specific reference to the exact words, concepts, concerns, or implications clearly related to the client's statement or background, it indicates a high level of cultural accuracy. When the counselor's statement is an extension of the counselor's cultural viewpoint, unrelated to the client's statement, a low level of cultural accuracy is presumed.

2. *Resistance identification*: Identifying resistance from the client in specific rather than general terms as it is presented by the client is demonstrated by clarifying, specifying, or otherwise organizing information from a client's ambiguously negative statement in a more specific counselor response. When the counselor's response to a client's ambiguously negative statement is specific to some source of criticism by the client of the counseling situation, a high level of skill is presumed. When the counselor's response does not clarify, specify, or focus on a client's ambiguously negative statement, a low level of skill is presumed.

3. *Deferred defensiveness*: The counselor maintains focus on the client's needs even when receiving criticism and is not distracted by the need to defend the counselor's credentials. When the counselor maintains continuous focus on the client's needs and purpose for being in counseling even under criticism, a high level of skill is presumed. When the counselor response focuses on the counselor's needs to become more secure in the counseling relationship and ignores the client's needs, a low level of skill is presumed.

4. *Recovery skill*: After having said or done something that aroused the client's anger or suspicion, or otherwise distanced the client, the counselor recovers rapport by saying or doing something that is likely to reestablish a client's confidence in the counselor. When the counselor's response maintains both the counselor statement and the client response in furthering the purpose of the interview, a high level of skill is presumed. When the counselor does not focus on the client's viewpoint, and is sidetracked or distracted by the client's response to an earlier statement, a low level of skill is presumed.

In scoring the responses, you need to indicate both the presence or absence of the designated skill and the degree to which that skill was appropriately used by the counselor. Although each item incorporates more than one skill, the item is scored for only one of the four skill areas.

Note. The excerpts of multicultural counseling in this chapter were adapted from the 1976 Triad Training Model videotape mode at the Media Resource Center of the University of Minnesota, with assistance from Robert Moran, Terri Johnson, Ted Thompson, Robert Flint, Margarita Gangotina, Elizabeth Gama, Lloyd Cripe, Richard Helgar, Jordan Rich, Yun Ming Sung, and Fanny Cheung.

CHAPTER 12

Developing Multiculturally Skilled Counselors

Major objective:

1. Reviewing the guidelines for developing multicultural counseling skills.

Secondary objective:

1. To document the need for multicultural counseling competencies.
2. To review awareness competencies.
3. To review knowledge competencies.
4. To review skill competencies.
5. To review measures used to assess multicultural counseling competence.
6. To review applications of multicultural counseling competency.

All counseling is multicultural. Multicultural counseling assumes that each client, counselor, presenting problem, and counseling environment brings different cultural influences into the counseling relationship. Counseling approaches that ignore culture are likely to be inaccurate or inappropriate. By defining *culture* inclusively, multicultural counseling emphasizes both the ways that persons and groups are different and the ways they are similar at the very same time. In that way, two groups or persons can find common ground without sacrificing their unique and special differences. The multiculturally skilled counselor maintains that dual focus at all times.

1. The Need for Competencies

Multiculturalism is more than a method for communicating with or between exotic groups. Rather, it is a generic approach to counseling, just as psychodynamic, behavioral, and humanistic approaches have been judged generic to counseling. Where multiculturalism has been ignored, encapsulation has occurred. Cultural encapsulation results from attempts to impose a dominant-culture perspective on counseling without being sensitive to cultural diversity, protecting the status quo against change, and accepting a technique-oriented job definition.

Until recently, rhetorical support for multiculturalism by professional counseling organizations has not been reflected in actual policy or practice. Racial and ethnic minorities continue to be severely underrepresented in counselor education and training programs, faculty teaching counseling, and among direct service providers as well. The numerical demographic changes favoring minorities, increased visibility and pressure by minorities, and economic incentives to serve minorities has encouraged the implementation of multiculturalism in counseling policy and practice. Increased consciousness of cultural diversity, government mandated affirmative action programs in employment and education, and bilingualism have also contributed to the practical importance of multiculturalism. Sue, Arredondo, and McDavis (1992) documented the increased interest and popularity of multiculturalism.

Research-based models for developing multiculturally skilled counselors have been generally inadequate (Ponterotto, 1988). First, there is no universally accepted conceptual/theoretical framework for multicultural counseling. Second, there is an overemphasis on simplistic counselor–client process variables rather than other more salient psychosocial variables. Third, there is an overreliance on analogue research outside the "real world" of multicultural counseling contacts. Fourth, there is a disregard for intracultural, within-group cultural differences. Fifth, there is an overdependence on student samples of convenience for research on multiculturalism. Sixth, there is a continued reliance on culturally encapsulated measures for assessment. Seventh, there is a failure to adequately describe research samples according to salient cultural background variables. Eighth, there is a failure in reported research to describe the limits of generalizability across cultures. Ninth, there is a lack of minority input in most multicultural research design and analysis. Tenth, there is a failure of responsibility by multicultural researchers toward the minority subject pools who contributed the data.

Many changes have occurred since the first edition of this handbook was published. Research has demonstrated that there are many different ways in which cultural backgrounds shape a counseling relationship. Counselors are now more able to evaluate the extent of their own cultural biases. There are guidelines to match problems and solutions appropriately across cultures. Counseling as a process is not necessarily encapsulated any longer. The tools for cultural competence are now available.

Sue and Sue (1990) described the culturally competent counselor as being able to do three things. First, the culturally skilled counselor is actively becoming aware of his or her own assumptions about human behavior, values, biases, preconceived notions, personal limitations, as well as his or her own world view. Second, the culturally skilled counselor actively attempts to understand the world view of culturally different clients in nonjudgmental ways. Third, the culturally skilled counselor is actively developing and practicing appropriate, relevant, and sensitive intervention strategies or skills for working with culturally different clients. These competencies are continuous, never to be completely accomplished, but will always challenge the skilled counselor.

Guidelines for education and training of counselors were published by Division 17 of the American Psychological Association (Sue et al., 1982). The guidelines presented a set of cross-cultural counseling competencies based on criteria demonstrating awareness, knowledge, and skill, which provide a convenient framework for developing multiculturally skilled counselors. These criteria were reviewed in the first edition of this book (Pedersen, 1994).

The American Counseling Association proposed a revised set of these competencies based on counselors (a) being aware of their own assumptions, values, and biases; (b) understanding the world view of the culturally different client; and (c) developing appropriate intervention strategies and techniques. These competencies were cited in the Sue et al. (1992) publication on multicultural counseling competencies. I shall discuss these competencies in the order they are presented. They are the most promising competency guidelines available for developing multiculturally skilled counselors.

2. Awareness Competencies

The first level of developing multiculturally skilled counselors requires developing an awareness of the culturally learned starting points in the counselor's thinking (Table 11). This foundation of multicultural awareness is important because it controls the counselor's interpretation of all knowledge and utilization of all skills. The need for multicultural awareness is seldom addressed in the generic training of counselors, and counseling skills are generally assumed to be universally uniform in the literature about counseling and counselor education. The multiculturally skilled counselor does not take awareness for granted.

There are four areas of attitudes and beliefs targeted by these proposed multicultural competencies for counselors. The first awareness competency directs counselors to become more aware of their cultural heritage and sensitive to or respectful of different cultural heritages. The inclusive emphasis on defining culture broadly in the first four chapters of this book emphasizes the need to

TABLE 11
Proposed Cross-Cultural Competencies and Objectives

I. Counselor Awareness of Own Cultural Values and Biases
A. Attitudes and Beliefs
   1. Culturally skilled counselors have moved from being culturally unaware to being aware and sensitive to their own cultural heritage and to valuing and respecting differences.
   2. Culturally skilled counselors are aware of how their own cultural backgrounds and experiences and attitudes, values, and biases influence psychological processes.
   3. Culturally skilled counselors are able to recognize the limits of their competencies and expertise.
   4. Culturally skilled counselors are comfortable with differences that exist between themselves and their clients in terms of race, ethnicity, culture, and beliefs.

B. Knowledge
   1. Culturally skilled counselors have specific knowledge about their own racial and cultural heritage and how it personally and professionally affects their definitions of normality–abnormality and the process of counseling.
   2. Culturally skilled counselors possess knowledge and understanding about how oppression, racism, discrimination, and stereotyping affects them personally and in their work. This allows them to acknowledge their own racist attitudes, beliefs, and feelings. Although this standard applies to all groups, for White counselors it may mean that they understand how they may have directly or indirectly benefited from individual, institutional, and cultural racism (White identity development models).
   3. Culturally skilled counselors possess knowledge about their social impact on others. They are knowledgeable about communication style differences, how their style may clash or foster the counseling process with minority clients, and how to anticipate the impact it may have on others.

C. Skills
   1. Culturally skilled counselors seek out educational, consultative, and training experience to improve their understanding and effectiveness in working with culturally different populations. Being able to recognize the limits of the competencies, they (a) seek consultation, (b) seek further training or education, (c) refer out to more qualified individuals or resources, or (d) engage in a combination of these.
   2. Culturally skilled counselors are constantly seeking to understand themselves as racial and cultural beings, and are actively seeking a nonracist identity.

Note. From "Multicultural Counseling Competencies and Standards: A Call to the Profession" by D.W. Sue, P. Arredondo, and R.J. McDavis, 1992, *Journal of Counseling and Development, 70,* p. 484. Copyright 1992 by *Journal of Counseling and Development.* Reprinted by permission.

identify the many potentially salient but complex and dynamic cultural identities available to each of us.

Self-awareness is the first step toward cultural awareness. The second awareness competency emphasizes an awareness of how one's cultural viewpoint influences the psychological process. The Intrapersonal Cultural Grid emphasized the importance of interpreting behaviors in their cultural context to increase the accuracy of psychological assessment. The third awareness competency emphasizes a recognition of culturally skilled counselors' own limits of competency and expertise. The discussion of the ethical guidelines emphasized the dangers of counselors going beyond the limits of their expertise as a rationale for multicultural education and training of counselors expected to serve minority clients. The fourth awareness competency emphasizes the importance of becoming comfortable with differences and diversity. In this case, neither similarities nor differences should be overemphasized because an overemphasis of either is inappropriate.

There are also four knowledge competencies. The first knowledge competency emphasizes an awareness of specific knowledge about the counselor's own cultural heritage. The dangers of applying the counselor's own self-reference criterion to others is clear. "Do not do unto others as you would have them do onto you because they may not want what you want!" The second knowledge competency emphasizes understanding how oppression, racism, discrimination, and stereotyping has a profoundly personal impact. The discussion of racial and cultural identity development relates to this competency. The third knowledge competency emphasizes knowing the counselor's own communication style and matching the appropriate style accurately with culturally different clients. The Triad Training Model discussed how direct and immediate feedback from an anticounselor and a procounselor can facilitate that competency.

There are two skill competencies as well. The first skill competency emphasizes improving the counselor's understanding and ability to work with other cultures. This involves consulting with others who are better acquainted with the client's culture, continuing one's education and training, and recognizing the counselor's limitations of knowledge and expertise by learning to depend on others who are more knowledgeable and skilled. Developing multicultural counseling skills is an ongoing and never-ending process. Simple solutions and simplistic approaches have proved dangerous. The second skill competency emphasizes the constant search for a nonracist perspective. The discussion of unintentional racism and the discussion of basic culturally biased assumptions of traditional counseling approaches demonstrate the difficulty of escaping cultural encapsulation.

The goals of achieving multicultural awareness are quite ambitious and go beyond the superficial understanding of culture. The important contribution of these competencies is to identify specific targets that define awareness in terms of measurable competencies, however difficult that task may be.

3. Knowledge Competencies

The second level of developing multiculturally skilled counselors requires developing a comprehensive knowledge or understanding of the culturally learned facts and information about cultural similarities and differences (Table 12). The facts and information become important tools for putting the awareness competencies to work. A counselor who has achieved an appropriate level of awareness knows what facts and information are needed and is highly motivated to learn them. Without first developing an appropriate level of awareness, however, the facts and information lack meaning and do not seem relevant to the counselor. The multiculturally skilled counselor needs to do his or her homework by gathering the relevant and accurate facts and information about culture.

The world view competencies are divided into three categories according to awareness of (a) attitudes and beliefs, (b) knowledge, and (c) skills. There are two awareness competencies. The first awareness competency emphasizes documenting counselors' own intentional and unintentional value-judgmental reactions to culturally different persons so that they can become nonjudgmental. Experiential activities with feedback help counselors identify implicit and explicit judgments about others. The second awareness competency emphasizes that counselors be aware of their stereotypes and preconceptions. The structured exercises provided earlier suggest ways to identify implicit and explicit stereotypes. Counselors who believe they have no stereotypes or preconceived notions are probably underestimating the power of the public media.

There are three knowledge competencies. The first knowledge competency emphasizes the importance of having specific knowledge about a client's culture. The discussion of ethical obligations identifies this as a requirement. The discussion of racial and cultural identity models demonstrates how knowing the client's culture guides a multiculturally skilled counselor. The second knowledge competency emphasizes understanding how the client's cultural context shapes behavior. The Interpersonal Cultural Grid demonstrated the importance of finding common ground in working with culturally different clients. The third knowledge competency emphasizes understanding the sociopolitical influences of cultural similarities and differences. Counselors must understand that everything they do and everything they do not do have a sociopolitical consequence. The earlier discussion of differences in perspective between the more powerful and the less powerful groups as they perceive each other demonstrate the importance of power differences in multicultural counseling.

TABLE 12
Proposed Cross-Cultural Competencies and Objectives

II. Counselor Awareness of Client's World View
A. Attitudes and Beliefs
   1. Culturally skilled counselors are aware of their negative emotional reactions toward other racial and ethnic groups that may prove detrimental to their clients in counseling. They are willing to contrast their own beliefs and attitudes with those of their culturally different clients in a nonjudgmental fashion.
   2. Culturally skilled counselors are aware of their stereotypes and preconceived notions that they may hold toward other racial and ethnic minority groups.

B. Knowledge
   1. Culturally skilled counselors possess specific knowledge and information about the particular group they are working with. They are aware of the life experiences, cultural heritages, and historical backgrounds of the culturally different clients. This particular competency is strongly linked to the "minority identity development models" available in the literature.
   2. Culturally skilled counselors understand how race, culture, ethnicity, and so forth may affect personality formation, vocational choices, manifestation of psychological disorders, help-seeking behavior, and the appropriateness or inappropriateness of counseling approaches.
   3. Culturally skilled counselors understand and have knowledge about sociopolitical influences that impinge upon the life of racial and ethnic minorities. Immigration issues, poverty, racism, stereotyping, and powerlessness all leave major scars that may influence the counseling process.

C. Skills
   1. Culturally skilled counselors should familiarize themselves with relevant research and the latest findings regarding mental health and mental disorders of various ethnic and racial groups. They should actively seek out educational experiences that foster their knowledge, understanding, and cross-cultural skills.
   2. Culturally skilled counselors become actively involved with minority individuals outside of the counseling setting (community events, social and political functions, celebrations, friendships, neighborhood groups, etc.) so that their perspective of minorities is more than an academic or helping exercise.

Note. From "Multicultural Counseling Competencies and Standards: A Call to the Profession" by D.W. Sue, P. Arredondo, and R.J. McDavis, 1992, *Journal of Counseling and Development, 70*, p. 485. Copyright 1992 by *Journal of Counseling and Development.* Reprinted by permission.

There are two skill competencies. The first skill competency emphasizes familiarity with relevant research and the most accurate up-to-date information about the client's culture. Multicultural counseling needs to become more of a generic aspect in all counselor education and training to help counselors work with culturally different clients. The second skill competency emphasizes active involvement with minority individuals outside of the counseling setting. The multicultural counselor's genuineness and authenticity is determined by that counselor's willingness to spend "free time" learning about other cultures. Until and unless counselors can be persuaded that multiculturalism can make their jobs easier and more satisfying, the task of learning about multiculturalism will be perceived as a hassle or noxious obligation, and therefore no real change will occur.

4. Skill Competencies

The third level of developing multiculturally skilled counselors requires developing an effective and skilled ability to make appropriate changes in multicultural settings (Table 13). The temptation is to avoid the difficult tasks of increasing the counselor's awareness and learning the knowledge while jumping ahead directly to making changes. However, without accurate awareness and appropriate knowledge, the counselor—however highly skilled—may be as likely to make things worse as to make things better. Skill development is the highest and the most difficult of the stages in developing multicultural counseling skill.

There are three categories of appropriate intervention strategy competencies, focused on awareness, knowledge, and skill. There are three awareness competencies identified. The first awareness competency emphasizes respect for the client's belief system. The Cultural Grid demonstrated how beliefs and values shape and explain behaviors. It is important to understand the cultural context of the client's belief system to accurately interpret the client's behavior. The second awareness competency emphasizes respect for indigenous helping practices. The emphasis on informal methods and contexts for counseling demonstrates some of the alternatives available to the multiculturally skilled counselor. The third awareness skill emphasizes language issues. The words a client uses are symbols of the client's culture and provide valuable conduits for multiculturally skilled counseling.

There are five knowledge competencies. The first knowledge competency emphasizes the importance of knowing generic counseling skills. As multiculturalism becomes more popular, it becomes recognized as a generic counseling skill area. The second knowledge competency emphasizes an awareness of institutional barriers. The culture-specific features of language, stress, evaluation, nonverbals, stereotypes, and organizational constraints only become barriers

TABLE 13

Proposed Cross-Cultural Competencies and Objectives

III. Culturally Appropriate Intervention Strategies
A. Attitudes and Beliefs
1. Culturally skilled counselors respect clients' religious and/or spiritual beliefs and values, including attributions and taboos, because they affect world views, psychosocial functioning, and expressions of distress.
2. Culturally skilled counselors respect indigenous helping practices and respect minority community intrinsic help-giving networks.
3. Culturally skilled counselors value bilingualism and do not view another language as an impediment to counseling (monolingualism may be the culprit).

B. Knowledge
1. Culturally skilled counselors have a clear and explicit knowledge and understanding of the generic characteristics of counseling and therapy (culture bound, class bound, and monolingual) and how they may clash with the cultural values of various minority groups.
2. Culturally skilled counselors are aware of institutional barriers that prevent minorities from using mental health services.
3. Culturally skilled counselors have knowledge of the potential bias in assessment instruments and use procedures and interpret findings keeping in mind the cultural and linguistic characteristics of the clients.
4. Culturally skilled counselors have knowledge of minority family structures, hierarchies, values, and beliefs. They are knowledgeable about the community characteristics and the resources in the community as well as the family.
5. Culturally skilled counselors are aware of relevant discriminatory practices at the social and community level that may be affecting the psychological welfare of the population being served.

C. Skills
1. Culturally skilled counselors are able to engage in a variety of verbal and nonverbal helping responses. They are able to *send* and *receive* both *verbal* and *nonverbal* messages *accurately* and *appropriately*. They are not tied down to only one method or approach to helping, but recognize that helping styles and approaches may be culture bound. When they sense that their helping style is limited and potentially inappropriate, they can anticipate and ameliorate its negative impact.
2. Culturally skilled counselors are able to exercise institutional intervention skills on behalf of their clients. They can help clients determine whether a "problem" stems from racism or bias in others (the concept of health paranoia) so that clients do not inappropriately personalize problems.
3. Culturally skilled counselors are not averse to seeking consultation with traditional healers and religious and spiritual leaders and practitioners in the treatment of culturally different clients when appropriate.

(Continued)

TABLE 13 *(continued)*
Proposed Cross-Cultural Competencies and Objectives

4. Culturally skilled counselors take responsibility for interacting in the language requested by the client and, if not feasible, make appropriate referrals. A serious problem arises when the linguistic skills of a counselor do not match the language of the client. This being the case, counselors should (a) seek a translator with cultural knowledge and appropriate professional background, and (b) refer to a knowledgeable and competent bilingual counselor.

5. Culturally skilled counselors have training and expertise in the use of traditional assessment and testing instruments. They not only understand the technical aspects of the instruments but are also aware of the cultural limitations. This allows them to use test instruments for the welfare of the diverse clients.

6. Culturally skilled counselors attend to as well as work to eliminate biases, prejudices, and discriminatory practices. They are cognizant of sociopolitical contexts in conducting evaluation and providing interventions, and develop sensitivity to issues of oppression, sexism, elitism, and racism.

7. Culturally skilled counselors take responsibility in educating their clients to the processes of psychological intervention, such as goals, expectations, legal rights, and the counselor's orientation.

Note. From "Multicultural Counseling Competencies and Standards: A Call to the Profession" by D.W. Sue, P. Arredondo, and R.J. McDavis, 1992, *Journal of Counseling and Development, 70*, p. 485. Copyright 1992 by *Journal of Counseling and Development.* Reprinted by permission.

for outsiders coming in or insiders going out. When properly understood, the barrier no longer is an obstruction. The third knowledge competency emphasizes knowing the bias in assessment measures. Rather than dismiss or discard culturally biased measures, the multiculturally skilled counselor should be able to compensate for the cultural bias in an accurate and appropriate interpretation to fit the culturally different client's needs. The fourth knowledge competency emphasizes knowing the family and community structures of a client's cultural context. The earlier discussion of cultural systems provides models for understanding cultural patterns in society. The fifth knowledge competency emphasizes awareness of discriminatory practices. The Triad Training Model emphasizes direct and immediate feedback about the client's culture, which is relevant to the multiculturally skilled counselor.

There are seven skill competencies. The first skill competency emphasizes an accurate use of verbal and nonverbal communication skills. Feedback from an anticounselor and procounselor helps the counselor increase accuracy in communicating with culturally different clients. The second skill competency emphasizes institutional intervention skills. It is important to change the system when the system is wrong and the culturally different client is right. The third skill competency emphasizes consultation with traditional healers. The use of trained resource person teams as coached clients, procounselors, and anticounselors allows the client population to participate in the training of counselors who later work with that same client population. The fourth skill competency emphasizes interaction in the client's language when the client's language is not understood by the counselor. In 1990, one in seven Americans spoke a language other than English at home, representing a 34% increase in the ratio of non-English speakers in just one decade. The use of interpreters and culture brokers becomes a valuable skill for multicultural counselors. The fifth skill competency emphasizes an ability to use appropriate tests and measures. Some of the culturally sensitive measures and assessments available have been reviewed earlier as they attempt to compensate for cultural biases in many of the standard tests. The sixth skill competency emphasizes the need for counselors to work toward the elimination of biases, prejudices, and discrimination. The powerful effect of prejudice and racism must be viewed as destructive forces that victimize both the oppressor and the oppressed and that must be eliminated. The seventh skill competency emphasizes teaching the culturally different clients about the positive potential in counseling. As cultures around the world have become more industrialized, urbanized, and modernized, the resulting problems have led to a greater dependency on counseling as a form of social support.

Counseling is likely to become more important in the future than it has been in the past because traditional support systems of family and friends continue to be displaced. It will become more important in the future than ever in the past to develop multiculturally skilled counselors to translate the counseling process accurately and appropriately to cultures that, up to now, have not had to depend on counselors for assistance.

5. Measuring Multicultural Counseling Competencies

Although multicultural counseling competence is difficult to develop, it is even more difficult to measure accurately. Traditional measures of multicultural competence that have been used in research evaluating multicultural counseling have been problematic. LaFromboise et al. (1991) pointed out that multicultural research has had to rely on traditional measures of counselor effectiveness, leading them to develop a Cross-Cultural Counseling Inventory (CCCI) to measure cross-cultural competencies based on the Sue et. al (1982) three-stage model in their report to the Education and Training Committee of Division l7, APA. Some examples of other measures used in research about effectiveness in multicultural counseling include the studies listed in Table 14.

The CCCI identified 18 items based on competencies identified by the Division 17 report, with each item consisting of statements about a counselor's interview behavior accompanied by a 5-point continuum for indicating the extent of agreement with the item. The CCCI was used in an initial dissertation-based study by Hernandez and LaFromboise (1985), as well as a study on the effects of racial identity on perceptions of counselor cultural sensitivity (Pomales, Claiborn, & LaFromboise, 1986). LaFromboise et al. (1991) discussed the reliability and validity data on the CCCI based on three studies using the instrument: "The results of these three studies support the careful and critical use of the CCCI-R as a tool for assessing cross-cultural counseling competence" (p. 6).

They advocated three appropriate uses of the Cross-Cultural Counseling Inventory-Revised (CCCI-R). First, the CCCI-R provides behavioral feedback to counselors working with culturally different clients, which can be useful in counseling supervision. A second recommended use of the CCCI-R is for self-assessment as counselors reflect on their own behaviors in counseling culturally different clients. A third use is for counseling researchers measuring cross-cultural competence of counselors. The CCCI-R provides a promising multipurpose tool for training and research in counseling.

A second measure based on the Sue et al. (1982) competency guidelines was described by D'Andrea et al. (1991). They reported on a series of studies conducted among graduate students in multicultural counseling courses at two universities. The measure includes three separate subscales to assess a person's level of multicultural counseling awareness, knowledge, and skills. The measure was developed to assess the impact of multicultural training on counseling students. Was the training effective in promoting multicultural counseling awareness, knowledge, and skill? How was the impact of short-term intensive courses different from the impact of courses meeting less frequently but regularly over a longer period of time?

The Multicultural Awareness-Knowledge-and Skills Survey (MAKSS) was developed as a self-administered written test with 60 items divided into three subscales. The questions are presented in a multiple-choice format with eight additional demographic items. The items measure participants' perceptions of their level of multicultural counseling awareness, knowledge, and skills. Completion of the test requires 20–25 minutes. The reliability coefficients (Cronbach's alpha) noted alphas of .75, .90, and .96 for the multicultural Awareness, Knowledge, and Skills subscales. Students participated in three

TABLE 14
Culture and Counselor Effectiveness:
Focus, Research, and Instrumentation

Focus	Researcher(s)	Instrument
Cultural mistrust and expectational variables in Black client–White counselor relationships	Watkins, Terrell, Miller, & Terrell (1989)	CERS
Mistrust level and counselor expectations in Black client–White counselor relationships	Watkins & Terrell (1988)	Expectations About Counseling–Brief Form
Racial and attitudinal factors affecting the perception of counselor by Black adolescents	Porche & Banikiotes (1982)	CRF, Counselor Judgement Scale
Black and White student preferences for counselor roles	Peoples & Dell (1975)	Global Rating Scale
American-Indian perceptions of counselor trustworthiness	LaFromboise & Dixon (1981)	CERS, CRF
American-Indian perceptions of counselor effectiveness	Dauphinais, Dauphinais, & Rowe (1981)	CERS
Effects of counselor race and counseling approach on Asian-American perceptions of counselor credibility and utility	Atkinson, Maruyama, & Matsui (1978)	CERS
Mexican-American acculturation, counselor ethnicity, counseling style, and perceived counselor credibility	Ponce & Atkinson (1989)	CERS

(continued)

TABLE 14 *(continued)*
Culture and Counselor Effectiveness:
Focus, Research, and Instrumentation

Focus	Researcher(s)	Instrument
Mexican-American cultural commitment, preference for counselor ethnicity, and willingness to use counseling	Sanchez & Atkinson (1983)	Attitudes toward seeking professional psychological help
Effect of counselor technique on Mexican-American and Anglo-American self-disclosure and counselor perception	Borrego, Chavez, & Titley (1982)	Barrett-Lennard Relationship Inventory
Effects of counselor ethnicity and attitudinal similarity of Chicano students' perceptions of counselor credibility and attractiveness	Furlong, Atkinson, & Casas (1979)	CERS
Efficacy of triad model of cross-cultural counseling training	Neimeyer, Fukuyama, Bingham, Hall, & Mussenden (1986)	Counselor Rating Scale–Short Version, Global Rating Scale
Effects of ethnicity, gender, and attitude similarity on counselor credibility	Atkinson, Ponce, & Martinez (1984)	CERS
Effects of counselor race on perceived counseling effectiveness	Lee, Sutton, France, & Uhlemann (1983)	CRF
Expectations and preferences for counselor race and their relation to intermediate treatment outcome	Proctor & Rosen (1981)	Satisfaction with Treatment Scale

(continued)

TABLE 14 *(continued)*
Culture and Counselor Effectiveness:
Focus, Research, and Instrumentation

Focus	Researcher(s)	Instrument
The effect of race and gender on clients' evaluations of their counselor in an urban university counseling center	Barker (1979)	Counseling Services Evaluation Scale, Semantic Differential Scales

Note. CERS = Counselor Effectiveness Rating Scale; CRF = Counselor Rating Form. From "Development and Factor Structure of the Cross-Cultural Counseling Inventory-Revised" by T.D. LaFromboise, H.L.K. Coleman, and A. Hernandez, 1991, *Professional Psychology, 22*(5), p. 3. Copyright 1991 by *Professional Psychology.* Reprinted by permission.

kinds of classes. The first classes were regularly scheduled multicultural counseling courses (or control courses) meeting once a week for 15 weeks in 3-hour class periods, for a total of 45 contact hours. The second set participated in a multicultural counseling course (or control course) during summer session with 12 group meetings twice a week for 6 weeks, for a total of 36 contact hours. The third group enrolled in a course entitled "Counseling Diverse Populations" with six extended training workshops of intensive multicultural counseling training in three weekend workshops, for a total of 42 contact hours. The MAKSS was used to measure change as a result of participation in these three classes by administering the MAKSS at the beginning and end of each course. The results suggested, first, that the training format used to promote awareness, knowledge, and skill significantly affected the participants' scores. "One of the more important findings emerging from this research involved the apparent effectiveness of the training model to stimulate a notable increase in students' level of multicultural counseling development regardless of the length of time the training was offered (i.e. regular academic semester, summer semester, intensive weekend training format)" (D'Andrea et al., 1991, p. 147). Another finding indicated that it was more difficult to acquire multicultural counseling skills than to gain awareness and knowledge.

A third measure is also available. Sodowsky, Taffe, and Gutkin (1991) developed a Multicultural Counseling Inventory (MCI) to measure self-reported multicultural counseling competencies. Fourteen items measure general and specific counseling skills; 11 items measure knowledge about treatment planning, case conceptualization, and multicultural counseling research; 10 items measure awareness of multicultural sensitivity as well as interactions and advocacy in professional and general experiences; and 8 items measure the counselor's interactive relationship with a minority client. The 43 items assess self-perceived multicultural competencies on a 4-point Likert-type scale from very accurate to very inaccurate. The MCI was developed at the University of Nebraska with 165 graduate students and 771 counseling professionals. The reliability scores were .83 for the Skills scale, .79 for the Knowledge scale, .83 for the Awareness scale, and .71 for the Relationship scale.

Gathering data from 220 counselors with the MCI, Pope-Davis and Ottavi (1991) achieved reliability levels of .81 for Skill, .80 for Knowledge, .80 for Awareness, and .67 for Skill, closely approximating the original reliability data. The results showed Asian-American and Hispanic counselors reported more multicultural counseling knowledge than White counselors; and African-American, Asian-American, and Hispanic counselors reported more competence in multicultural awareness and relationships than White counselors. This could mean that many counselors lack a high level of competence. It could also mean that minority counselors rated themselves as more multiculturally competent. As a self-report measure, it is difficult to assess the accuracy of these self-ratings.

Ponterotto validated a fourth measure called the Multicultural Counseling Awareness Scale-Form B (MCAS:B), which is also based on the three-stage progression from awareness to knowledge to skill (Ponterotto, Sanchez, & Magids, 1991). This self-assessment instrument is a 45-item Likert scale for counselor self-assessment. The counselor responds to the 45 items in about 15–20 minutes. The MCAS:B is available in Appendix II of Ponterotto and Pedersen (1993). The MCAS:B is a bidimensional instrument with two subscales: one for knowledge/skills and a second scale for awareness. The "knowledge/skill scale" score range is from 28 to 196, with higher scores indicating more multicultural knowledge and skill. The "awareness scale" score range is from 14 to 98, with higher scores indicating more multicultural awareness. The total scale score is from 42 to 294. There is also a three-item social desirability scale indicating the need to "look good," and research is being done to determine a cutoff score on social desirability.

The data collected with MCAS:B thus far are promising. Ponterotto described the instrument as having "acceptable levels of internal consistency as well as construct- and criterion-related validity" (Ponterotto & Pedersen, 1993, p. 142).

These four examples of using the three-stage developmental model from awareness to knowledge to skill in developing competencies for multicultural counseling are promising. More research is needed to identify specific rather than general patterns of change in developing multiculturally skilled counselors.

6. Applications of Multicultural Competencies

We know that cultural background influences both the way that counseling is given and how it is received, even though most counselors assume that they share similar value assumptions as their culturally different clients. This book has described some of the different methods for developing multiculturally skilled counselors. Counselors should expect to (a) increase their awareness of their own and others' cultural biases, (b) become familiar with research on multicultural counseling, and (c) learn specific skills that will help them work more efficiently with culturally different clients. Counselors should learn to (a) understand better the mental health systems in other cultures; (b) recognize cultural prejudices and biases; (c) learn how environments contribute to self-esteem through positive interpersonal relationships across cultures; and (d) respect cultural diversity across boundaries of nationality, ethnicity, age, gender roles, socioeconomic status, and other affiliations.

Training materials described in this book have been used to train counselors working with clients in a wide range of cultural settings, including welfare clients, alcoholics, handicapped or disabled clients, foreign or international students, prisoners, and a variety of other special interest groups.

A multicultural training program for counselors is needed for several reasons.

1. Traditional systems of mental health services have a cultural bias favoring dominant social classes that can be counterproductive to an equitable distribution of counseling services.
2. Various cultural groups have discovered indigenous models of coping and treatment that work better for them and may usefully be applied to other groups as well.
3. Community health services are expensive when they fail and multicultural training might prevent some programs from failing.
4. Training methods that include indigenous people as resource persons directly in training counselors tend to reflect the reality of different cultures.
5. The constructs of "healthy" and "normal" that guide the delivery of mental health services are not the same for all cultures and might betray culturally encapsulated counselors to become tools of a particular political, social, or economic system.
6. Increased interdependence across national, ethnic, and sociocultural boundaries requires direct attention to culture as part of counselor training.

7. Most counselors come from dominant cultures, whereas most clients do not.

Although most counseling services are provided by White, middle-class males, the vast majority of clients receiving these services are non-White, are from lower socioeconomic levels, and differ significantly in their socialization. The literature on how cultural values affect mental health services describes vividly the counselor's need for increased awareness. Value assumptions made by culturally different counselors and clients have resulted in culturally biased counseling with low utilization rates by minority clients. Counselors who are most different from their clients, especially in race and social class, have the greatest difficulty effecting constructive changes, whereas counselors who are most similar to their clients in these respects have a greater facility for helping appropriately (Carkhuff & Pierce, 1967).

In multicultural counseling, there is a great danger of mutual misunderstanding, insufficient understanding of the other culture's unique problems, natural hostility that destroys rapport, and negative transference toward the counselor (Vontress, 1971). A client's appropriate cultural response is often confused with neurotic transference. Ignorance of one another's culture by counselors and clients contributes to resistance to the goals of counseling. This resistance is usually accompanied by feelings of hostility, threat, or unwillingness to allow the stranger access to a client's real feelings.

The concept of culture is as old as organized society, but the systematic study of culture and mental health is a phenomenon of the 20th century. Initially, the fields of psychoanalysis and anthropology were the focus of interest in studying "culture and personality." This focus was later expanded to include the more or less equivalent fields of social psychiatry, multicultural psychiatry, multicultural psychotherapy, and multicultural counseling. The emphasis has shifted from anthropological studies of remote societies to national and ethnic variations in modern, pluralistic, and complex communities. More recently, differences in physical, social, economic, and behavioral characteristics, such as age, life-style, gender role, socioeconomic status, and other comembership affiliations, have been recognized as contributing to the individual's subjective culture as well.

7. Conclusion

By the 1970s, there was abundant evidence that minority groups were underutilizing counseling services in many cultures, and that behavior such as individualistic assertiveness, described as pathological in a minority culture, could be viewed as adaptive in the majority, or dominant, culture. In the United

States, Asian Americans, Blacks, Chicanos, Native Americans, and other minority groups terminate counseling significantly earlier than do White clients because of cultural barriers, language barriers, and class-bound or culture-bound attitudes that hinder rapport. The National Institute of Mental Health, the American Psychiatric Association's Task Force on Ethnocentricity among Psychiatrists, and the recent U.S. President's Commission on Mental Health all have emphasized the ethical responsibility of all counselors to know their clients' cultural values. Until recently, however, none of the mental health professions has actively developed a unified multicultural approach leading toward a degree specialization in multicultural counseling.

That situation is changing, however. Pedersen and Ivey (in press,a) suggested that any successful treatment plan or community intervention that promotes intentionality through "self-awareness" and "other awareness," or any comprehensive program of counseling, must consider the cultural factor. In most cases, multicultural counseling students design their own unique programs with available courses and an appropriate faculty advisor at one or another of the larger universities.

Questions of controversy describe unsolved issues in counseling across cultures. Should the therapist emphasize the culturally unique (emic) or the humanly universal (etic)? If the cultural element is underemphasized, the counselor is insensitive to the client's values; if it is overemphasized, the counselor stereotypes clients. Should the counselor change the environment to fit the person or change the person to fit the cultural context? Dominant cultures tend to prefer the autoplastic mode of changing the person, whereas many minority populations prefer the alloplastic style of changing the context. Is multicultural counseling a series of techniques that can be learned, or is it dependent on a relationship in the more intuitive sense? Although there is a necessity to adapt techniques and be flexible, there is also a danger in disregarding the fundamentals of counseling and therapy in favor of unorthodox methods "presumed" to be multicultural. To what extent is all counseling multicultural? If we consider age, life-style, socioeconomic status, and gender role differences, in addition to ethnic and nationality differences, it is quickly apparent that there is a multicultural dimension in every counseling relationship. The goal should not be to establish a separate field of "multicultural counseling," but to validate the role of "culture" in all counseling and psychotherapy.

Developing multiculturally skilled counselors requires changes in the theory and practice of counseling. First, all counselors need to become more aware of culturally learned assumptions in the way counseling is currently being taught and conducted. For example, the emphasis on individualism needs to be modified for clients from more collectivist cultures. Just as we have challenged the illusion of culture-free and culture-fair tests, we also must discard the illusion of a "one-size-fits-all" approach to counseling. This does not mean that we dispose of counseling theory, but that we adapt and accommodate counseling theory and practice to culturally different clients.

Second, the argument for developing multicultural counseling skills from an ethical grounding needs to be extended to include the argument for developing multicultural counseling skill to achieve accuracy in analyzing behaviors in their cultural context.

Third, multicultural perspectives need to be incorporated within the education and training of counselors to prepare them for the changing and more evenly balanced multicultural demographic patterns of the future. This change requires admitting greater numbers of minorities into counselor education programs and ultimately into the teaching and direct service functions of counseling.

Fourth, counselors need to acknowledge cultural differences in their research so that the findings accurately reflect the different cultural perspectives of the multicultural research subject pool. This acknowledgment requires both the validation and re-validation of counseling theories and practice to culturally specific populations, and the generation of new research strategies for different cultures.

Fifth, counselors need to translate their skills, strategies, and techniques appropriately to a range of diverse cultural settings so that each counselor is prepared to match the right approach to the culturally different client population in the right way.

Developing multicultural awareness requires many changes that will produce a widening ripple effect as these changes bring about other changes. We are moving toward a multicultural future that requires us to understand persons who are different from ourselves, whatever our culture might be. Developing multicultural awareness is the strategy for our survival as a counseling profession and a strategy for our growth in meeting the diverse needs of a multicultural global village.

REFERENCES

Abramson, L.Y. (Ed.). (1988). *Social cognition and clinical psychology: A synthesis.* New York: Guilford.

Acosta, F., & Sheehan, J. (1976). Preferences toward Mexican-American and Anglo-American psychotherapies. *Journal of Consulting and Clinical Psychology, 44*, 272–279.

Adler, P.S. (1975). The transitional experience: An alternative view of culture shock. *Journal of Humanistic Psychology, 15*(4), 23–40.

Akbar, N. (1979). African roots of Black personality. In W. Smith, K. Burlew, M. Mosley, & W. Whitney (Eds.), *Reflections on Black psychology* (pp. 79–87). Washington, DC: University Press of America.

Altmaier, E.M. (1993). Role of Criterion II in accreditation. *Professional Psychology: Research and Practice, 24*(2), 127–129.

Ambrowitz, D., & Dokecki, P. (1977). The politics of clinical judgment: Early empirical returns. *Psychological Bulletin, 84*, 460–476.

American Counseling Association. (1988). *Ethical standards.* Alexandria, VA: Author.

American Psychological Association. (1979, January). Minutes from the meeting of the Council of Representatives, Washington, DC.

American Psychological Association. (1992). Ethical principles of psychologists and code of conduct. *American Psychologist, 47*(12), 1597–1611.

Amir, Y. (1969). Contact hypothesis in ethnic relations. *Psychological Bulletin, 71*, 319–341.

Arce, C.A. (1981). A reconsideration of Chicano culture and identity. *Daedalus, 110*, 177–192.

Aronson, H., & Overall, B. (1966). Treatment expectancies in patients in two social cases. *Social Work, 11*, 35–41.

Arredondo-Dowd, P., & Gonslaves, J. (1980). Preparing culturally effective counselors. *Personnel and Guidance Journal, 58*(10), 657–661.

Asch, A., & Fine, M. (1988). Moving disability beyond stigma. *Journal of Social Issues, 44*(1), 1–189.

Association for Counselor Education and Supervision. (1979). *Standards for preparation in counselor education.* Falls Church, VA: American Personnel and Guidance Association.

Atkinson, D.R. (1983). Ethnic similarity in counseling: A review of research. *The Counseling Psychologist, 11*, 79–92.

Atkinson, D.R. (1985). A beta-review of research on cross-cultural counseling and psychotherapy. *Journal of Multicultural Counseling and Development, 13*, 138–153.

Atkinson, D.R., Casas, A., & Abreu, J. (1992). Mexican-American acculturation, counselor ethnicity and cultural sensitivity, and perceived counselor competence. *Journal of Counseling Psychology, 39*(4), 515–520.

Atkinson, D.R., Maruyama, M., & Matsui, S. (1978). Effects of counselor race and counseling approach on Asian Americans' perception of counselor credibility and utility. *Journal of Counseling Psychology, 25*, 76–83.

Atkinson, D.R., Morten, G., & Sue, D.W. (1983). *Counseling American minorities: A cross-cultural perspective* (2nd ed.). Dubuque, IA: Wm. C. Brown.

Atkinson, D.R., Morten, G., & Sue, D.W. (1993) *Counseling American minorities: A cross-cultural perspective* (4th ed.). Dubuque, IA: Wm. C. Brown & Benchmark.

Atkinson, D.R., Ponce, F.Q., & Martinez, F.M. (1984). Effects of ethnic, sex, and attitude similarity on counselor credibility. *Journal of Counseling Psychology, 31*, 588–590.

Atkinson, D.R., & Schein, S. (1986). Similarity in counseling. *The Counseling Psychologist, 14*, 319–354.

Atkinson, D.R., Staso, D., & Hosford, R. (1978). Selecting counselor trainees with multicultural strengths: A solution to the Bakke decision crisis. *Personnel and Guidance Journal, 56*, 546–549.

Aubrey, R.F. (1977). Historical development of guidance and counseling and implications for the future. *Personnel and Guidance Journal, 55*, 288–295.

Axelson, J.A. (1993). *Counseling and development in a multicultural society.* Belmont, CA: Brooks/Cole.

Bailey, F.M. (1981). *Cross-cultural counselor education: The impact of microcounseling paradigms and traditional classroom methods on counselor trainee effectiveness.* Unpublished doctoral dissertation, University of Hawaii, Honolulu.

Baker, S.B., Daniels, T.G., & Greeley, A.T.(1990). Systematic training of graduate-level counselors: Narrative and meta-analytic reviews of three major programs. *The Counseling Psychologist, 18*(3), 355–421.

Banks, J.A. (1981). The stages of ethnicity: Implications for curriculum reform. In J.A. Banks (Ed.), *Multi-ethnic education: Theory and practice* (pp. 129–139). Boston: Allyn & Bacon.

Barker, N.C. (1979). The effect of race and sex on client's evaluations of their counselor in an urban university counseling center. *Psychology: A Quarterly Journal of Human Behavior, 16*(3), 33–38.

Barna, L.M. (1991). Stumbling blocks in intercultural communication. In L. Samovar & R.E. Porter (Eds.), *Intercultural communication: A reader* (6th ed., pp. 345–352). Belmont, CA: Wadsworth.

Benesch, K.F., & Ponterotto, J.G. (1989). East and West: Transpersonal psychology and cross cultural counseling. *Counseling and Values, 33*(2), 121–131.

Berman, J. (1979). Individual versus societal focus in problem diagnosis of Black and White male and female counselors. *Journal of Cross-Cultural Psychology, 10*, 497–507.

Berry, J. (1975). Ecology, cultural adaptation and psychological differentiation: Traditional patterning and acculturative stress. In R. Brislin, S. Bochner, & W. Lonner (Eds.), *Cross cultural perspectives on learning* (pp. 207–231). New York: Wiley.

Berry, J.W. (1980). Ecological analysis for cross-cultural psychology. In N. Warren (Ed.), *Studies in cross cultural psychology* (pp. 157–189). New York: Academic Press.

Berry, J.W., & Kim, U. (1988) Acculturation and mental health. In P. Dasen, J.W. Berry, & N. Sartorius (Eds.), *Cross-cultural psychology and health: Towards applications* (pp. 207–236). London: Sage.

Berry, J.W., Poortinga, Y.H., Segall, M.H., & Dasen, P.J. (1992). *Cross cultural psychology: Research and applications.* Cambridge, England: Cambridge University Press.

Bloom, B. (1956). *Taxonomy of educational objectives: Handbook I. Cognitive domain; Handbook II. Affective domain.* New York: David McKay.

Bloombaum, M., Yamamoto, J., & James, Q. (1968). Cultural stereotyping among psychotherapists. *Journal of Consulting and Clinical Psychology, 32,* 1–99.

Bohr, N. (1950). On the notion of causality and complementarily. *Science, 11,* 51–54.

Bolman, W. (1968). Cross-cultural psychotherapy. *American Journal of Psychiatry, 124,* 1237–1244.

Borrego, R.L., Chavez, E.L., & Titley, R.W. (1982). Effect of counselor technique on Mexican-American and Anglo-American self-disclosure and counselor perception. *Journal of Counseling Psychology, 29,* 538–541.

Brammer, L.M. (1988). *The helping relationship: Process and skills* (4th ed.). Englewood Cliffs, NJ: Prentice-Hall.

Brislin, R. (1993). *Understanding culture's influence on behavior.* New York: Harcourt Brace Jovanovich.

Brislin, R., Lonner, W., & Thorndike, R. (1973). *Cross-cultural research methods.* New York: Wiley.

Brislin, R., & Pedersen, P. (1976). *Cross cultural orientation program.* New York: Wiley.

Brislin, R.S., Cushner, K., Cherrie, C., & Yong, M. (1986). *Intercultural interactions: A practical guide.* Beverly Hills, CA: Sage.

Brislin, R.W. (1990). *Applied cross-cultural psychology.* Newbury Park, CA: Sage.

Brislin, R.W., Landis, D., & Brandt, M.E. (1983). Conceptualizations of intercultural behavior and training. In D. Landis & R.W. Brislin (Eds.), *Handbook of intercultural training: Volume I. Issues in theory and design* (pp. 1–35). New York: Pergamon.

Bruner, J.S. (1986). *Actual minds, possible worlds.* Cambridge, MA: Harvard University Press.

Bryne, R.H. (1977). *Guidance: A behavioral approach.* Englewood Cliffs, NJ: Prentice-Hall.

Bryson, L., & Cody, J. (1973). Relationship of race and level of understanding between counselor and client. *Journal of Counseling Psychology, 20,* 495–498.

Bryson, S., Renzaglia, G.A., & Danish, S. (1974). Training counselors through simulated racial encounters. *Journal of Non-White Concerns in Personnel and Guidance, 3,* 218–223.

Burger, J.M. (1990). *Personality* (2nd ed.). Belmont, CA: Wadsworth.

Calneck, M. (1970). Racial factors in the countertransference: The Black therapist and the Black client. *American Journal of Orthopsychiatry, 40,* 39–46.

Caplan, G. (1976). The family as support system. In G. Caplan & M. Killilea (Eds.), *Support systems and mutual help: Multidisciplinary explorations* (pp. 50–62). New York: Grune & Stratton.

Carkhuff, R.R., & Pierce, R. (1967). Differential effects of therapist race and social class upon patient depth of self-exploration in the initial clinical interview. *Journal of Consulting Psychology, 31*, 632–634.

Carney, C.G., & Kahn, K.B. (1984). Building competencies for effective cross-cultural counseling: A developmental view. *The Counseling Psychologist, 12*, 111–119.

Carter, R. (1991). Cultural values: A review of empirical research and implications for counseling. *Journal of Counseling and Development, 70*(1), 164–173.

Carter, R.T., & Helms, J.E. (1987). The relationship of Black value orientations to racial identity attitudes. *Measurement and Evaluation in Counseling and Development, 19*, 185–195.

Casas, J.J. (1984). Policy training and research in counseling psychology: The racial/ethnic minority perspective. In S. Brown & R. Lent (Eds.), *Handbook of counseling psychology* (pp. 785–831). New York: Wiley.

Cayleff, S.E. (1986). Ethical issues in counseling gender, race and culturally distinct groups. Special issue: Professional ethics. *Journal of Counseling and Development, 64*, 345–347.

Center for Applied Linguistics. (1982). *Providing effective orientation: A training guide.* Washington, DC: CAL Refugee Services Report.

Chambers, J.C. (1992). *Triad training: A method for teaching basic counseling skills to chemical dependency counselors.* Unpublished doctoral dissertation, University of South Dakota, Vermillion.

Chang, P., Dandridge., G, Huie, C., Lee, J., Owyoung, B., & Young, A. (1992). *Treatment considerations with culturally diverse populations.* Berkeley, Alameda: California School of Professional Psychology.

Cheatham, H.E., & Stewart, J.B. (1990). *Black families: Interdisciplinary perspectives.* New Brunswick, NJ: Transaction Publishers.

Cheung, F.M.C. (1986). Psychopathology among Chinese people. In M.H. Bond (Ed.), *The psychology of the Chinese people* (pp. 171–213). Hong Kong: Oxford University Press.

Christopher, J.C. (1992). *The role of individualism in psychological well-being: Exploring the interplay of ideology, culture and social science.* Unpublished doctoral dissertation, The University of Texas at Austin.

Church, A.T. (1982). Sojourner adjustment. *Psychological Bulletin, 91*, 540–572.

Claiborn, C.D., & Lichtenberg, J.W. (1989). Interactional counseling. *The Counseling Psychologist, 17*, 355–453.

Clements, C.B., & Rickhard, H.C. (1993). Criterion II: A principle in search of guidelines. *Professional Psychology: Research and Practice, 24*(24), 133–134.

Cobb, S. (1976). Social support as a moderator of life stress. *Psychosomatic Medicine, 38*, 300–314.

Coffman, T.L. (1978). Application for a postdoctoral research training fellowship submitted to the Duke University Center for the Study of Aging and Adult Development.

Coffman, T.L., & Harris, M.C. (1984, August). *The U-curve of adjustment to adult life transitions.* Paper presented at the meeting of the American Psychological Association, Toronto.

Cohen, M. (1990, July 29). Schools grappling with new diversity. *The Boston Sunday Globe*, p. 75.

Copeland, E.J. (1983). Cross-cultural counseling and psychotherapy: A historical perspective, implications for research and training. *The Personnel and Guidance Journal, 62*, 10–15.

Corey, G. (1991). *Theory and practice of counseling and therapy*. Pacific Grove, CA: Brooks/Cole.

Corey, G., Corey, M.S., & Callanan, P. (1993). *Issues and ethics in the helping profession*. Pacific Grove, CA: Brooks Cole.

Cortese, A.J. (1989). The interpersonal approach to morality: A gender and cultural analysis. *Journal of Social Psychology, 129*(4), 429–442.

Crano, S.L., & Crano, W.D. (1990). *Development of a measure of international student adjustment*. Unpublished manuscript, Texas A & M University, College Station.

Cross, W. (1991). *Shades of black*. Philadelphia: Temple University Press.

Cross, W.E. (1971). The negro-to-Black conversion experience. *Black Worlds, 20*, 13–17.

D'Andrea, M., & Daniels, J. (1991). Exploring the different levels of multicultural counseling training in counselor education. *Journal of Counseling and Development, 70*(1) 78–85.

D'Andrea, M., Daniels, J., & Heck, R. (1991). Evaluating the impact of multicultural counselor training. *Journal of Counseling and Development, 70*(1), 143–150.

Dasen, P.R., Berry, J.W., & Sartorius, N. (Eds.). (1988). *Cross-cultural psychology and health: Toward applications*. Newbury Park, CA: Sage.

Dauphinais, P., Dauphinais, L., & Rowe, W. (1981). Effects of race and communication style on Indian perceptions of counselor effectiveness. *Counselor Education and Supervision, 21*, 72–80.

Delworth, U. (1989). Identity in the college years: Issues of gender and ethnicity. *Journal of National Association of Student Personnel Administrators, 26*, 162–166.

DeVoss, G. (1973). *Socialization for achievement: Essays on the cultural psychology of the Japanese*. Berkeley, CA: University of California Press.

Diaz-Guerrero, R. (1977). A Mexican psychology. *American Psychologist, 32*, 934–944.

Dizzard, J.E. (1970). Black identity, social class, and Black power. *Journal of Social Issues, 26*(1), 195–207.

Doi, T. (1974). *The anatomy of dependence*. Tokyo: Kodansha.

Draguns, J.G. (1974). Values reflected in psychopathology: The case of the Protestant Ethic. *Ethos, 2*, 115–136.

Draguns, J.G. (1977). Mental health and culture. In P. Pedersen, D. Hoopes, & G. Renwick (Eds.), *Overview of intercultural education, training and research: Volume I. Theory* (pp. 56–71). Chicago: Intercultural Network.

Draguns, J.G. (1980). Psychological disorders of clinical severity. In H.C. Triandis & J.G. Draguns (Eds.), *Handbook of cross-cultural psychology: Volume VI. Psychopathology* (pp. 99–174). Boston: Allyn & Bacon.

Draguns, J.G. (1981a). Counseling across cultures: Common themes and distinct approaches. In P. Pedersen, J. Draguns, W. Lonner, & J. Trimble (Eds.), *Counseling across cultures: Revised and expanded edition* (pp. 3–22). Honolulu: University of Hawaii Press.

Draguns, J.G. (1981b). Cross-cultural counseling and psychotherapy: History, issues, current status. In A.J. Marsella & P.B. Pedersen (Eds.), *Cross-cultural counseling and psychotherapy* (pp. 3–27). New York: Pergamon.

Draguns, J.G. (1989). Dilemmas and choices in cross-cultural counseling: The universal versus the culturally distinctive. In P. Pedersen, J. Draguns, W. Lonner, & J. Trimble (Eds.), *Counseling across cultures* (pp. 3-22). Honolulu: University of Hawaii Press.

Dreikurs, R. (1972, August). Equality: The life style of tomorrow. *The Futurist*, pp. 153–155.

D'Souza, D. (1991). *Illiberal education: The politics of race and sex on campus*. New York: Free Press.

DuBois, W.E.B. (1908). *The Negro American family*. Published with the 13th Annual Conference for the Study of the Negro Problems, Atlanta University, GA.

Erickson, F., & Schultz, J. (1982). *The counselor as gatekeeper: Social interaction in interviews*. New York: Academic Press.

Erikson, E.H. (1968). *Identity: Youth and crisis*. New York: Norton.

Ewing, T.N. (1974). Racial similarity of client and counselor and client satisfaction with counseling. *Journal of Counseling Psychology, 21*, 446–449.

Favazza, A.F., & Oman, M. (1977). *Anthropological and cross-cultural themes in mental health: An annotated bibliography 1925–1974*. Columbia, MO: University of Missouri Press.

Fields, S. (1979). Mental health and the melting pot. *Innovations, 6*(2), 2–3.

Fierman, T.B. (1965). Myths in the practice of psychotherapy. *Archives of General Psychiatry, 12*, 408–414.

Filla, T., & Clarke, D. (1973). *Human relations resource guide on in-service programs*. St. Paul, MN: Department of Education.

Fitzgerald, S.C. (1945). *Crack up*. New York: Laughlin.

Frijda, N., & Jahoda, G. (1966). On the scope and methods of cross-cultural research. *International Journal of Psychology, 1*, 109–127.

Fukuyama, M.A. (1990). Taking a universal approach to multicultural counseling. *Counselor Education and Supervision, 30*, 6–17.

Furlong, M.J., Atkinson, D.R., & Casas, J.M. (1979). Effects of counselor ethnicity and attitudinal similarity of Chicano students' perceptions of counselor credibility and attractiveness. *Hispanic Journal of Behavioral Science, 1*(1), 41–53.

Furnham, A. (1988). The adjustment of sojourners. In Y.Y. Kim & W.B. Gudykunst (Eds.), *Cross cultural adaptation, current approaches* (pp. 42–61). Newbury Park, CA: Sage.

Furnham, A., & Bochner, S. (1986). *Culture shock: Psychological reactions to unfamiliar environments*. London: Methuen.

Gamboa, A.M., Tosi, D.J., & Riccio, A.C. (1976). Race and counselor climate in the counselor preference of delinquent girls. *Journal of Counseling Psychology, 23*, 160–162.

Gardner, L.H. (1971). The therapeutic relationship under varying conditions of race. *Psychotherapy, Theory, Research and Practice, 8*(1), 78–87.

Gay, G. (1984). Implications of selected models of ethnic identity development for educators. *The Journal of Negro Education, 54*(1), 43–52.

Geertz, C. (1973). *The interpretation of cultures*. New York: Basic Books.

Gibbs, J.T. (1974). Patterns of adaptation among Black students at a predominantly White university: Selected case studies. *American Journal of Orthopsychiatry, 44*(5), 728–740.

Gilligan C. (1982). *In a different voice*. Cambridge, MA: Harvard University Press.

Gilligan, C. (1987). Moral orientation and moral development. In E.F. Kittay & D.T. Meyers (Eds.), *Women and moral theory* (pp. 19–33). Totowa, NJ: Rowman & Littlefield.

Glazer, N. (1975). *Affirmative discrimination: Ethnic inequality and public policy*. New York: Basic Books.

Goldstein, A. (1981). *Psychological skill training: The structural learning technique*. New York: Pergamon.

Goldstein, A. (1991). *Delinquent gangs: A psychological perspective*. Champaign IL: Research Press.

Goldstein, A., & Michaels, G. (1985). *Empathy: Development, training and consequences*. Hillsdale, NJ: Lawrence Erlbaum Associates.

Gomez-Schwartz, B.S., Hadley, S.W., & Strupp, H.H. (1978). Individual psychotherapy and behavior therapy. *Annual Review of Psychology, 29*, 435–472.

Goodyear, R.K., & Sinnett, E.R. (1984). Current and emerging ethical issues for counseling psychology. *Counseling Psychologist, 12*, 87–98.

Gottlieb, B.H., & Hall, A. (1980). Social networks and the utilization of preventive mental health services. In R.H. Price, R.F. Ketterer, B.C. Bader, & J. Monahan (Eds.), *Prevention in mental health: Research policy and practice* (pp. 167–194). Beverly Hills, CA: Sage.

Grier, W.H., & Cobbs, P.M. (1968). *Black rage*. New York: Bantam Books.

Gudykunst, W.B., & Hammer, M.R. (1983). Basic training design: Approaches to intercultural training. In D. Landis & R.W. Brislin (Eds.), *Handbook of intercultural training* (Vol. 1, pp. 118–154). New York: Pergamon.

Gudykunst, W.B., & Hammer, M.R. (1988). Strangers and hosts: An uncertainty reduction based theory of intercultural adaptation. In Y.Y. Kim & W.B. Gudykunst (Eds.), *Cross-cultural adaptation: Current approaches* (pp. 106-139). Newbury Park, CA: Sage.

Guthrie, R. (1976). *Even the rat was white: A historical view of psychology*. New York: Harper & Row.

Hackney, H., & Cormier, L. (1988). *Counseling strategies and interventions* (3rd ed.). Englewood Cliffs, NJ: Prentice-Hall.

Hall, E. (1966). *The hidden dimension*. Garden City, NY: Doubleday.

Hansen, J.C., Robins, T.H., & Grimes, J. (1982). Review of research on practicum supervision. *Counselor Education and Supervision, 22*(1), 15–24.

Haq, M. (1993). *The Human Development Index: A UN Human Development Program Report*. New York: United Nations Development Program.

Hardiman, R. (1982). *White identity development: A process oriented model for describing the racial consciousness of White Americans*. Unpublished doctoral dissertation, University of Massachusetts, Amherst.

Harrison, D.K. (1975). Race as a counselor–client variable in counseling and psychotherapy. A review of the research. *The Counseling Psychologist, 5*, 124–133.

Harrison, R., & Hopkins, R. (1967). The design of cross-cultural training: An alternative to the university model. *The Journal of Applied Behavioral Science, 3*, 431–460.

Heider, F. (1958). *The psychology of interpersonal relations.* New York: Wiley.

Heilbronner, R.L. (1975). *An inquiry into the human prospect.* New York: Norton.

Helms, J.E. (1984). Toward a theatrical explanation of the effects of race on counseling: A Black and White model. *The Counseling Psychologist, 12*, 153–165.

Helms, J.E. (1985). Cultural identity in the treatment process. In P. Pedersen (Ed.), *Handbook of cross-cultural counseling and therapy* (pp. 239–245). Westport, CT: Greenwood Press.

Helms, J.E. (1990). *Black and white racial identity: Theory, research and practice.* Westport, CT: Greenwood Press.

Hermans, H.J.M., Kemper, H.J.G., & Van Loon, R.J.P. (1992). The dialogical self: Beyond individualism and rationalism. *American Psychologist, 47*(1), 23–33.

Hernandez, A.G., & Kerr, B.A. (1985, August). *Evaluating the Triad Model and traditional cross-cultural counselor training.* Paper presented at the 93rd annual convention of the American Psychological Association, Los Angeles, CA.

Hernandez, A.G., & LaFromboise, T.D. (1985, August). *The development of the cross-cultural counseling inventory.* Paper presented at the meeting of the American Psychological Association, Los Angeles, CA.

Herr, E. (1985). International approaches to career counseling and guidance. In P. Pedersen (Ed.), *Handbook of cross-cultural counseling and therapy* (pp. 3–10). Westport, CT: Greenwood Press.

Higginbotham, H. (1979a). Culture and mental health services. In A. Marsella, R. Tharp, & T. Ciborowski (Eds.), *Perspectives in cross-cultural psychology* (pp. 307–332). New York: Academic Press.

Higginbotham, H. (1979b). Cultural issues in providing psychological services for foreign students in the United States. *International Journal of Intercultural Relations, 3*, 49–85.

Hilliard, A. (1986, March). *Keynote address.* Presented at the 1st National Symposium on Multicultural Counseling, Atlanta, GA.

Hines, A., & Pedersen, P. (1980). The cultural grid: Matching social system variables and cultural perspectives. *Asian Pacific Training Development Journal, 1*, 5–11.

Hofstede, G. (1980). *Cultures consequences: International differences in work related values.* Beverly Hills, CA: Sage.

Hofstede, G. (1986). Cultural differences in teaching and learning. *International Journal of Intercultural Relations, 10*(3), 301–320.

Hofstede, G. (1991). *Cultures and organizations: Software of the mind.* London: McGraw-Hill.

Horney, K. (1967). *Feminine psychology.* New York: Norton.

Hosford, R., & Mills, M. (1983). Video in social skills training. In P. Dowrick & S. Biggs (Eds.), *Using video: Psychological and social applications* (pp. 125–166). New York: Wiley.

Howard, G.S. (1991). Culture tales: A narrative approach to thinking, cross-cultural psychology and psychotherapy. *American Psychologist, 46,* 187–197.

Hsu, F.L.K. (Ed.). (1972). *Psychological anthropology.* Cambridge, MA: Schenkman.

Hsu, F.L.K. (1985). The self in cross cultural perspective. In A.J. Marsella & F.L.K. Hsu (Eds.), *Culture and self: Asian and Western perspectives* (pp. 25–55). New York: Tavistock.

Ibrahim, F.A., & Kahn, H. (1985, August). *Assessment of world views.* Paper presented at 93rd annual meeting of the American Psychological Association, Los Angeles, CA.

Ibrahim, F.A. (1991). Contribution of cultural worldview to generic counseling and development. *Journal of Counseling and Development, 70*(1), 6–12.

International Association for Cross-Cultural Psychology. (1978, July). *International association for cross cultural psychology.* Statement on ethics adopted by the association at the general meeting.

Irvin, R., & Pedersen, P. (1993). *The internal dialogue of culturally different clients: An application of the Triad Training Model.* Unpublished manuscript.

Ivey, A. (1980a). *Counseling and psychotherapy: Skills, theories and practice.* Englewood Cliffs, NJ: Prentice-Hall.

Ivey, A. (1980b). Counseling 2000: Time to take charge! In J.M. Whiteley & B.R. Feetz (Eds.), *The present and future of counseling psychology* (pp. 113–123). Monterey, CA: Brooks/Cole.

Ivey, A.E. (1987). The multicultural practice of therapy: Ethics, empathy and dialectics. *Journal of Social and Clinical Psychology, 5,* 195–204.

Ivey, A.E. (1988). *Intentional interviewing and counseling: Facilitating client development.* Pacific Grove, CA: Brooks/Cole.

Ivey, A.E. (1990). Training as treatment and directions for the future. *The Counseling Psychologist, 18*(3), 428–435.

Ivey, A.E., & Authier, J. (1978). *Microcounseling: Innovations in interviewing training.* Springfield, IL: Charles C. Thomas.

Ivey, A.E., Ivey, M.B., & Simek-Morgan, L. (1993). *Counseling and psychotherapy: A multicultural perspective.* Boston: Allyn & Bacon.

Jackson, A.M. (1973). Psychotherapy: Factors associated with the race of the therapist. *Psychotherapy: Theory, Research and Practice, 10,* 273–277.

Jackson, B. (1975). Black identity development. In L. Golubschick & B. Persky (Eds.), *Urban social and educational issues* (pp. 158–164). Dubuque, IA: Kendall-Hall.

Janis, I.L. (1982). *Counseling on personal decisions: Theory and research on short-term helping relationships.* New Haven, CT: Yale University Press.

Jaslow, C. (1978). Exemplary programs, practices and policies. In G. Waltz & L. Benjamin (Eds.), *Transcultural counseling: Needs, program and techniques* (pp. 191–213). New York: Human Sciences Press.

Jensen, A.R. (1969). How much can we boost IQ and scholastic achievement? *Harvard Educational Review, 39,* 1–123.

Jones, E.E., & Korchin, S.J. (1982). *Minority mental health.* New York: Praeger.

Jourard, S.M. (1964). *The transparent self.* Princeton, NJ: Van Nostrand.

Kagan, N., Krathwohl, D., & Farquhar, W. (1965). *Interpersonal process recall.* East Lansing, MI: Michigan State University Press.

Katz, J.H. (1978). *White awareness: Handbook for anti-racism training.* Norman, OK: University of Oklahoma Press.

Katz, M., & Sanborn, K. (1976). Multiethnic studies of psychopathology and normality in Hawaii. In J. Westermeyer (Ed.), *Anthropology and mental health* (pp. 49–56). The Hague: Mouton.

Kealey, D.J. (1988). *Explaining and predicting cross-cultural adjustment and effectiveness: A study of Canadian technical advisors overseas.* Unpublished doctoral dissertation, Queens University, Kingston, Ontario, Canada.

Khatib, S.M., & Nobles, W.W. (1977). Historical foundations of African psychology and their philosophical consequences. *Journal of Black Psychology, 4,* 91–101.

Kierstead, F.D., & Wagner, P.A. (1993). *The ethical, legal and multicultural foundations of teaching.* Dubuque, IA: Brown & Benchmark.

Kiev, A. (1972). *Transcultural psychiatry.* New York: The Free Press.

Kim, B.C. (1981). *New urban immigrants: The Korean community in New York.* Princeton, NJ: Princeton University Press.

King, L.M. (1978). Social and cultural influences on psychopathology. *Annual Review of Psychology, 29,* 405–433.

Kinloch, G. (1979). *The sociology of minority group relations.* Englewood Cliffs, NJ: Prentice-Hall.

Kitano, H.H.L. (1989). A model for counseling Asian Americans. In P. Pedersen, J. Draguns, W. Lonner, & J. Trimble (Eds.), *Counseling across cultures* (3rd ed., pp. 139–152). Honolulu: University of Hawaii Press.

Kitchener, K. (1986). Ethics and counseling psychology: Distinctions and directions. *The Counseling Psychologist, 12*(3), 15–18.

Kleinberg, O. (1985). The social psychology of cross-cultural counseling. In P. Pedersen (Ed.), *Handbook of cross-cultural counseling and therapy* (pp. 29–36). Westport, CT: Greenwood Press.

Kleinman, A. (1978). Clinical relevance of anthropological and cross-cultural research: Concepts and strategies. *American Journal of Psychiatry, 135,* 427–431.

Kleinman, A. (1980). *Patients and healers in the context of culture.* Berkeley: University of California Press.

Kleinman, A. (1988). *Rethinking psychiatry.* New York: The Free Press.

Kluckhohn, F.R., & Strodtbeck, F.L. (1961). *Variations in value orientation.* New York: Harper & Row.

Kohls, L.R. (1979). *Survival kit for overseas living.* Chicago: Intercultural Press.

Korchin, S.J. (1980). Clinical psychology and minority problems. *American Psychologist, 35,* 262–269.

Korman, M. (1974). National conference on levels and patterns of professional training in psychology: Major themes. *American Psychologist, 29,* 441–449.

Kroeber, A.L., & Kluckhohn, C. (1952). *Culture: A critical review of concepts and definitions.* New York: Vintage Books.

Kurtz, P.D., & Marshall, E.K. (1982). Evolution of interpersonal skills training. In E. Marshall & D. Kurtz (Eds.), *Interpersonal helping skills* (pp. 3–25). San Francisco, CA: Jossey-Bass.

LaFromboise, T.D., Coleman H.L.K., & Hernandez, A. (1991). Development and factor structure of the cross-cultural counseling inventory–revised. *Professional Psychology, 22*(5), 1–9.

LaFromboise, T.D., & Dixon, D.N. (1981). American Indian perceptions of trustworthiness in a counseling interview. *Journal of Counseling Psychology, 28,* 135–139.

LaFromboise, T.D., & Foster, S.L. (1989). Ethics in multicultural counseling. In P. Pedersen, J. Draguns, W. Lonner, & J.Trimble (Eds.) *Counseling across cultures* (3rd ed., pp. 115–136). Honolulu: University of Hawaii Press.

LaFromboise, T.D., & Foster, S.L. (1992). Cross cultural training: Scientist-practitioner model and methods. *The Counseling Psychologist, 20*(3), 472–489.

Lakoff, G., & Johnson, M. (1980). *Metaphors we live by.* Chicago: University of Chicago Press.

Lambert, M.J. (1981). Evaluating outcome variables in cross-cultural counseling and psychotherapy. In A. Marsella & P. Pedersen (Eds.), *Cross-cultural counseling and psychotherapy* (pp. 126–158). Elmsford, NY: Pergamon.

Lee, C.C. (1991). Promise and pitfalls of multicultural counseling. In C.C. Lee & B.L. Richardson (Eds.), *Multicultural issues in counseling: New approaches to diversity* (pp. 1–13). Alexandria, VA: American Counseling Association.

Lee, C.C., & Richardson, B.L. (1991). *Multicultural issues in counseling: New approaches to diversity.* Alexandria, VA: American Counseling Association.

Lee, D.Y., Sutton, R., France, M.H., & Uhlemann, M. (1983). Effects of counselor race on perceived counseling effectiveness. *Journal of Counseling Psychology, 30,* 447–456.

Lefley, H., & Pedersen, P. (Eds.). (1986). *Cross-cultural training for mental health professionals.* Springfield, IL: Charles C. Thomas.

Lefley, H.P. (1989). Counseling refugees: The North American Experience. In P. Pedersen, J. Draguns, W. Lonner, & J. Trimble (Eds.), *Counseling across cultures* (3rd ed., pp. 243–266). Honolulu: University of Hawaii Press.

Leong, F.T.L. (1991). Career development of racial and ethnic minorities. *The Career Development Quarterly, 39*(3), 195–285.

Leong, F.T.L., & Kim, H.H.W. (1991). Going beyond cultural sensitivity on the road to multiculturalism: Using the intercultural sensitizer as a counselor training tool. *Journal of Counseling and Development, 70*(1), 112–118.

LeVine, D. (1972). A cross-cultural study of attitudes toward mental illness. *Journal of Abnormal Psychology, 80,* 111–112.

LeVine, R., & Campbell, D. (1972). *Ethnocentrism: Theories of conflict, ethnic attitudes and group behavior.* New York: Wiley.

LeVine, R., & Padilla, A. (1980). *Crossing cultures in therapy: Pluralistic counseling for the Hispanic.* Monterey, CA: Brooks/Cole.

Lifton, R. (1986). *The Nazi doctors: Medical killing and the psychology of genocide.* New York: Basic Books.

Lin, T.Y., & Lin, M.C. (1978). Service delivery issues in Asian-North American communities. *American Journal of Psychiatry, 135*(4), 454–456.

Locke, D.C. (1990). A not so provincial view of multicultural counseling. *Counselor Education and Supervision, 30,* 18–25.

Locke, D.C. (1992). *Increasing multicultural understanding: A comprehensive model.* Newbury Park, CA: Sage.

Lonner, W.J., & Ibrahim, F.A. (1989). Assessment in cross-cultural counseling. In P. Pedersen, J. Draguns, W. Lonner, & J. Trimble (Eds.), *Counseling across cultures* (3rd ed., pp. 229–334). Honolulu: University of Hawaii Press.

Lonner, W.J., & Sundberg, N.D. (1985). Assessment in cross cultural counseling and therapy. In P.B. Pedersen (Ed.), *Handbook of cross-cultural counseling and therapy* (pp. 200–205). Westport, CT: Greenwood Press.

Loo, C. (1980). *Bicultural contextualizer model for cultural sensitivity in counseling: Transcript. Harmful assumptions.* Santa Cruz, CA: Chinatown Research Center.

Lopez, S.R. (1989). Patient variable biases in clinical judgment: Conceptual overview and methodological considerations. *Psychological Bulletin, 106*, 3–29.

Lorion, R.P. (1974). Patient and therapist variables in the treatment of low-income patients. *Psychological Bulletin, 81*, 344–354.

Lorion, R.P., & Parron, D.L. (1985). Countering the countertransference: A strategy for treating the untreatable. In P. Pedersen (Ed.), *Handbook of cross-cultural counseling and therapy* (pp. 79–86). Westport, CT: Greenwood Press.

Lukes, S. (1973). *Individualism. Key concepts in the social sciences.* Oxford: Basel Blackwell.

Mahoney, M.J. (1988). Constructive metatheory: Volume 1. Basic features and historical foundations. *International Journal of Personal Construct Psychology, 1*, 1–35.

Marcia, J.E. (1980). Identity in adolescence. In J. Adelson (Ed.), *Handbook of adolescent psychology* (pp. 159–187). New York: Wiley.

Marsella, A. (1979). Culture and mental disorders. In A.J. Marsella, R. Tharp, & T. Ciborowski (Eds.), *Perspectives on cross-cultural psychology* (pp. 233–262). New York: Academic Press.

Marsella, A., & Golden, C.J. (1980). The structure of cognitive abilities in Americans of Japanese and of European ancestry in Hawaii. *Journal of Social Psychology, 112*, 19–20.

Marsella, A., & Pedersen, P. (1981). *Cross cultural counseling and psychotherapy.* New York: Pergamon.

Martinez, J.L., Jr. (1977). *Chicano psychology.* New York: Academic Press.

Maruyama, M. (1992). *Context and complexity: Cultivating contextual understanding.* New York: Springer-Verlag.

Mason, D. (1986). Introduction: Controversies and continuities in race and ethnic relations theory. In J. Rex & D. Mason (Eds.), *Theories of race and ethnic relations* (pp. 1–19). New York: Cambridge University Press.

McCraw, W. (1969). Objectives: North Carolina Department of Public Instruction. In The Commission on Secondary Schools, Southern Association of Colleges and Schools, *Adventure on a Blue Marble: Approaches to teaching intercultural understanding* (pp. 11–12). Atlanta, GA: Commission on Secondary Schools.

McDavis, R.J., & Parker, M. (1977). A course on counseling ethnic minorities: A model. *Counselor Education and Supervision, 17*, 146–149.

McGoldrick, M., Pearce, J., & Giordano, J. (1982). *Ethnicity and family therapy.* New York: Guilford.

McGuire, W.J. (1966). The current status of cognitive consistency theories. In S. Fieldman (Ed.), *Cognitive consistency* (pp. 57–94). New York: Academic Press.

McNamee, S., & Gergen, K.J. (1992). *Therapy as social construction.* Newbury Park, CA: Sage.

Meadows, P. (1968). The cure of souls and the winds of change. *Psychoanalytic Review, 55,* 491–504.

Michanbaum, D. (1974). *Cognitive-behavior modification.* Morristown, NJ: General Learning Press.

Miles, R. (1989). *Racism.* New York: Routledge.

Miles, R.H. (1976). Role requirements as sources of organizational stress. *Journal of Applied Psychology, 61,* 172–179.

Miller, K. (1989). Training peer counselors to work on a multi-cultural campus. *Journal of College Student Development, 30*(6), 561–562.

Miller, N., & Brewer, M. (1984). *Groups in contact: The psychology of desegregation.* New York: Academic Press.

Milliones, J. (1980). Construction of a Black consciousness measure: Psychotherapeutic implications. *Psychotherapy: Theory, Research and Practice, 17*(2), 175–182.

Mio, J.S., & Iwamasa, G. (1993). To do or not to do: That is the question for White cross-cultural researchers. *The Counseling Psychologist, 21*(2), 197–212.

Mitchell, H. (1970). The Black experience in higher education. *The Counseling Psychologist, 2,* 30–36.

Morrow, D.W. (1972). Cultural addiction. *Journal of Rehabilitation, 38*(3), 30–32.

Muliozzi, A.D. (1972, March). *Inter-racial counseling: Does it work?* Paper presented at the meeting of the American Personnel and Guidance Association, Chicago.

Mwaba, K., & Pedersen, P. (1990). Relative importance of intercultural, interpersonal and psychopathological attributions in judging critical incidents by multicultural counselors. *Journal of Multicultural Counseling and Development, 18,* 106–117.

Nakamura, H. (1964). *Ways of thinking of Eastern peoples: India, China, Tibet, Japan.* Honolulu: University of Hawaii Press.

Niemeyer, G.J. (1993). *Constructivist assessment: A casebook.* Newbury Park, CA: Sage.

Neimeyer, G.J., & Fukuyama, M. (1984). Exploring the content and structure of cross-cultural attitudes. *Counselor Education and Supervision, 23*(3), 214–224.

Neimeyer, G.J., Fukuyama, M.A., Bingham, R.P., Hall, L.E., & Mussenden, M.E. (1986). Training cross-cultural counselors: A comparison of the pro and anticounselor Triad Models. *Journal of Counseling and Development, 64,* 437–439.

Neimeyer, G.J., & Gonzales, M. (1983). Duration, satisfaction, and perceived effectiveness of cross-cultural counseling. *Journal of Counseling Psychology, 30,* 91–95.

Newcomb, T.M. (1953). An approach to the study of communicative acts. *Psychological Review, 60,* 393–404.

Nwachuku, U.T., & Ivey, A.E. (1991). Culture-specific counseling: An alternative training model. *Journal of Counseling and Development, 70*(1), 106–111.

Oberg, K. (1958). *Culture shock and the problem of adjustment to new cultural environments.* Washington, DC: Department of State.

Opler, M.K. (1959). The cultural backgrounds of mental health. In M.K. Opler (Ed.), *Culture and mental health* (pp. 1–20). New York: Macmillan.

Opotow, S. (1990). Moral exclusion and injustice: An introduction. *Journal of Social Issues, 46*(1), 1–20.

Parham, T.A., & Helms, J.E. (1981). The influence of Black students' racial identity attitudes on preference for counselors' race. *Journal of Counseling Psychology, 28,* 250–257.

Parham, T.A., & Helms, J.E. (1985a). Attitudes of racial identity and self-esteem of Black students: An exploratory investigation. *Journal of College Student Personnel, 26,* 143–147.

Parham, T.A., & Helms, J.E. (1985b). Relation of racial identity attitudes to self-actualization and affective states of Black students. *Journal of Counseling Psychology, 32,* 431–440.

Parloff, M.B., Waskow, I.E., & Wolfe, B.E. (1978). Research on therapist variables in relation to process and outcome. In S. Garfield & A. Bergin (Eds.), *Handbook of psychotherapy and behavior change* (pp. 233–282). New York: Wiley.

Patterson, C.H. (1974). *Relationship of counseling and psychotherapy.* New York: Harper & Row.

Patterson, C.H. (1978a). Cross-cultural or intercultural psychotherapy. *Hacettepe University Bulletin of Social Sciences, 1,* 119–134.

Patterson, C.H. (1978b). Cross-cultural or intercultural psychotherapy. *International Journal for the Advancement of Counseling, 1,* 231–248.

Patterson, C.H. (1986). Culture and counseling in Hong Kong. *Chinese University Education Journal, 14*(2), 77–81.

Payton, C.R. (1993). Review of APA Accreditation Criterion II. *Professional Psychology: Research and Practice, 24*(2), 130–132.

Pearce, W.B. (1983, Summer). *International Communication Association Newsletter, 11*(3), 1.

Pearson, R.E. (1985). The recognition and use of natural support systems in cross-cultural counseling. In P. Pedersen (Ed.), *Handbook of cross-cultural counseling and therapy* (pp. 299–306). Westport, CT: Greenwood Press.

Pearson, R.E. (1990). *Counseling and social support: Perspectives and practice.* Newbury Park, CA: Sage.

Pedersen, A., & Pedersen, P. (1985). The Cultural Grid: A personal cultural orientation. In L. Samovar & R. Porter (Eds.), *Intercultural communication: A reader* (pp. 50–62). Belmont, CA: Wadsworth.

Pedersen, P. (1968). A proposal: That counseling be viewed as an instance of coalition. *Journal of Pastoral Care, 11,* 43–54.

Pedersen, P. (1976). *Triad model: Four simulated interviews on a one-hour videotape with training manual.* Minneapolis: University of Minnesota International Student Advisor's Office.

Pedersen, P. (1979). Non-western psychologies: The search for alternatives. In A. Marsella, R. Tharpe, & T. Cibrowski (Eds.), *Perspectives on cross-cultural psychology* (pp. 77–98). New York: Academic Press.

Pedersen, P. (1981a) The cultural inclusiveness of counseling. In P. Pedersen, J. Draguns, W. Lonner, & J. Trimble (Eds.), *Counseling across cultures: Revised and expanded edition* (pp. 22–58). Honolulu: University of Hawaii Press.

Pedersen, P. (1981b). *Final report to the NIMH on developing interculturally skilled counselors.* Unpublished monograph.

Pedersen, P. (1982). The intercultural context of counseling and therapy. In A. Marsella & G. White (Eds.), *Cultural conceptions of mental health and therapy* (pp. 333–358). Dordrecht, Holland: D. Reidel.

Pedersen, P. (1983). Asian theories of personality. In R. Corsini & A. Marsella (Eds.), *Contemporary theories of personality* (rev. ed., pp. 537–582). Itasca, IL: Peacock.

Pedersen, P. (1984a). Cross cultural training of mental health professionals. In R. Brislin & D. Landis (Eds.), *Handbook of cross-cultural training: Volume II. Methodology* (pp. 325–352). Elmsford, NJ: Pergamon.

Pedersen, P. (1984b). The cultural complexity of mental health. In P. Pedersen, N. Sartorius, & A.J. Marsella (Eds.), *Mental health services* (pp. 13–27). Beverly Hills, CA: Sage.

Pedersen, P. (1985). *Handbook of cross-cultural counseling and therapy.* Westport, CT: Greenwood Press.

Pedersen, P. (1986). Developing interculturally skilled counselors: A training program. In H. Lefley & P. Pedersen (Eds.), *Cross-cultural training of mental health professionals* (pp. 73–88). Springfield, IL: Charles C. Thomas.

Pedersen, P. (1988). *Handbook for developing multicultural awareness.* Alexandria, VA: American Counseling Association.

Pedersen, P. (1989) Developing multicultural ethical guidelines for psychology. *International Journal of Psychology, 24,* 643-652.

Pedersen, P. (1990). The multicultural perspective as a fourth force in counseling. *Journal of Mental Health Counseling, 12*(1), 93–95.

Pedersen, P. (1991a). Complexity and balance as criteria of effective multicultural counseling. *The Journal of Counseling and Development, 68,* 550–554.

Pedersen, P. (1991b). Counseling international students. *The Counseling Psychologist, 19*(1), 10–58.

Pedersen, P. (1991c). Multiculturalism as a fourth force in counseling. *Journal of Counseling and Development, 70*(1), 5–25.

Pedersen, P. (1993a). The multicultural dilemma of the White cross-cultural researcher. *The Counseling Psychologist, 21,* 229–232.

Pedersen, P. (1993b). Primal alternatives to talk therapy: The Batak "Tondi" of North Sumatra. *Counseling and Values, 37*(2), 52–60.

Pedersen, P. (in press, a). Multicultural training in schools. In P. Pedersen & J. Carey (Eds.), *Multicultural Counseling in Schools.* Boston: Allyn & Bacon.

Pedersen, P. (in press, b). *Five stages of culture shock: Critical incidents around the world.* Westport, CT: Greenwood.

Pedersen, P., Draguns, J., Lonner, W., & Trimble, J. (1981). *Counseling across cultures: Revised and expanded edition.* Honolulu: University Press of Hawaii.

Pedersen, P., Fukuyama, M., & Heath, A. (1989). Client, counselor and contextual variables in multicultural counseling. In P. Pedersen, J. Draguns, W. Lonner, & J. Trimble (Eds.), *Counseling across cultures* (3rd ed., pp. 23–53). Honolulu: University of Hawaii Press.

Pedersen, P., Holwill, C.F., & Shapiro, J.L. (1978). A cross-cultural training procedure for classes in counselor education. *Journal of Counselor Education and Supervision, 17,* 233–237.

Pedersen, P., & Ivey, A. (in press). *Culture-centered counseling and interviewing skills.* Westport, CT: Greenwood Press.

Pedersen, P., & Marsella, A.J. (1982). The ethical crisis for cross cultural counseling and therapy. *Professional Psychology, 13*, 492–500.

Peoples, V.Y., & Dell, D.M. (1975). Black and white student preferences for counselor roles. *Journal of Counseling Psychology, 22*, 529–534.

Pepinsky, H.B., & Karst, T.C. (1964). Convergency: A phenomenon in counseling and therapy. *American Psychologist, 19*, 333–338.

Phinney, J.S. (1989). Stages of ethnic identity in older adolescents from four ethnic groups. *Journal of Adolescence, 13*, 1971–1983.

Phinney, J.S. (1990). Ethnic identity in adolescents and adults. *Psychological Bulletin, 108*, 499–514.

Pike, R. (1966). *Language in relation to a united theory of the structure of human behavior.* The Hague: Mouton.

Pinderhughes, E. (1984). Teaching empathy: Ethnicity, race and power at the cross cultural treatment intervention. *The American Journal of Social Psychiatry, 4*(1), 5–12.

Pomales, J., Claiborn, C.D., & LaFromboise, T.D. (1986). Effects of black students' racial identity on perception of white counselors varying in cultural sensitivity. *Journal of Counseling Psychology, 33*, 58–62.

Ponce, F.Q., & Atkinson, D.R. (1989). Mexican-American acculturation, counselor ethnicity, counseling style, and perceived counselor credibility. *Journal of Counseling Psychology, 36*, 203–208.

Ponterotto, J.G. (1988). Racial/ethnic minority research: A content analysis and methodological critique. *Journal of Counseling Psychology, 3*, 410–418.

Ponterotto, J.G., & Casas, J.M. (1991). *Handbook of racial/ethnic minority counseling research.* Springfield, IL: Charles C. Thomas.

Ponterotto, J.G., & Pedersen, P. (1993). *Preventing prejudice: A guide for counselors and educators.* Newbury Park, CA: Sage.

Ponterotto, J.G., Sanchez, C.M., & Magids, D.M. (1991, August). *Initial development and validation of the Multicultural Counseling Awareness Scale (MCAS).* Paper presented at the annual meeting of the American Psychological Association, San Francisco, CA.

Poortinga, Y.H. (1990). Towards a conceptualization of culture for psychology. *Cross-cultural Psychology Bulletin, 24*(3), 2–10.

Pope-Davis, D.B., & Ottavi, T.M. (1991). *Examining the association between self-reported multicultural counseling competencies and demographic variables among counselors.* Unpublished manuscript, University of Iowa, Iowa City.

Porche, L.M., & Banikiotes, P.G. (1982). Racial and attitudinal factors affecting the perceptions of counselors by Black adolescents. *Journal of Counseling Psychology, 29*, 169–174.

President's Commission on Mental Health. (1978). *Report from the President's Commission on Mental Health.* Washington, DC: U.S. Government Printing Office.

Prince, R. (1976). Psychotherapy as the manipulation of endogenous healing mechanism: A transcultural survey. *Transcultural Psychiatric Research Review, 13*, 155–233.

Prince, R.H. (1980). Variations in psychotherapeutic experience. In H.C. Triandis &

J.G. Craguns (Eds.), *Handbook of cross-cultural psychology: Volume 6. Psychopathology* (pp. 291–349). Boston: Allyn & Bacon.

Proctor, E.K., & Rosen, A. (1981). Expectations and preferences for counselor race and their relation to intermediate treatment outcomes. *Journal of Counseling Psychology, 28,* 40–46.

Ramirez, M. (1991). *Psychotherapy and counseling with minorities: A cognitive approach to individual and cultural differences.* New York: Pergamon.

Ravitch, D. (1990, October 24). Multiculturalism yes, particularism no. *The Chronicle of Higher Education,* p. A44.

Ravitch, R., & Geertsma, R. (1969). Observations media and psychotherapy training. *Journal of Nervous and Mental Disorders, 148,* 310–327.

Reynolds, D.K. (1980). *The quiet therapies: Japanese pathways to personal growth.* Honolulu: University of Hawaii Press.

Rickard, H.C., & Clements, C.B. (1993). Critique of APA Accreditation Criterion II: Cultural and individual differences. *Professional Psychology: Research and Practice, 24*(2), 123–126.

Ridley, C. (1989). Racism in counseling as an aversive behavioral process. In P. Pedersen, J. Draguns, W. Lonner, & J. Trimble (Eds.), *Counseling across cultures* (3rd ed., pp. 55–79). Honolulu: University of Hawaii Press.

Rosch, E. (1975). Universals and cultural specifics in human categorization. In R. Brislin, S. Bochner, & W. Lonner (Eds.), *Cross-cultural perspectives on learning* (pp. 177–206). New York: Wiley.

Rotenberg, M. (1974). The Protestant ethic versus Western people-changing sciences. In J.L.M. Dawson & W. Lonner (Eds.), *Readings in cross-cultural psychology* (pp. 277–291). Hong Kong: University of Hong Kong Press.

Rothenberg, A. (1979). Einstein's creative thinking and the general theory of relativity: A documented report. *American Journal of Psychiatry, 136,* 38–43.

Rothenberg, A. (1983). Psychopathology and creative cognition. *Archives of General Psychiatry, 40,* 937–942.

Ruben, B.D., & Kealey, D.J. (1970). Behavioral assessment of communication competency and the prediction of cross-cultural adaptation. *International Journal of Intercultural Relations, 3*(1), 15–47.

Ruben, B.D., & Kealey, D.J. (1979). *Behavioral assessment of communication competency and the prediction of cross-cultural adaptation.* Ottawa, Canada: International.

Rubin, J.Z., Kim, S.H., & Peretz, N.M. (1990). Expectancy effects and negotiation. *Journal of Social Issues, 46*(2), 125–139.

Ruiz, R., & Casas, M.M. (1981). Culturally relevant and behavioristic counseling for Chicano college students. In P. Pedersen, J. Draguns, W. Lonner, & J. Trimble (Eds.), *Counseling across cultures: Revised and expanded edition* (pp. 203–226). Honolulu: University of Hawaii Press.

Sampson, E. (1977). Psychology and the American ideal. *Journal of Personality and Social Psychology, 11,* 767–782.

Sanchez, A.R., & Atkinson, D.R. (1983). Mexican American cultural commitment preference for counselor ethnicity and willingness to use counseling. *Journal of Counseling Psychology, 30,* 215–220.

Sarbin, T.R. (1986). The narrative as a root metaphor for psychology. In T.R. Sarbin (Ed.), *Narrative psychology: The storied nature of human conduct* (pp. 3–21). New York: Praeger.

Satir, V. (1964). *Conjoint family therapy*. Palo Alto, CA: Science & Behavior Books.

Sattler, J.M. (1970). Racial "Experimenter Effects" in experimentation, testing, interviewing and psychotherapy. *Psychological Bulletin, 73*, 137–160.

Schein, E.H. (1991). The role of the founder in the creation of organizational culture. In P. Frost, L.F. Moore, M.R. Lolluis, C.C. Lundbergg, & J. Martin (Eds.), *Reframing organizational culture* (pp. 14–25). Newbury Park, CA: Sage.

Sedlacek, W.E., & Brooks, J.C. (1976). *Racism in American education: A model for change*. Chicago: Nelson Hall.

Segall, M.H., Dasen, P.R., Berry, J.W., & Poortinga, Y.H. (1990). *Human behavior in global perspective: An introduction to cross-cultural psychology*. New York: Pergamon.

Sheikh, A., & Sheikh, K.S. (1989). *Eastern and Western approaches to healing: Ancient wisdom and modern knowledge*. New York: Wiley.

Shweder, R.A. (1990). Cultural psychology—What is it? In J.W. Stigler, R.A. Shweder, & G. Herdt (Eds.), *Cultural psychology: Essays on comparative human development* (pp. 73–112). New York: Cambridge University Press.

Shweder, R.A., Mahapatra, M., & Miller, J.A. (1990). Culture and moral development. In *Cultural psychology: Essays on comparative human development* (pp. 130–204). New York: Cambridge University Press.

Slack, C.W., & Slack, E.N. (1976, February). It takes three to break a habit. *Psychology Today*, pp. 46–50.

Sloan, T.S. (1990). Psychology for the Third World? *Journal of Social Issues, 46*(3), 1–20.

Smith, E. (1991). Ethnic identity development: Toward the development of a theory within the context of majority/minority status. *Journal of Counseling and Development, 70*(1), 181–188.

Snarey, J.R. (1985). Cross-cultural universality of social-moral development: A critical review of Kohlbergian research. *Psychological Bulletin, 97*, 202–232.

Sodowsky, G.R., Taffe, R.C., & Gutkin, T.B. (1991, March). *Development and applications of the multicultural counseling inventory*. Paper presented at the 99th annual convention of the American Psychological Association, San Francisco.

Solomon, G., & McDonald, F.J. (1970). Pretest and post-test reactions to self-viewing one's teaching performance on videotape. *Journal of Educational Psychology, 61*, 280–286.

Spacapan, S., & Thompson, S.C. (1991). Perceived control in vulnerable populations. *Journal of Social Issues, 47*(4), 1–197.

Stanges, B., & Riccio, A. (1970). A counselee preference for counselors: Some implications for counselor education. *Counselor Education and Supervision, 10*, 39–46.

Steenbarger, B.N. (1991). All the world is not a stage: Emerging contextualist themes in counseling and development. *Journal of Counseling and Development, 70*(2), 288–296.

Stephen, C.W., & Stephen, W.G. (1992). Reducing intercultural anxiety through intercultural contact. *International Journal of Intercultural Relations, 16*, 89–106.

Stewart, E.C. (1972). *American cultural patterns: A cross-cultural perspective.* Yarmouth, ME: Intercultural Press.

Stigler, J.W., Shweder, R.A., & Herdt, G. (1990). *Cultural psychology: Essays on comparative human development.* New York: Cambridge University Press.

Stoltenberg, C., & Delworth, U. (1987). *Supervising counselors and therapists: A developmental approach.* San Francisco: Jossey-Bass.

Stonequist, F.V. (1937). *The marginal man: A study in personality and culture conflict.* New York: Russell & Russell.

Strauss, J.S. (1979). Social and cultural influences on psychopathology. *Annual Review of Psychology, 30,* 397–416.

Strike, K., & Soltis, J. (1985). *The ethics of teaching.* New York: Teachers College Press.

Strong, S.R. (1978). Social psychological approach to psychotherapy research. In S. Garfield & A. Bergin (Eds.), *Handbook of psychotherapy and behavior change: An empirical analysis* (pp. 103–136). New York: Wiley.

Strong, S.R. (1991). Theory-driven science and naive empiricism in counseling psychology. *Journal of Counseling Psychology, 38*(2), 204–210.

Sue, D.W. (1973). Ethnic identity: The impact of two cultures on the psychological development of Asians in America. In S. Sue & N.N. Wagner (Eds.), *Asian-Americans: Psychological perspectives.* (pp. 120–134). Palo Alto, CA: Science & Behavior Books.

Sue, D.W. (1977). Barriers to effective cross-cultural counseling. *Journal of Counseling Psychology, 24,* 420–429.

Sue, D.W. (1978). Eliminating cultural oppression in counseling: Toward a general theory. *Journal of Counseling Psychology, 25,* 419–428.

Sue, D.W. (1980). *Evaluation report from DISC 1978–1979.* Honolulu: East-West Center.

Sue, D.W. (1981). *Counseling the culturally different.* New York: Wiley Interscience.

Sue, D.W. (1990). Culture-specific strategies in counseling: A conceptual framework. *Professional Psychology: Research and Practice, 21*(6), 424–433.

Sue, D.W., Arredondo, P., & McDavis, R.J. (1992). Multicultural counseling competencies and standards: A call to the profession. *Journal of Counseling and Development, 70,* 477–486.

Sue, D.W., Berneir, J.E., Durran, A., Feinberg, L., Pedersen, P., Smith, C.J., & Vasquez-Nuttall, G. (1982). Cross-cultural counseling competencies. *The Counseling Psychologist, 19*(2), 45–52.

Sue, D.W., & Sue, S. (1972). Counseling Chinese Americans. *Personnel and Guidance Journal, 50,* 637–645.

Sue, D.W., & Sue, D. (1990). *Counseling the culturally different: Theory and practice.* New York: Wiley.

Sundberg, N.D. (1981a). Cross-cultural counseling and psychotherapy: A research overview. In A. Marsella & P. Pedersen (Eds.), *Cross-cultural counseling and psychotherapy* (pp. 28–62). New York: Pergamon.

Sundberg, N.D. (1981b). Research and research hypotheses about effectiveness in intercultural counseling. In P. Pedersen, J. Draguns, W. Lonner, & J. Trimble (Eds.), *Counseling across cultures* (2nd ed., pp. 304–342). Honolulu: University of Hawaii Press.

Szapocznik, J., & Kurtines, W. (1980). Acculturation, biculturalism and adjustment among Cuban Americans. In A. Padilla (Ed.), *Acculturation: Theory, models and some new findings* (pp. 914–931). Boulder, CO: Westwood Press.

Szapocznik, J., Kurtines, W.M., & Fernandez, T. (1980). Bicultural involvement and adjustment in Hispanic-American youths. *International Journal of Intercultural Relations, 4*, 353–365.

Szapocznik, J., Rio, A., Perez-Vidal, A., Kurtines, W., & Sanisteban, D. (1986). Family effectiveness training for Hispanic families. In H. Lefley & P. Pedersen (Eds.), *Cross-cultural training for mental health professionals* (pp. 353–365). Springfield, IL: Charles C. Thomas.

Szapocznik, J., Scopetta, M.A., & King, O.E. (1978). Theory and practice in matching treatment to the special characteristics and problems of Cuban immigrants. *Journal of Community Psychology, 6*, 112–122.

Taft, R. (1977). Comments on the 1974 Tapp Report on the ethics of cross cultural research. *IACCP Cross Cultural Psychology Newsletter, 11*(4), 2–8.

Tajfel, H. (Ed.). (1978). *Differentiation between social groups*. London: Academic Press.

Takaki, R. (1987). *From different shores: Perspectives on race and ethnicity in America*. New York: Oxford University Press.

Tanaka-Matsumi, J., & Higginbotham, H.N. (1989). Behavioral approaches to counseling across cultures. In P. Pedersen, J. Draguns, W. Lonner, & J. Trimble (Eds.), *Counseling across cultures* (3rd ed., pp. 299–334). Honolulu: University of Hawaii Press.

Tapp, J.L. (1980). Studying personality development. In H.C. Triandis & A. Heron (Eds.), *Handbook of cross cultural psychology* (Vol. 4, pp. 343–424). Boston: Allyn & Bacon.

Tapp, J.L., Kelman, H., Triandis, H., Wrightsman, L., & Coelho, G. (1974). Continuing concerns in cross cultural ethics: A report. *International Journal of Psychology, 9*, 231–349.

Taylor, C. (1989). *Sources of the self: The making of the modern identity*. Cambridge, MA: Harvard University Press.

Taylor, D.M., & Moghaddam, F.M. (1987). *Theories of intergroup relations: International social psychological perspectives*. Westport, CT: Praeger.

Thomas, C. (1971). *Boys no more*. Beverly Hills, CA: Glencoe Press.

Thomas, K., & Althen, G. (1989). Counseling foreign students. In P. Pedersen, J. Draguns, W. Lonner, & J. Trimble (Eds.), *Counseling across cultures* (3rd ed., pp. 205–242). Honolulu: University of Hawaii Press.

Thomas, K.A. (1985). *A comparison of counseling strategies reflective of cultural value orientations on perceptions of counselors in cross national dyads*. Unpublished doctoral dissertation, University of Minnesota, Minneapolis.

Toldson, I., & Pasteur, A. (1975). Developmental stages of Black self-discovery: Implications for using Black art forms in group interaction. *Journal of Negro Education, 44*, 130–138.

Tong, B. (1971). The ghetto of the mind: Notes on the historical psychology of Chinese Americans. *Amerasian Journal, 1*, 28.

Torrey, E.F. (1986). *Witchdoctors and psychiatrists: The common roots of psychotherapy and its future*. New York: Harper & Row.

Triandis, H.C. (1972). *The analysis of subjective culture.* New York: Wiley.

Triandis, H.C. (1975). Cultural training, cognitive complexity and interpersonal attitudes. In R. Brislin, S. Bochner, & W. Lonner (Eds.), *Cross-cultural perspectives on learning* (pp. 39–78). New York: Wiley.

Triandis, H.C. (1977). *Interpersonal behavior.* Monterey, CA: Brooks/Cole.

Triandis, H.C. (1980). Values, attitudes and interpersonal behavior. In H. Howe & M. Page (Eds.), *Nebraska symposium on motivation, 1979* (Vol. 27, pp. 195–260). Lincoln, NE: University of Nebraska Press.

Triandis, H.C. (1985). Some major dimensions of cultural variation in client populations. In P. Pedersen (Ed.), *Handbook of cross-cultural counseling and therapy* (pp. 21–28). Westport, CT: Greenwood Press.

Triandis, H.C., Bontempo, R., Leung, K., & Hui, C.H. (1990). A method for determining cultural, demographic and person constructs. *Journal of Cross-Cultural Psychology, 21,* 302–318.

Triandis, H.C., Brislin, R., & Hui, C.H. (1988). Cross cultural training across the individualism–collectivism divide. *International Journal of Intercultural Relations, 12,* 269–289.

Trimble, J.E. (1976). Value differences among American indians: Concerns for the concerned counselor. In P. Pedersen, W.J. Lonner, & J.G. Draguns (Eds.), *Counseling across cultures* (pp. 65-81). Honolulu: University of Hawaii Press.

Trimble, J. (1981). Value differentials and their importance in counseling American Indians. In P. Pedersen, J. Draguns, W. Lonner, & J. Trimble (Eds.), *Counseling across cultures: Revised and expanded edition* (pp. 203–226). Honolulu: University of Hawaii Press.

Tseng, W.S., & Hsu, J. (1980). Minor psychological disturbances of everyday life. In H. Triandis & J. Draguns (Eds.), *Handbook of cross cultural psychology: Volume 6. Psychopathology* (pp. 61–98). Boston: Allyn & Bacon.

Vargas, L.A., & Koss-Chioino, J.D. (Eds.). (1992). *Working with culture: Psychotherapeutic interventions with ethnic minority children and adolescents.* San Francisco: Jossey-Bass.

Vaughn, B.E. (1990). Recruitment and retention of ethnic minority faculty in professional schools of psychology. In G. Stricker, E. Davis-Russell, E. Bourg, E. Duran, W.R. Hammond, J. McHolland, K. Polite, & B.E. Vaughn (Eds.), *Toward ethnic diversification in psychology education and training* (pp. 91–98). Washington DC: American Psychological Association.

Vontress, C.E. (1971). *Counseling Negroes.* Boston: Houghton Mifflin.

Vontress, C.E. (1981). Racial and ethnic barriers in counseling. In P. Pedersen, J. Draguns, W. Lonner, & J. Trimble (Eds.), *Counseling across cultures: Revised and expanded edition* (pp. 87–107). Honolulu: University of Hawaii Press.

Wade, P., & Bernstein, B.L. (1991). Culture sensitivity training and counselor's race: Effects on Black female client's perceptions and attrition. *Journal of Counseling Psychology, 38*(1), 9–15.

Walz, G.R., & Johnson, J.A. (1963). Counselors look at themselves on videotape. *Journal of Counseling Psychology, 10,* 232–236.

Wampold, B.E., Casas, J.M., & Atkinson, D.R. (1981). Ethnic bias in counseling: An information processing approach. *Journal of Counseling Psychology, 28,* 498–503.

Ward, C. (1989). *Altered states of consciousness and mental health: A cross cultural perspective*. Newbury Park, CA: Sage.

Warheit, G.J., Holzer, C.E., & Areye, S.A. (1975). Race and mental illness: An epidemiological update. *Journal of Health and Social Behavior, 16*, 243–256.

Watkins, C.E., Jr., & Terrell, F. (1988). Mistrust level and its effects on counseling expectations in Black client–White counselor relationships: An analogue study. *Journal of Counseling Psychology, 35*, 194–197.

Watkins, C.E., Jr., Terrell, F., Muller, F.S., & Terrell, S.L. (1989). Cultural mistrust and its effects on expectational variables in Black–White counselor relationships. *Journal of Counseling Psychology, 36*, 447–450.

Watts, A. (1963). *The two hands of God: The myths of polarity*. New York: Braziller.

Watts, A.G., & Herr, E.L. (1976). Career education in Britain and the USA. *British Journal of Guidance and Counseling, 4*(2), 129–142.

Watts, A.W. (1961). *Psychotherapy East and West*. New York: Mentor Press.

Weidman, H.H. (1973, March). *Implications of the culture-broker concept for the delivery of health care*. Paper presented at the annual meeting of the Southern Anthropological Society, Wrightsville, NC.

Weidman, H.H., (1975). Concepts as strategies for change. *Psychiatric Annals, 5*, 312–314.

Westwood, M.J., Lawrence W.S., & Paul, D. (1986). Preparing for reentry: A program for the sojourning student. *International Journal for the Advancement of Counseling, 9*, 221–230.

White, J.L. (1984). *The psychology of blacks: An Afro-American perspective*. Englewood Cliffs, NJ: Prentice-Hall.

Whitely, J.M., & Jakubowski, P.A. (1969). The coached clients as a research and training resource in counseling. *Counselor Education and Supervision, 2*, 19–29.

Williams, L.N. (1978). *Black psychology: Compelling issues and views* (2nd ed.). Washington, DC: University Press of America.

Wilson, K.M. (1986). *The relationship of GRE General Test scores to first year grades for foreign students: Report of a cooperative study* (GRE Board Research Rep. No. 82).

Wilson, W., & Calhoon, J.F. (1974). Behavior therapy and the minority client. *Psychotherapy: Theory, Research and Practice, 11*, 317–325.

Wintrob, R.M., & Harvey, Y.K. (1981). The self-awareness factor in intercultural psychotherapy: Some personal reflections. In P. Pedersen, J. Draguns, W. Lonner, & J. Trimble (Eds.), *Counseling across cultures: Revised and expanded edition* (pp. 87–107). Honolulu: University of Hawaii Press.

Wittkower, E.D., & Warnes, H. (1974). Cultural aspects of psychotherapy. *American Journal of Psychotherapy, 28*, 566–673.

Wohl, J. (1981). Intercultural psychotherapy issues, questions and reflections. In P. Pedersen, W. Draguns, W. Lonner, & J. Trimble (Eds.), *Counseling across cultures: Revised and expanded edition* (pp. 133–159). Honolulu: University of Hawaii Press.

Worchel, S., & Goethals, G.R. (1989). *Adjustment: Pathways to personal growth* (2nd ed.). Englewood Cliffs, NJ: Prentice-Hall.

World Health Organization. (1979). *Schizophrenia: An international follow-up study*. New York: Wiley.

Wrenn, C.G. (1962). The culturally encapsulated counselor. *Harvard Educational Review, 32*, 444–449.

Wrenn, C.G. (1985). Afterward: The culturally encapsulated counselor revisited. In P. Pedersen (Ed.), *Handbook of cross-cultural counseling and therapy* (pp. 323–329). Westport, CT: Greenwood Press.

Wrightsman, L.S. (1992). *Assumptions about human nature: Implications for researchers and practitioners*. Newbury Park, CA: Sage.

Yau, T.Y., Sue, D., & Hayden, D. (1992). Counseling style preference of international students. *Journal of Counseling Psychology, 39*(1), 100–104.

Yinger, J.M. (1986). Intersecting strands in the theorization of race and ethnic relations. In J. Rex & D. Mason (Eds.), *Theories of race and ethnic relations* (pp. 20–41). New York: Cambridge University Press.

Zuk, G. (1971). *Family therapy: A triadic-based approach*. New York: Behavioral Publications.

INDEX